Boston Beverley. A fresher stern trawler.

D0875274

Orsino. A freezer trawler.

Fishermen's Handbook

Edited by
Captain W H Perry MRIN

for the
UK Trawlers Mutual Insurance Company Limited

Published by
Fishing News Books Ltd
Farnham, Surrey, England

© UK Trawlers Mutual Insurance Company Limited 1980

British Library Cataloguing in Publication Data

Fishermen's handbook.
  1. Trawls and trawling
  2. Seamanship
  I. Perry, W H   II. UK Trawlers
  Mutual Insurance Company
  623.88'2'8   SH344.6.T7

ISBN 0 85238 106 9

Typeset by Inforum Ltd, Portsmouth
Printed by The Pitman Press Ltd, Bath

Contents

	Page
List of illustrations	ix
Tables of weights and measures *etc*	xiv
Preface	xix

Part I Practical seamanship

Chap	1	Bends and hitches	1
	2	Knots and splices	11
	3	Tackles	18
	4	Slings and spans	25
	5	Anchors and cables	28
	6	Rigging and working bottom trawl gear	40
	7	Seine net fishing	49
	8	Care of the fish	53

Part II Safety and survival at sea

9	Distress and rescue procedures	56
10	Visual signals, ships in distress, and shore stations, United Kingdom	74
11	Inflatable rafts	80
12	Fire prevention and fire fighting	86
13	Emergencies at sea	96

Part III Navigation

14 Buoyage systems: combined lateral and cardinal 112
15 Tides and tidal streams 121
16 Navigational instruments and appliances 131
17 Coastal navigation 151
18 Astronomical navigation 165
19 Electronic navigational aids and equipment 183

Part IV Watchkeeping, shiphandling

20 Officer of the watch 202
21 Shiphandling 210
22 Basic elements of stability 232
23 Meteorology 249
24 Collision avoidance regulations 266
25 International code of signals 297
26 Submarine telegraph cables 301

List of useful publications 309
Index 311

List of Illustrations

Frontispiece   *Page*

An inshore fishing vessel	ii
Glen Rushen. A seine net, multi-purpose vessel	ii
Boston Beverley. A fresher stern trawler	iii
Orsino. A freezer trawler	iii
Fig 1 Terms used in ropework	2
Fig 2 Half-hitch, round turn, overhand knot	2
Fig 3 Reef knot	2
Fig 4 Figure-of-eight knot	2
Fig 5 Round turn and two half-hitches	2
Fig 5a Fisherman's bend	2
Fig 6 Timber hitch	3
Fig 6a Timber hitch and a half-hitch	3
Fig 7 Clove hitch on the end	3
Fig 7a Clove hitch on the bight	3
Fig 8 Rolling hitch	3
Fig 9 Sheet bend, double sheet bend	5
Fig 10 Fisherman's knot	5
Fig 11 Bowline	5
Fig 12 Running bowline	5
Fig 13 Bowline on the bight	7
Fig 14 French bowline	7
Fig 15 Butterfly knot	7
Fig 16 Midshipman's hitch	7

Fig 17	Blackwall hitch	7
Fig 18	Double blackwall hitch	8
Fig 19	Mousing a hook	8
Fig 20	Catspaw	8
Fig 21	Marline spike hitch, on a marline spike and on a hook	8
Fig 22	Marling hitch	9
Fig 23	Hawser bend	9
Fig 24	Joining two wire hawsers with a grommet strop	9
Fig 25	Fibre rope stopper	9
Fig 26	Chain stopper	9
Fig 27	Chain check stopper	9
Fig 28	Cod end knot	10
Fig 29	Heaving line knot	12
Fig 30	Wall knot	12
Fig 31	Crown knot	12
Fig 32	Crown and wall knot	12
Fig 33	Crown knot and back splice	12
Fig 34	Long splice	13
Fig 35	Selvagee strop	13
Fig 36	Making an eye splice	14
Fig 37	Short splice finished by dogging the strands	14
Fig 38	Use of a strop	14
Fig 39	Common whipping	15
Fig 40	Bend whipping	15
Fig 41	Tucking order for a wire splice	17
Fig 42	Single whip	19
Fig 43	Runner	19
Fig 44	Double whips	19
Fig 45	Luff	20
Fig 46	Two-fold purchase	20
Fig 47	Three-fold purchase	20
Fig 48	Runner and tackle	22
Fig 49	Luff on luff	22
Fig 50	Dutchman's purchase	22
Fig 51	Racking a tackle	23
Fig 52	Choking a luff	23
Fig 53	Parbuckling	23

Fig 54 Variation of stresses in the legs of a span   26
Fig 55 Variation of the tensions in a span   26
Fig 56 Right way to sling a case   27
Fig 57 Wrong way to sling a case   27
Fig 58 An open moor   33
Fig 59 Light anchor stowed on the transom and over
      the stern   35
Fig 60 Heavy anchor slung beneath a boat   35
Fig 61 Heavy anchor slung between two boats   36
Fig 62 Check stopper stoppering a hawser in a boat   37
Fig 63 A deep sea demersal trawl   41
Fig 64 Mouth of a pelagic trawl   47
Fig 65 Shooting, pursing, hauling and brailing the purse
      seine.

(a) The shooting operation, showing (i) the buoy, (ii)
the upper edge rope shackled to the buoy as well as
the purse line, (iii) running through the rings and
(iv) the net flowing off the upper dory deck
      50

(b) The pursing operation showing (i) the retrieving
ropes of the wing, (ii) the pursing gallow and (iii) the
purse line
      51

(c) The hauling operation, showing (i) the pursing
gallow, (ii) the pursing winch and (iii) the rings
unshackled from the purse line and reshackled on a
leading line towards the powerblock
      51

(d) The brailing operation, showing (i) the boom on
which the breast is hooked and general arrangement
of brailing
      52

Fig 66 Fibreglass container, raft stowage   81
Fig 67 A canvas liferaft valise   81
Fig 68 Collapsible wooden box, raft stowage   81
Fig 69 Leak stopper   83
Fig 70 Use of fire extinguisher   90

Fig 71	Air supporting combustion drawn in at low level	91
Fig 72	Spreading foam across surface of liquid fire to avoid dispersement	93
Fig 73	Small and large powder extinguishers	93
Fig 74	Loss of stability from use of water when fire fighting	95
Fig 75	Approaching a ship at anchor	103
Fig 76	Connecting a tow when anchor and cable are to be used	105
Fig 77	Conventional buoyage direction	114
Fig 78	Influence of moon and sun on tides (a) springs (b) neaps	123
Fig 79	Cast of lead compared with sounding on chart	126
Fig 80	Correcting a sounding	127
Fig 81	Mean tide level, regular/semi diurnal tide	129
Fig 82	Patent log	132
Fig 83	Graduated magnetic compass card	134
Fig 84	The aneroid barometer	140
Fig 85	The sextant	144
Fig 86	Station pointer	147
Fig 87	Two cross bearings	153
Fig 88	Vertical sextant angle	153
Fig 89	Fix by station pointer	155
Fig 90	Horizontal safety angle	155
Fig 91	Running fix	157
Fig 92	Three cross bearings	158
Fig 93	Two ranges	159
Fig 94	Angles on the bow	160
Fig 95	Effect and allowance for tide on course	161
Fig 96	Mercator chart, showing rhumb line and great circle tracks	162
Fig 97	Gnomic chart, showing great circle and rhumb line	163
Fig 98	The celestial sphere with the earth at its centre	166
Fig 99	The PZX, celestial triangle	167
Fig 100	Meridian altitude of the sun	173
Fig 101	Applying zenith distance and declination to find latitude	174

Fig 102   Transferring position line to the noon latitude   175
Fig 103   Position line obtained by DF bearing   186
Fig 104a   Right handed propellor going ahead   213
Fig 104b   Right handed propellor going astern   213
Fig 105   Going alongside, right handed screw
           (a) port side to (b) starboard side to   214
Fig 106   Going alongside, left handed screw
           (c) port side to (d) starboard side to   215
Fig 107   Correct mooring of a vessel   216
Fig 108   Use of anchor when swinging in a tideway   217
Fig 109a   Centre of gravity and buoyancy   233
Fig 109b   Righting lever GZ when heeled by an
           outside force   233
Fig 110   Suspended weight loss of GM   237
Fig 111   Effect of a moved weight creating a list   239
Fig 112a   Loll, unstable equilibrium   241
Fig 112b   Stable at angle of loll, owing to increased
           waterplane area   241
Fig 113a   Loss of stability due to slack tanks
           (b) & (c) show reduction in stability loss with the
           greater number of tanks   242
Fig 114   Path of low pressure systems in the north Atlantic   251
Fig 115   Storm centre, giving three ship positions relative
           to the centre   252
Fig 116   Typical frontal system of a storm   253
Fig 117   Path of a typical storm in the southern hemisphere   256
Fig 118   Locating ship's position relative to storm centre
           in the southern hemisphere   257
Fig 119   Coastal weather forecast areas   265
Fig 120   Approximate position of submarine cables normally
           shown as magenta wavy lines on admiralty charts   302

           Endpapers
           International code of flag signals   *front*
           Buoys and beacons   *front*
           Lights and shapes to be shown   *back*

Tables of weights and measures

Nautical Miles, Statute Miles, Kilometres

Nautical Miles	Statute Miles	Kilo-Metres	Statute Miles	Nautical Miles	Kilo-Metres	Kilo-Metres	Nautical Miles	Statute Miles
1	1·15	1·85	1	0·87	1·61	1	0·54	0·62
2	2·30	3·71	2	1·74	3·22	2	1·08	1·24
3	3·45	5·56	3	2·61	4·83	3	1·62	1·86
4	4·61	7·41	4	3·47	6·44	4	2·16	2·49
5	5·76	9·27	5	4·34	8·05	5	2·70	3·11
6	6·91	11·12	6	5·21	9·66	6	3·24	3·73
7	8·06	12·97	7	6·08	11·27	7	3·78	4·35
8	9·21	14·82	8	6·95	12·87	8	4·32	4·97
9	10·36	16·68	9	7·82	14·48	9	4·86	5·59
10	11·52	18·53	10	8·86	16·09	10	5·40	6·21
50	57·58	92·65	50	43·42	80·47	50	26·98	31·07
100	115·15	185·30	100	86·84	160·93	100	53·96	62·14
500	575·75	926·50	500	434·20	804·65	500	269·80	310·69
1000	1151·50	1853·00	1000	868·40	1609·30	1000	539·60	621·38

Metric measures

Kilo-(1000) kg.Km.Kl	Hecto-(100) Hg.Hm.Hl.	Deca-(10) Dg.Dm.Dl.	Gramme (g) Metre (m) Litre (l)	Deci-1/10 dg.dm.dl.	Centi-1/100 cg.cm.cl.	Milli-1/1000 mg.mm.ml.

(Note: dm. with a small "d" is a *deci*metre = 1/10 of a metre.
Dm. with a capital "D" is a *Deca*metre = 10 metres).

There are certain connections between the metric system and the British measures. (They are only approximate)

1 cm. = rather less than $^2/_5$ in

1 m. = 39·37 in (rather more than a yd)

1 g. (·032 oz) is the weight of 1 cc of water

1 cu ft of water = $6^1/_4$ galls (approx)

1Km = $^5/_8$ mile or 5 furlongs

1 l. = $1^3/_4$ pt (rather less than 1 quart)

1 Kg = $2^1/_5$ lb

1 Hl = 22 gals (approx)

Shackles of cable to metres

Shackles		Metres	Shackles		Metres
1 = 15 fathoms	=	27·432	6 = 90 fathoms	=	165 approx.
2 = 30 fathoms	=	55 approx.	7 = 105 fathoms	=	192 approx.
3 = 45 fathoms	=	82 approx.	8 = 120 fathoms	=	220 approx.
4 = 60 fathoms	=	110 approx.	9 = 135 fathoms	=	246 approx.
5 = 75 fathoms	=	140 approx.	10 = 150 fathoms	=	274 approx.

Lengths in British units

12 inches = 1 foot   3 feet = 1 yard   6 feet = 1 fathom

1 cable = 608 feet (which is roughly 100 fathoms or 200 yards).

10 cables = 1 nautical or 1 sea mile.

1 nautical mile = 6080 feet (roughly 2000 yards) = 1·15 statute miles.

1 statute mile (or land mile) = 5280 feet = 1760 yards = 0·87 sea miles.

The range of metric units

1 metre = 1·094 yards = 3·28 feet = 39·37 inches.

10 millimetres	=	1 centimetre	10 dekametres	=	1 hectometre
10 centimetres	=	1 decimetre	10 hectometres	=	1 kilometre
10 decimetres	=	1 metre	10 kilometres	=	1 myriameter
10 metres	=	1 dekametre	1 kilometre	=	0·62 land miles
				=	0·54 sea miles

Comparative tables of weight

Avoirdupois

16 drams	=	1 ounce
16 ounces	=	1 pound
14 pounds	=	1 stone
28 pounds	=	1 quarter
4 quarters	=	1 hundred-weight (112lb)
20 hundred-weights	=	1 ton (2240 lb)

Metric

10 milligrams	=	1 centigram
10 centigrams	=	1 decigram
10 decigrams	=	1 gram*
10 grams	=	1 dekagram
10 dekagrams	=	1 hectogram
10 hectograms	=	1 kilogram
10 kilograms	=	1 myriagram
1000 kilograms	=	1 tonne

* *The weight of one cubic centimetre of pure water.*

Other measures of weight

1 pig of ballast = 56 lb. ∴ 2 pigs = 1 cwt. and 40 pigs = 1 ton

1 long ton (British) = 2,240 lb. = 1·12 short tons = 1·016 metric tonnes.

1 short ton (USA and Canada) = 20 centals of 100 lb. each = 2,000 lb. = 0·893 long tons = 0·907 metric tonnes.

1 metric tonne = 2204·62 lb = 1·1023 short tons = 0·9842 long tons.

Comparative tables of measure or capacity

British			Metric		
4 gills	=	1 pint	10 millilitres	=	1 centilitre
2 pints	=	1 quart	10 centilitres	=	1 decilitre
4 quarts	=	1 gallon	10 decilitres	=	1 litre*
2 gallons	=	1 peck	10 litres	=	1 dekalitre
4 pecks	=	1 bushel	10 dekalitres	=	1 hectolitre
8 bushels	=	1 quarter	10 hectolitres	=	1 kilolitre
5 quarters (approx.)	=	1 load	1 litre	=	$1\frac{3}{4}$ pints
36 bushels	=	1 chaldron	* 1000 *cubic centimetres*		

Note:—British measure is used for both liquid and dry goods. Metric units are not used for solid content.

NAUTICAL MEASURES

1 ton (displacement) = 35 cu. feet of Salt Water or 36 cu. feet of Fresh Water
1 ton (register) = 100 cu. feet   **1 ton (measurement)** = 40 cu. feet

Fresh Water

1 cubic foot = $6\frac{1}{4}$ gallons and weighs 62·5 lb (1000 oz.)
36 cubic feet = 224 gallons and weighs 1 ton
1 gallon = 4·536 litres and weighs 10 lb
10 British gallons = 12 American gallons (approx.)

Salt Water

1 cubic foot weighs 64 lb.   35 cubic feet weigh 1 ton.

MEASUREMENT OF TIME

Days

1 Mean Solar Day = 24 Mean Solar hours.
1 Sidereal Day = 23h. 56m. 04·1s. of Mean Solar Time.
1 Lunar Day averages approximately 24h. 50m. of Mean Solar Time.

Months

A Calendar Month = 28, 29, 30 or 31 days, depending on which month.

A Lunar Month (or Lunation, or Synodical Month) is the time interval between successive New Moons, i.e. one revolution of the Moon with reference to the Sun—about $29\frac{1}{2}$ Mean Solar Days.

A Sidereal Month. The average time taken for the Moon to complete one orbit with reference to a star, a period of approximately $27^{1}/_{3}$ Mean Solar Days.

Years

The **common year** has 365 calendar days.

Leap Years, which have 366 calendar days, are those years which are divisible by 4 (as 1976, 1980, etc) *except* those century years not divisible by 400 (e.g. 1900). The year 2000 A.D. will be a leap year, and 2100 A.D. a common year.

If without leap years, calendar date would gradually fall out of step with the seasons and, gradually, midsummer would occur in January.

One complete cycle of the **Gregorian Calendar** takes 400 years, viz.—in 400 years there are:—

97 *(leap) years of 366 days, each*	=	35,502 days
and 303 years of 365 days each	=	110,595 days
Thus the total number of days is	=	146,097

and hence, the **Civil Year** is $\frac{146,097}{400}$ or **365·2425 Days.**

Feet to metres 1ft = 0·3048 m.

Feet	Metres	Feet	Metres	Feet	Metres	Feet	Metres
1	0·30	26	7·92	51	15·54	76	23·16
2	0·61	27	8·23	52	15·85	77	23·47
3	0·91	28	8·53	53	16·15	78	23·77
4	1·22	29	8·84	54	16·46	79	24·08
5	1·52	30	9·14	55	16·76	80	24·38
6	1·83	31	9·45	56	17·07	81	24·69
7	2·13	32	9·75	57	17·37	82	24·99
8	2·44	33	10·06	58	17·68	83	25·30
9	2·74	34	10·36	59	17·98	84	25·60
10	3·05	35	10·67	60	18·29	85	25·91
11	3·35	36	10·97	61	18·59	86	26·21
12	3·66	37	11·28	62	18·90	87	26·52
13	3·96	38	11·58	63	19·20	88	26·82
14	4·27	39	11·89	64	19·51	89	27·13
15	4·57	40	12·19	65	19·81	90	27·42
16	4·88	41	12·50	66	20·12	91	27·74
17	5·18	42	12·80	67	20·42	92	28·04
18	5·49	43	13·11	68	20·73	93	28·35
19	5·79	44	13·41	69	21·03	94	28·65
20	6·10	45	13·72	70	21·34	95	28·96
21	6·40	46	14·02	71	21·64	96	29·26
22	6·71	47	14·33	72	21·95	97	29·57
23	7·01	48	14·63	73	22·25	98	29·87
24	7·32	49	14·94	74	22·56	99	30·18
25	7·62	50	15·24	75	22·86	100	30·48

Metres to feet 1 metre = 3.2808 ft.

Metres	Feet	Metres	Feet	Metres	Feet	Metres	Feet
1	3·28	26	85·30	51	167·32	76	249·34
2	6·56	27	88·58	52	170·60	77	252·62
3	9·84	28	91·86	53	173·88	78	255·91
4	13·12	29	95·14	54	177·17	79	259·19
5	16·40	30	98·43	55	180·45	80	262·47
6	19·69	31	101·71	56	183.73	81	265·75
7	22·97	32	104·99	57	187·01	82	269·03
8	26·25	33	108·27	58	190·29	83	272·31
9	29·53	34	111·55	59	193·57	84	275·59
10	32·81	35	114·83	60	196·86	85	278·87
11	36·09	36	118·11	61	200·13	86	282·15
12	39·37	37	121·39	62	203·41	87	285·43
13	42·65	38	124·67	63	206·69	88	288·71
14	45·93	39	127·95	64	209·97	89	291·99
15	49·21	40	131·23	65	213·25	90	295·28
16	52·49	41	134·51	66	216·54	91	298·56
17	55·77	42	137·80	67	219·82	92	301·84
18	59·06	43	141·08	68	223·10	93	305·12
19	62·34	44	144·36	69	226·38	94	308·40
20	65·62	45	147·64	70	229·66	95	311·68
21	68·90	46	150·92	71	232·94	96	314·96
22	72·18	47	154·20	72	236·22	97	318·24
23	75·46	48	157·48	73	239·50	98	321·52
24	78·74	49	160·76	74	242·78	99	324·80
25	82·02	50	164·04	75	246·06	100	328·08

Preface

Deep-sea fishing has always been a very demanding art. The successful fisherman has traditionally possessed a sound knowledge of the sea and "all that therein is", good judgement, and courage. Today he sails in increasingly sophisticated vessels, equipped with valuable technical aids; yet the traditional qualities are still required as are a proper understanding of seamanship and navigation.

The sea will always be a hard taskmaster and an unforgiving one. Few men can have learned all the lessons it teaches at first hand so that even an experienced seaman should not be ashamed to seek advice. Certainly no fisherman can afford to neglect basic rules in meeting his responsibilities for the safety and efficiency of the vessel in which he sails.

There has been an impressive continuity of sound and helpful advice set out over the years in the compact manuals produced for fishermen from the days of the 'Fishermen's Handy Billy' to the 'Trawlermen's Handbook'. I hope the present volume will prove a worthy successor and as useful to the present generation of fishermen as earlier ones have been to their predecessors.

Captain W. Perry has been at pains to reflect the changing pattern of the industry in his recompilation of this manual, ably assisted by several willing hands, all anxious to maintain the original aim of the "Handy Billy", namely that of compiling a book to create amongst our fishermen, especially the younger men, a greater interest in their duties, setting forth hints which are friendly offers of help from one sailor to another.

C.R.P.C. Branson, C.B.E., M.B.I.M.,
Managing Director,
U.K. Trawlers Mutual Insurance Company Limited.

Part I Practical seamanship

1 Bends and hitches

The rope in the diagram (*Fig 1*) has a whipping at one end to prevent it unlaying. One bight of the rope is 'lying Judas' (idle) in a bight on the deck and is stopped by twine to the rail. The rope is hanging in bights, while the standing part is 'hanging Judas' and ends in an eye (or bight) with the bare end seized back on the standing part.

It is dangerous to stand in the bight or to put a hand or any part of the body in a bight without first being certain that the rope – whether it be wire or fibre or large or small – cannot be worked.

Half-hitch, round turn, overhand knot

These three knots (*Fig 2*) enter into the make-up of a large number of bends and hitches

Reef knot

The reef knot (*Fig 3*) consists of two overhand knots with the ends passed opposite to each other. It will not easily come undone by itself but can be untied. If it is used on ropes of unequal size or on slippery ropes the ends must be stopped to their own standing parts. If the reef knot is not formed correctly a 'granny' will result which will slip and jam and consequently be very difficult to undo when required. A seaman should not use a 'granny' knot.

Figure-of-eight knot

This knot (*Fig 4*) is used to prevent a rope unreeving through a block and for use with a log rotator.

Round turn and two half-hitches, fishermen's bend

Both of these knots (*Fig 5* and *5a*) are used for securing weights to a standing object, but the former is preferred as not being liable to jam. More than one round turn can be taken if desired.

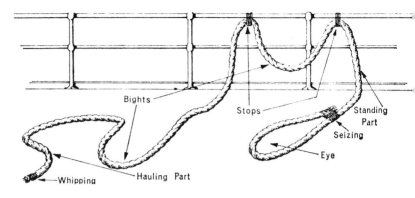

Fig 1   Terms used in ropework

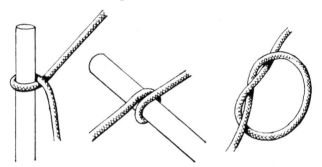

Fig 2   Half-hitch, round turn, overhand knot

Fig 3   Reef knot

Fig 4   Figure of eight knot

Fig 5   Round turn and two half hitches
Fig 5a   Fisherman's bend

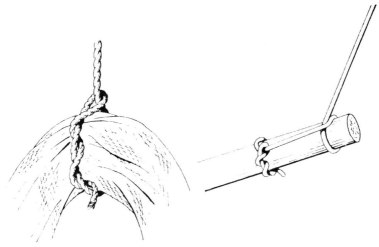

Fig 6   Timber hitch   *Fig 6a*   Timber hitch and a half hitch

Fig 7   Clove hitch on the end

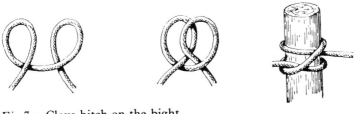

Fig 7a   Clove hitch on the bight

Fig 8   Rolling hitch

Timber hitch and half-hitch

The timber hitch (*Fig 6*) by itself is merely a quick means of making a running eye and is of some use on soft objects but not as useful on hard ones. With the addition of a half-hitch (*Fig 6a*) the hold is improved. Generally speaking, the hitch and half-hitch would be used only on tapering objects with the half-hitch at the larger end. When lowering something like a spar, a length of piping or a plank into the hold, over the side or down a cliff, see that the timber hitch does not catch anywhere. It could slide towards the half-hitch which could then come off the end of the load and allow it to slip clear of the running eye. The load would then fall.

Clove hitch on the end, clove hitch on the bight

A most useful hitch for general purposes but it will not resist a sideways pull. (*Figs* 7 and 7a).

Rolling hitch

The rolling hitch (*Fig 8*) is also useful for general purposes but especially where it must resist a sideways pull. Note that in the diagram, the hitch is made to resist a pull to the right.

Sheet bend or swab hitch, double sheet bend

The knot (*Fig 9*) is used to secure a rope's end to an eye or a small rope to a larger one.

Fishermen's knot

The fishermen's knot (*Fig 10*) is used to join two smaller ropes together. When strain comes on, the two overhand knots slide together and if made as illustrated will fit snugly. The ends can then be stopped to the standing part.

Bowline, running bowline, bowline on the bight, French bowline

A bowline makes a reliable temporary eye, as shown in the diagram (*Fig 11*). A running bowline (*Fig 12*) makes a sliding eye. The bowline on the bight (*Fig 13*) can be used for lowering a man from aloft or over

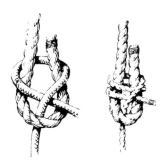

Fig 9   Sheet bend, double sheet bend

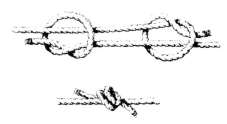

Fig 10   Fisherman's knot

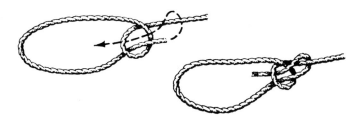

Fig 11   Bowline

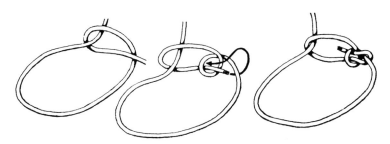

Fig 12   Running bowline

the side with the short bight under his arms and the long one under his seat.

The French bowline (*Fig 14*) is better for the above purpose than the bowline on the bight as the weight in the main bight keeps the arm bight taut. Form the small bight and pass the end up through it as if starting a bowline, then bring the end round (to form the arm bight) and pass it up through the small bight again and continue the bowline.

Butterfly knot

A party having to be roped together to climb a cliff can secure the first and last man with a bowline and each remaining man with a butterfly knot (*Fig 15*).

Midshipman's hitch, blackwall hitch, double blackwall hitch

All three hitches (*Figs 16, 17* and *18*) are used to secure a rope to a hook. The double blackwall hitch is preferred.

Mousing

Mousing (*Fig 19*) is used to prevent a hook from unhooking.

Catspaw

The catspaw (*Fig 20*) is used to shorten a sling.

Marline spike hitch

This hitch (*Fig 21*) is used to assist in hauling taut.

Marling hitch

The marling hitch (*Fig 22*) is used when lashing hammocks and similar long bundles, and as a temporary repair for chafed rope.

Hawser bend

The hawser bend (*Fig 23*) is used to join two large ropes together. Note the seizings.

6

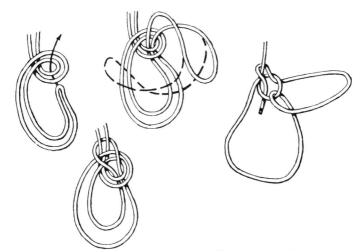

Fig 13   Bowline on the bight   Fig 14   French bowline

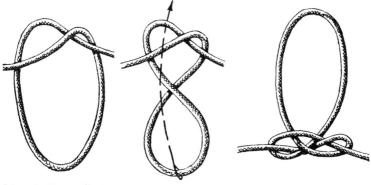

Fig 15   Butterfly knot

Fig 16   Midshipman's hitch

Fig 17   Blackwall hitch

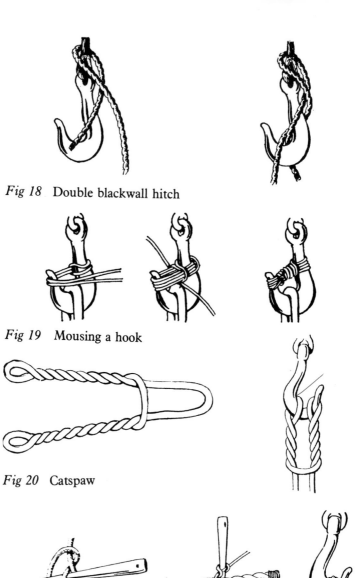

Fig 18 Double blackwall hitch

Fig 19 Mousing a hook

Fig 20 Catspaw

Fig 21 Marline spike hitch, on a marline spike and on a hook

Fig 22 Marling hitch

Fig 23 Hawser bend

Fig 24 Joining two wire hawsers with a grommet strop

Fig 25 Fibre rope stopper

Fig 26 Chain stopper

Fig 27 Chain check stopper

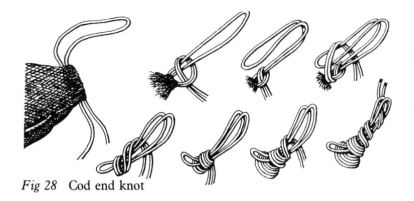

Fig 28   Cod end knot

Wire rope join

This diagram (*Fig 24*) shows the use of a wire strop in joining wire ropes.

Fibre rope stopper

The fibre rope stopper (*Fig 25*) is used to hold a fibre rope or wire rope temporarily when it is under stress.

Chain stopper

To make a chain stopper (*Fig 26*), one end of the chain is secured on to the rope using either a half-hitch or the first two parts of a rolling hitch. The bight of the hitch should be against the lay of the rope when a fibre rope is used and with the lay when a wire rope is used. The end should then be extended with the lay on a fibre rope or against the lay on a wire rope and finally stopped to the rope.

Chain check stopper

The chain check stopper (*Fig 27*) is used to control the speed of paying out a wire.

Cod end knot

The cod end knot (*Fig 28*) is used to close the cod end before shooting the trawl.

2   Knots and splices

Heaving line knot

This knot (*Fig 29*) is for use at the end of heaving lines because it is heavy enough to carry the line the maximum distance (about 60 ft) that a man can throw. The use of weights such as steel nuts or bolts is strictly forbidden because of possible injury to persons at the other end of the throw. After the heaving line is passed, the inboard end should be bent to the hawser, which may be a mooring rope, by means of a bowline with a long eye. This will enable the eye on the hawser to be handled by the men on shore while the bowline is pulled clear of any bollard or other mooring.

Wall knot, crown knot

These knots (*Figs 30, 31* and *32*) form the basis of many of the knots commonly used. The crown knot by itself is used to commence a back splice.

Back splice

To make a back splice (*Fig 33*), first form a crown knot and tuck each strand along the rope over one laid-up strand and under the next. Two tucks of whole and one tuck of halved strands is sufficient.

Long splice

To make a long splice (*Fig 34*), unlay each rope approximately one foot for every inch in size, *ie* 2ft for a 2in rope. Marry the ropes and further unlay a strand of one and lay up a strand of the other in its place. Separate a third of the yarns of each of the two strands and tie the two-thirds portion in an overhand knot left over right. Tuck these two portions over one and under one. Carry out the same for the other end. Separate, knot and tuck the two remaining strands. Stretch the

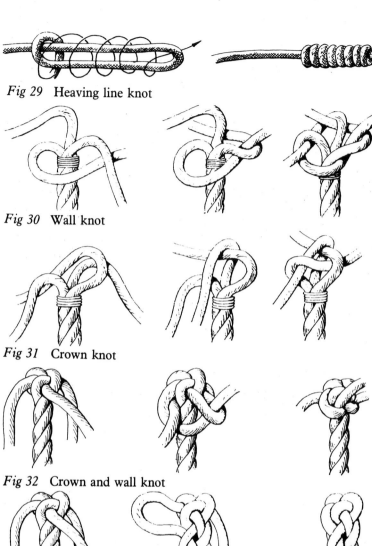

Fig 29 Heaving line knot

Fig 30 Wall knot

Fig 31 Crown knot

Fig 32 Crown and wall knot

Fig 33 Crown knot and back splice

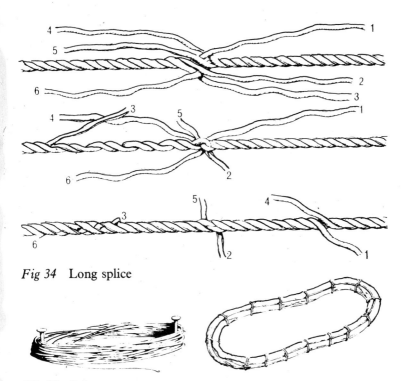

Fig 34   Long splice

Fig 35   Selvagee strop

splice and cut off the yarns remaining. This splice will allow the rope
to pass through a block.

Selvagee strop

The selvagee strop (*Fig 35*) is made of spun yarn and will grip a larger
rope or wire much better than will a strop made from laid-up rope. Fix
two nails at the required distance apart and pass turns with a ball of
spun yarn till the strop is of the required thickness and then marl it
down with marling hitches.

Eye splice

To make an eye splice (*Fig 36*), unlay the end of the rope and form a
bight. Tuck the strands over one and under one. Do this three times,
then stop the ends.

13

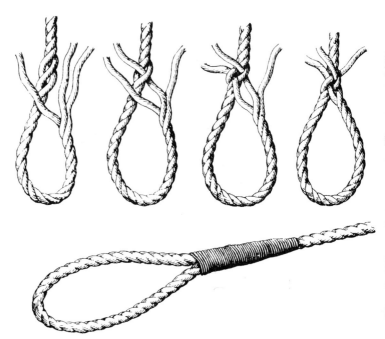

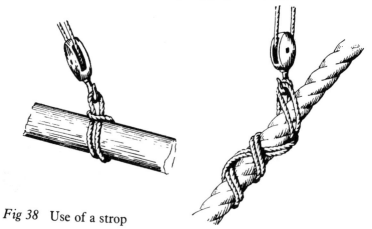

Fig 36   Making an eye splice

Fig 37   Short splice finished by dogging the strands

Fig 38   Use of a strop

14

Short splice

To make a short splice (*Fig 37*), unlay the end of each rope and marry them together. Tuck each strand over one and under one on either end. Repeat three times.

Common strop, bale sling strop

A strop (*Fig 38*) is a length of rope with its ends spliced together. A short strop is called a common strop and is used to pass round a rope or spar *etc* to provide an eye to take a hook or shackle. A longer strop is called a bale sling strop and is used for general purposes such as slinging, hoisting, *etc*.

Whipping

A whipping (*Figs 39* and *40*) is used on any bare end of rope in order to prevent the unlaying of the strands.

Wire splicing

Flexible steel wire rope is six-stranded, right handed, and has a hemp heart. Each strand also has a hemp heart. Before working wire rope good stops should be placed where the rope is to be cut and at the point to which it will be unlaid.

Fig 39   Common whipping

Fig 40   Bend whipping

There are several methods for tucking the strands. The following is one example: (See *Fig 41*)

(*1*) Allow approximately 1ft of wire per inch circumference for splicing wire rope.

(*2*) Bend wire to shape the required eye and clamp in vice with the eye to the left hand side of vice if left handed and to the right if right handed.

(*3*) Put on a tight whipping to hold eye in position and prevent wire from unlaying

(*4*) Take out of vice and hang up with loose wires to the left and reclamp in vice.

(*5*) Bend over wire from each strand.

(*6*) Cut off whipping at the end of wires to be tucked.

(*7*) Take out the small hearts for about 2in.

(*8*) Whip each strand tightly.

(*9*) Take the main heart between the centre of the six loose strands away from the standing wire and to the left.

(*10*) The wire nearest to you on the right is No 1 and counting clockwise from this wire they are numbered 2, 3, then main heart, 4, 5 and 6, and they are tucked in this order.

(*11*) Pass spike through the centre of the standing wire away from you, leaving the main heart and three strands on the left hand side.

(*12*) Pass No 1 wire through in the same direction as the spike, remove spike and pull wire down tight.

(*13*) Pass spike in through the same place as for No 1 but only through two wires, pass No 2 after spike and pull tight.

(*14*) Pass spike in through the same place as for No 1 but only through one wire, pass No 3 after spike and pull tight.

(*15*) Pass spike through the next wire (still working in a clockwise direction), pass wire No 4 after it, take out spike and pull tight.

(*16*) Pass spike through the next wire (still working clockwise), pass wire No 5 through and pull tight.

(*17*) Pass spike through the next wire (still working clockwise), pass wire after it, take out spike and pull tight.

(*18*) All wires have now been tucked once. Take out small hearts and cut off main heart.

(*19*) The loose wires are now run up the standing wires 'Liverpool fashion' in the following manner, working from 6 to 1.

(*a*) No 6 loose strand is held in left hand. Spike is then passed back

16

through the standing wire through which the loose wire has already been passed.

(b) Loose wire No 6 is then passed through one wire under the spike and against the spike. Tighten by turning spike clockwise, then without withdrawing spike twist anti-clockwise one turn. Pass loose wire through against spike. Tighten as before. This is done until four tucks have been taken with each wire.

(c) No 5 as No 6
No 4 as No 6
No 3 as No 6
No 2 as No 6
No 1 as No 6

(d) Take off loose ends and serve.

Wire splices should be parcelled with oily canvas and served. Broken wires should not be allowed to protrude; break them off by bending backwards and forwards but do not cut.

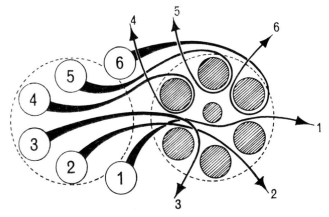

Fig 41 Tucking order for a wire splice

3   Tackles

A tackle is a system of blocks through which is rove a rope. It is used to move heavy weights.

The mechanical advantage (MA) of a tackle is estimated by counting the number of parts of the rope at the moving block. It is not always possible to use a tackle to advantage, *ie* to have the hauling part of the fall coming away from the moving block, but the seaman should try to make the block with the greater number of sheaves to be the moving block.

The greater the MA the less will be the load on the standing block which is calculated by adding the pull required to the weight being moved. Friction is mentioned later and is not taken into account in the following examples.

Single whip

The single whip (*Fig 42*) has one standing block and no moving block. (No MA) The load on the standing block is twice the weight to be moved.

Runner

A runner (*Fig 43*) consists of a rope rove through a single moving block. (MA = 2).

Double whip

The double whip (*Fig 44*) consists of two single blocks with the standing part of the rope made fast to the upper block. (MA = 2).

Luff

The luff (*Fig 45*) uses a three inch rope or larger. It consists of a double and a single block with the standing part made fast to the single block

18

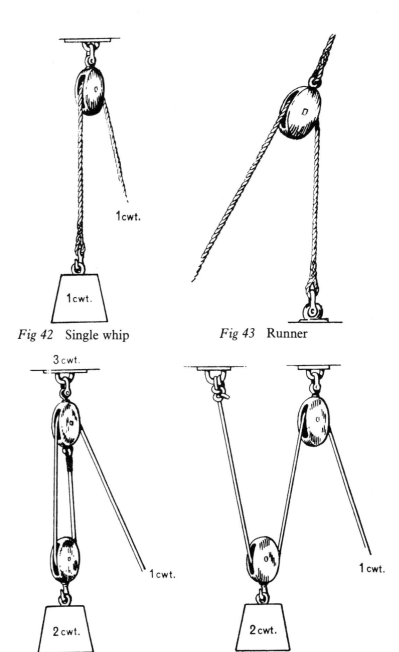

1 cwt.

1 cwt.

Fig 42 Single whip

Fig 43 Runner

3 cwt.

1 cwt.

2 cwt.

1 cwt.

2 cwt.

Fig 44 Double whips

19

(The MA = 4 if the tackle is rove to advantage or 3 if rove to disadvantage.)

Jigger

The jigger is the same as a luff using a 2 to $2\frac{1}{2}$ in rope.

Handy billy

This is a small tackle like a luff but using a smaller rope than 2 in.

Two-fold purchase

The two-fold purchase (*Fig 46*) uses two double blocks. (MA = 5 or 4)

Three-fold purchase

The three-fold purchase (*Fig 47*) uses two treble blocks. (MA = 7 or 6) The purchase in the illustration is rove to disadvantage and has six parts at the moving block.

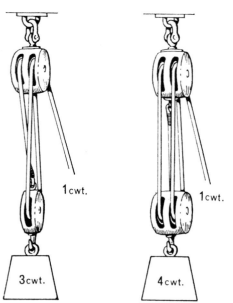

1 cwt.

1 cwt.

1 cwt.

3 cwt.

4 cwt.

6 cwt.

Fig 45 Luff   *Fig 46* Two-fold purchase

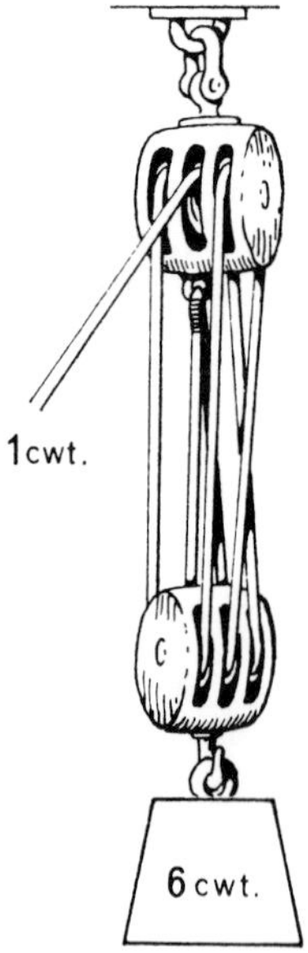

Fig 47
Three-fold purchase

Runner and tackle

$(MA = 2 \times 4 = 8) (Fig\,48)$

Luff upon luff

The name describes the combined use of two tackles. The two luffs in the illustration $(Fig\,49)$ are rove to advantage. $(MA = 4 \times 4 = 16)$

Dutchman's purchase

The Dutchman's purchase $(Fig\,50)$ is a tackle used in reverse to drive a light whip at a fast speed from a slow source of great power. Useful in salvage work.

Friction

In all the assessments of mechanical advantage the effects of friction have been ignored. Friction has to be overcome in the lifting of weights and it is therefore sensible for any tackles or other blocks and sheaves in the ship to be regularly attended and to have the pins of the sheaves well greased at all times.

A rough rule for finding the pull (P) required on the hauling part of a tackle is as follows:

Add the weight to be moved (W) to $1/10$ of W for each sheave (S) in the system, ie $W + (S/10 \times W)$. Divide the result by the number of parts of fall (F) at the moving block. Thus,

$$P = \frac{W + (S/10 \times W)}{F}$$

In luff upon luff to best advantage, the pull required to move a weight of half-a-ton is found as follows:

$$P = \frac{1120 + (^6/_{10} \times 1120)}{8} = 224 \text{ lb}$$

By this formula, using one luff only, the sum works as follows:

$$P = \frac{1120 + (^3/_{10} \times 1120)}{4} = 364 \text{ lb}$$

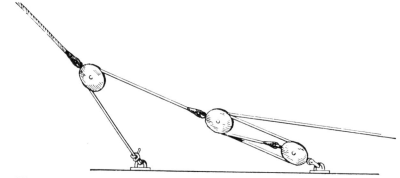

Fig 48   Runner and tackle

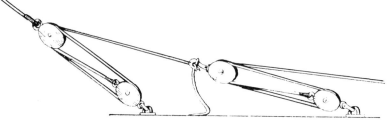

Fig 49   Luff on luff

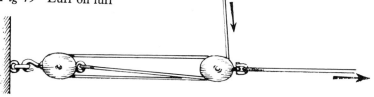

Fig 50   Dutchman's purchase

Racking a tackle

If for any reason it is found necessary to move the hauling part of a tackle *ie* from a winch drum to belaying pins or bollards, the tackle may be racked or stopped off by the use of a light rope or seizing cross-whipped around the standing part and a moving part as shown in *Fig 51*.

Choking the luff

Another method of stoppering off a tackle temporarily by allowing the hauling part to jam under a moving part at the sheave. The luff is

22

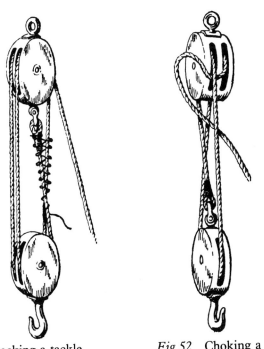

Fig 51   Racking a tackle   *Fig 52*   Choking a luff

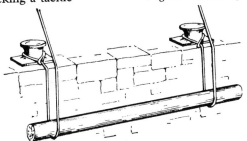

Fig 53   Parbuckling

choked by the weight on the hook (see *Fig 52*). This method should only be used in an emergency when reasonably light weights are being lifted by hand.

Parbuckling

Parbuckling is a method by which a pole, cask or other suitably rounded object may be raised or lowered down a ramp, quayside or

23

bulkhead. No blocks are used but a similar principle applies and as illustrated in *Fig 53* the weight can be lowered under control.

The mechanical advantage is 2 but there is a greater frictional loss when lifting because the ropes move around the weight itself and not through a sheave.

4 Slings and spans

Frequent causes of serious accidents are the misuse and overloading of slings and spans. The following diagrams show that the wider the angle of the slings at the lifting hook the greater the stress. Slings at a small angle share the load being lifted while slings at a wide angle share a load four times the weight being lifted.

The same applies to strops and spans where the angles between the legs should be kept as small as possible. Slings and spans should be examined before use with these facts in mind (see *Figs 54, 55, 56* and *57*).

Strength of ropes

It is not possible to give a definite rule for finding the amount of stress which a rope will sustain. Supposing it to be a rope in good, but not new, condition a rough rule is:

Breaking stress of fibre cordage $= \dfrac{\text{circumference squared}}{3}$ tons.

Therefore breaking stress of 4 in quarter rope $= \dfrac{4 \times 4}{3} = 5^1/_3$ tons.

If the rope is spliced its strength is reduced by $^1/_6$.
Therefore breaking strain of a spliced 4 in quarter rope
$$= {}^5/_6 \times 5^1/_3 = 4.45 \text{ say } 4^1/_2, \text{ tons.}$$
If the rope is knotted its strength may be reduced by $\frac{1}{2}$.
To find the safe working load divide the breaking stress by 6. Breaking stress of wire rope up to $4\frac{1}{2}$ in = circumference squared $\times$ 2 tons. Breaking stress of wire rope above $4\frac{1}{2}$ in = circumference squared $\times$ $2\frac{1}{2}$ tons.
Safe working load of wire rope is $^1/_6$ of its breaking stress for slings and running gear.

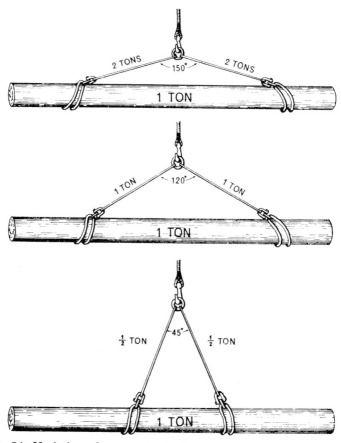

Fig 54 Variation of stresses in the legs of a span

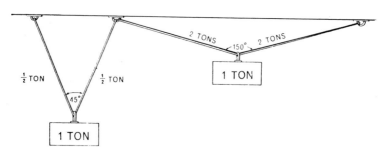

Fig 55 Variations of the tensions in a span

26

Fig 56
Right way to sling a case

Fig 57
Wrong way to sling a case

Artificial fibre ropes

For artificial fibre ropes such as Nylon, Terylene, Ulstron, *etc*, the breaking stresses are greater than for equal sizes of sisal or manila, while the knotted strengths are about half the unknotted strengths.

Artificial ropes stretch under strain and it is advisable to stand well clear when they are under heavy loads as they tend to 'fly' rather more than natural fibre ropes when they part under these conditions. They also slip more easily round bollards and winch drums, making it necessary to take extra turns when using these ropes. They also tend to melt when subjected to heavy friction.

They can be spliced like manila or sisal, but the end of each strand must be whipped before starting the splice and after the standard four tucks have been taken it is as well to halve the strands and seize the halves together in the manner known as 'shouldering' or 'dogging' to prevent them from drawing under strain.

Each kind of artificial fibre rope has its own advantages over ropes made of natural fibres. Some of them are considerably lighter and some will float and will not absorb water. All those made for work at sea in ships, given normal care, will give good service.

It is imperative to stand well clear of fibre ropes or wires under strain. Man-made fibre ropes, in particular, like nylon, terylene, ulstron, *etc*, have a very severe whip-lash effect when they part and fatal accidents have occurred. When attempting to tow-off a grounded ship, or other difficult tow requiring maximum power, the towing vessel(s) should never lunge into the effort. The two lines must be tautened steadily so as to avoid parting.

5   Anchors and cables

Following is a list of terms used in anchor work:

Weigh anchor.   To heave in the cable until the anchor is broken out of the ground and clear of the water. The anchor is aweigh when it has broken out of the ground but is not clear until out of the water and it can be seen that there is nothing attached to it. Otherwise it is foul.

Lead or grow.   The direction in which the cable leads between the hawse-pipe and the anchor. It is indicated by the anchor officer pointing in the direction in which the cable leads, *ie* ahead, astern, abeam, *etc*. When the cable is underfoot and leading vertically it is said to be 'up and down'. A slowing down of the windlass usually indicates the breaking out of the anchor from the ground at this stage, when weighing anchor.

Short or long stay.   The cable is at short stay when it leads downwards from the hawse-pipe towards the vertical and is at long stay when taut and leading close to the horizontal.

Brought-up or come-to.   A ship has brought-up or come-to when the operation of dropping the anchor has been completed, the cable has tightened, the anchor has held, and the ship has come towards the anchor with the cable lying along the bottom and the ship lying comfortably at rest.

Veer or walk back.   To pay out the cable by using the windlass in gear and power. The cable cannot thus run out.

Surge.   To let the cable run out off the brake and without power.

Snub.   To brake sharply when surging.

Clear hawse. When both anchors are out and the respective cables are clear of each other.

Foul hawse. When both anchors are out and the cables are crossed or turned round each other.

Windrode. A vessel is said to be windrode when she is lying head to wind regardless of any tide that there may be.

Tiderode. A vessel is tiderode when she is lying head to tide regardless of any wind.

Leetide. Wind and tide together acting on the anchored ship. Surface water appears unbroken or calm.

Weathertide. Tide against wind. Surface water broken and choppy.

A-cock-bill. Or anchor clear to let go, means an anchor 'walked back' so that the shank is clear of the hawse-pipe and ready to let go.

Cocked anchor. An anchor is said to be cocked when it has been weighed and the shank has entered the hawse-pipe either at an angle (with a part turn in the cable) with one or both of the flukes pointing inboard and on the ship's side. If, by walking back, the anchor does not clear then a wire messenger round the flukes should be used to correct. *Do not* continue to heave in with the flukes pointing inboard.

Anchoring

Before anchoring, choose a suitable position on a large scale chart with a line of approach and tide right ahead if possible. If the tide is on one bow or the other allowance will have to be made on the approach run. Choose the anchoring position bearing in mind the vessel's draught in relation to low water depths, swinging room and length.

Note the direction of the wind, see if there are any other ships at anchor and the direction in which they lie to their cables. This will give guidance on how to position the vessel when letting go the anchor. Having chosen a position seek out a conspicuous object or light ahead of the approach line and if possible another mark abeam of the anchoring position.

With engine room and hands at stations, proceed along the approach line, losing headway as the anchoring position is neared. Be sure that the anchor is ready to let go and when the desired position is reached, either put the engines to slow astern or let the tide carry the ship back so that a little sternway has been gathered. Just before the required amount of cable is paid out put the engines ahead in order that the ship is brought up easily by the cable. Do not let the cable become bar-tight between the anchor and the hawse-pipe, because of sternway; you may break out the anchor from the ground or part the cable at the hawse-pipe.

Never drop the anchor when moving ahead over the ground, except in an emergency or when making a pre-arranged running moor. Remember that the cable will stand a tremendous strain when taut and straight, but when nipped in a hawse-pipe or around the stem, it will weaken or break.

There is no firm rule of thumb method on the amount of cable to use when anchoring that will meet all conditions. A popular guide is that the amount of cable to use should be about five times the depth. This is a very rough and haphazard guide and would only be sufficient for ideal conditions such as: (*1*) Good holding ground; (*2*) Fine weather and little tide; (*3*) Deep waters and heavy cable.

Bad holding ground is usually of rock, stone or very soft mud. Good holding ground is of sand, shingle or soft clay. The most important point to emphasize is that an anchor is most efficient when subjected to a horizontal pull along the sea bed. Consequently, sufficient cable must be used so that a bight or catenary is made between the ship and the anchor, resulting in a length of cable lying along the sea bed and exerting a horizontal pull on the crown of the anchor. It will be apparent why the heavier cable of wrought iron used on older vessels is better for anchoring than the stronger but lighter forged steel cable now widely used on the more modern ships. All these various factors should be allowed for when deciding just how much cable to use when anchoring, *eg* if anchoring in a river with a muddy bottom (bad holding ground) and a strong tide, the '5 × depth' rule may quite easily become the '8 or 9 × depth' rule.

At anchor

The ship, having been brought up, should now be left to ride to the anchor with the cable secured by the compressor or cable stopper with the brake screwed up as a preventer. If possible the cable should be secured so that the shackle is available inboard from the compressor or stopper. The anchor cable may then be easily buoyed and slipped in case of emergency.

Anchor bearings should be taken, entered in the log book and put on the chart. Convenient bearings abeam should be noted for visual checks against dragging, and a radar bearing and distance should also be taken in the event that visibility deteriorates. Watches on deck and in the engine room should be maintained as if the vessel is at sea, and officers should be particularly alert when the vessel is about to swing. Apart from the fact that the anchor may be broken out of the ground when swinging rapidly, the engines may be needed, because of other vessels at anchor or because of a lack of swinging room. At night a sure sign that the vessel is dragging will be continuous vibration noises coming from the cable between the outboard end of the hawse-pipe and the windlass. Vibrations can be felt by placing a hand on the chain.

Weighing anchor

With engines ready, the operations of heaving away should begin with the mate in charge forward. A man should be stationed in the chain locker to stow the cable as it comes inboard. Failure to stow the cable properly may result in the chain piling up until it reaches the spurling pipe, thus creating a blockage at the deck head just under the windlass. If the chain locker is too deep for this to happen, the next time the ship rolls the cable will fall over to one side of the locker and may become foul on its own parts. This will cause a blockage and will probably not be discovered until the next occasion on which the anchor is dropped.

If it becomes necessary to veer the cable or if after weighing anchor it is decided to drop the anchor again, then it is the mate's responsibility to make sure that the man stowing the cable is out of the locker before any cable is paid out. When heaving in, the mate should indicate to the skipper on the bridge the direction in which the cable leads, so that the engines and helm can be moved appropriately allowing the cable to come into the hawse-pipe without being turned around the bow or subjected to any form of strain.

Losing an anchor

If for any reason an anchor and cable are lost, the position should be buoyed. If it cannot be buoyed, accurate bearings of the position should be taken to assist in the recovery of the lost anchor. The loss should be reported to the owners and, if within the precincts of a port, to the harbour authority. Repeated and expensive attempts to recover the lost gear may be made if an accurate position is not reported.

Mooring

The mooring of a ship becomes necessary when there is a lack of swinging room. If it is assumed that a ship is to anchor where four lengths of cable are necessary but there is a lack of swinging room, she would have to be moored with one anchor leading ahead with four lengths out and the other anchor leading astern with the same length of cable. The ship would turn with the tide from one anchor to the other and pivot in one position.

Standing moor

The vessel should be brought head to the tide and if she has a right handed propeller, the port anchor be let go at the appropriate time and place. With the ship falling astern and head to the tide, eight lengths of cable should be paid out until she has been brought up. The starboard anchor should then be let go and, with the engines put ahead, it should be paid out to four lengths.

Simultaneously, the port anchor should be hove in until the vessel is riding on the port anchor and there are four lengths out to each anchor.

Running moor

Assuming the same conditions and requirements as before, the running moor is carried out by dropping the starboard anchor first and then paying out eight lengths while going ahead against the tide before dropping the port anchor. The vessel is then allowed to fall back on the tide until she is middled between the two anchors and rides to the upstream or port anchor.

If one had a choice on which moor to carry out, the standing moor should be used in preference to the running moor. The running moor requires that the lee or downstream anchor be dropped first making it necessary to render out astern double the amount of cable finally required while the ship is steamed ahead against the tide. The leeward cable can quite easily be nipped or strained when it is being snubbed out and running astern from the hawse-pipe, and may be damaged or parted if not handled very carefully.

When at anchor on either a standing or running moor, steps should be taken to ensure that the ship swings within the same arc on consecutive tides to avoid crossing the cables. Engines and helm should be used as necessary when swinging from the riding anchor to the lee anchor.

Open moor

This moor is different from those described previously in that the vessel rides to two anchors lying ahead and angled outward, one from each bow. It is used where it is known that the wind or current will come strongly from one direction and it is necessary to use two anchors.

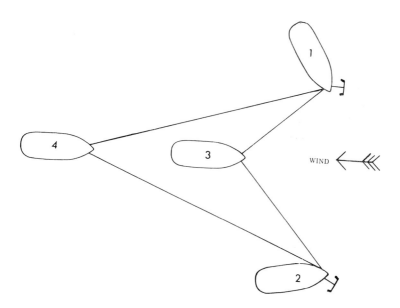

Fig 58 An open moor

33

If we assume that the wind or current comes from the north and the ship is approaching from the west, then the port anchor should be dropped with the vessel headed at a slow speed in a NE-ENE direction, so that an easterly course will be made good in the prevailing wind or current.

With the engine working easily ahead and the use of helm to maintain an easterly direction, pay out about one third or one half of the required length of cable on the port anchor, and hold on. With little or no headway, bring the ship's head up towards the wind or current and let go the starboard anchor. With the engines stopped, allow the ship to fall back and pay out the starboard cable until it equals the scope of the port cable, then pay out the required lengths on both, until properly brought up.

It will be seen from *Fig 58* that as more cable is paid out on both anchors from position 3, to position 4, the angle between the cables becomes less. The stress on the cables reduces directly with the angle of the cables at the bow so that it can be seen that two anchors, spread sufficiently to avoid fouling, will share the stress better than anchors which are spread too far apart.

Sea anchors

A sea anchor is used to lessen drift to leeward and to keep the vessel out of the trough of the sea when the engines or steering gear are out of action. When such circumstances arise, consideration should be given to anchoring the vessel by her main anchors and not by sea anchors, but if there is no danger of the ship driving ashore and the water is comparatively shallow, it may be possible to keep the vessel out of the trough by unshackling the anchor and paying out the cable until two or three lengths are dragging along the bottom. The drag on the cable should keep the ship head to sea. This method has been used with good results on numerous occasions. In deeper water, warp may be used to veer sufficient cable to the bottom in the same way.

A string of bobbins through the bow fairlead or from the fore gallows will act as a sea anchor; a trawl door may be used similarly.

Laying out an anchor to assist in refloating

The kedge anchor may be taken away from the ship by boat and will serve to move the ship from one spot to another providing she is afloat and not hard aground. The bower or 'snow' anchor will prove much more efficient in the latter case.

Having decided on which bearing to lay out the big anchor, the kedge anchor should be taken away in the boat, together with plenty of dan wire and a buoy or some pellets. The small anchor should be dropped on the bearing selected for the big anchor, but at a much greater distance from the ship. The buoy or pellets should be made fast to the dan wire in order to mark the position of the anchor and to keep some of the wire from the bottom. The boat should then return to the ship paying out the dan wire, the end of which should be passed back on board the ship and secured. In returning, the boat must make plenty of allowance for wind and tide because, with a bight of wire on the bottom, it may be difficult to reach the ship. In modern trawlers which do not have suitable boats, shore boats should be used for this work. (See *Fig 59*)

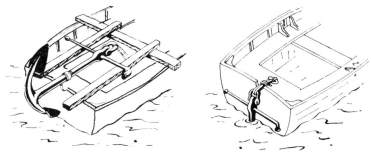

Fig 59 Light anchor stowed on the transom and over the stern

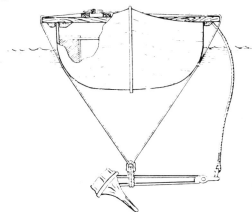

Fig 60 Heavy anchor slung beneath a boat

From now on the boat can be hauled to and fro on this wire and the use of oars should not be necessary. Thus much time and effort will be saved.

Meanwhile, the big anchor, warps, wire cables, suitable shackles, dan wire, float pellets, pound boards, spars, small line, hangers, seizing wire, hammers, spikes, chisels, saws, nails, wedges, knives, axes and all else should be prepared.

Much depends on the depth of water as to how the anchor should be carried, but in a ship which has only a single (Class C) boat it will be best, if possible, to sling the anchor under the boat either horizontally or vertically (*Fig 60*). If two boats are available the anchor may be carried between the boats (*Fig 61*). Great care is necessary in the slinging of the anchor and preparation of the gear and there must be a wire cable on the anchor with the other end buoyed with dan wire and pellets before the anchor leaves the ship. This makes recovery much easier if the anchor should accidentally be slipped.

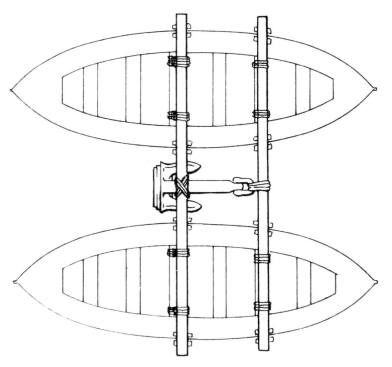

Fig 61   Heavy anchor slung between two boats

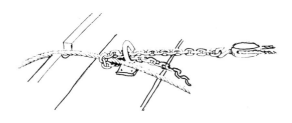

Fig 62 Check stopper stoppering a hawser in a boat

Some bower anchors are too large to be carried by a Class C boat. It may be possible to use a shore boat instead.

While the preparations are being made, the boat should be employed in laying out wire towards the spot where the anchor is to be let go.

A certain amount of warp can be coiled in the boat and some can be paid out from the ship as the boat hauls along the dan wire. When the boat has gone as far as she can in this way (and it will not be very far) the coils in her can be paid out, the end being buoyed with dan wire and pellets. There is some danger to personnel in this manoeuvre as the coils in the boat are liable to take charge unless suitably secured and the wire controlled in its run-out by means of a check stopper (*Fig 62*).

A trawler commonly carries several wires in lengths of 25 fathoms and upwards to 50 fathoms, such as the wire cables used in fishing. It will be a fairly simple matter to lay out these wires one by one, buoying each length until the next one is brought to it and shackled on.

It may seem laborious to have the boat going to and fro so many times and to shift the dan wire and pellets from length to length but in 200 yards there are only two 50-fathom lengths or four 25-fathom lengths and the job will be done safely and more quickly than if the men have to struggle with the weight of warp involved in the other method. Light loads and quick work is the best rule here.

Having laid out the wire to a distance of not less than 200 yards, the boat must now take out the big anchor.

First, a strongback must be fitted across the boat to prevent the gunwhales being squeezed in by the weight of the anchor. (See *Fig 60* on page 35) The pound board may be cut either to fit snugly inside the gunwhale or to lay across the boat and to have a notch cut in each end to accommodate the anchor sling. In this case, wedges or blocks of wood are nailed on to the strongback to fit inside the gunwhale. This latter system is recommended as being easier to fit but the wedges must be very firmly fixed and the strongback lashed securely to the thwarts so that it cannot move.

The anchor will have been lifted horizontally by its point of balance where, if there is no special provision for lifting, a good lashing and two strops will have been placed. One strop is for use with the sling round the boat described later and the second and much longer strop is for taking the whip or tackle hook. The lashing must be prevented from sliding along the shank of the anchor by passing a line from the lashing and across the crown of the anchor. If the water abreast the fore derrick is not deep enough, the anchor must be slung from the after gallows or boat's davit and if the water is not deep enough anywhere alongside, arrangements must be made to lay the anchor on the boat following the same plan as is outlined for the light anchor.

If the anchor is to be slung vertically under the boat the work will be a little easier but the depth of water alongside and all the way to the place of dropping the anchor must be checked. (See *Fig 60*).

Before the anchor is swung outboard a wire cable must be shackled to the ring and the other end buoyed with dan wire and pellets. Then, in case of accident, the anchor will not be lost. Also, the strop into which is hooked the whip or tackle to lift the anchor must be capable of being cut unless the hook can be tripped.

As the anchor is lowered to the water line, those in the boat will pass a suitable rope or wire round the boat and through the shorter strop and work it around the strongback and secure it by a suitable bend or by slip and shackle so that the anchor is slung horizontally and centrally under the boat. The tackle may then be disengaged, perhaps by cutting the strop, and the wire cable with its buoyed end passed into the boat, which is then hauled out to the spot where the anchor is to be dropped.

On its way out, the boat will arrive at the pellets marking the end of the connected wire cables already laid out. This end can be hauled up by means of the dan wire on it and can be shackled to the end of the buoyed wire cable in the boat. The cable can be paid out as the boat is hauled further out and then the sling around the boat can be slipped or chopped and the anchor will go to the bottom.

The dan wire and pellets on the last length will serve to mark the spot and make recovery easier.

Steady taut by winch and the anchor will prevent the ship from going further on shore and may pull her off when the tide serves. An anchor so used will stand more pull than two good tugs. If time permits, another anchor can be laid out similarly.

It may be possible to lay out the kedge anchor and to have on it a block through which is rove a dan wire, one end of which can be made fast to the buoyed end of the warp and the other end taken to the winch and used to haul the warp out to the kedge anchor. The boat could then take out the big anchor and one length as before, haul up the warp, shackle up, pay out and then slip the anchor.

Reference has been made to shore boats because the ship's boats may be too small to carry a large anchor in any of the methods suggested. Larger boats, suitable fishing vessels or other craft may be available on hire from near by. The terms of hire should be agreed through the stranded vessel's agents but if the ship is in any danger, immediate assistance should be obtained by the skipper.

The wire cables or warps led out from the ship may be taken to a suitably placed large rock or big tree on the other side of the river, fjord or harbour, or a special holdfast may be constructed on shore. The laying out of an anchor may thus not always be necessary.

6   Rigging and working bottom trawl gear

A distant water trawler usually carries three or four trawls, one or two fully made up and the rest in pieces. The trawl is made up of the top part and the belly and baitings, the lengtheners and the cod ends (*Fig 63*). These joined together make a full trawl. The top part is made up of the top wings, the lower wings, the bosom and the square. The belly and baitings are two bellies joined together by lacing them together down the edges to form a selvedge and the lengtheners are joined to the bellies at the narrowest end. The cod end is formed by lacing two sides of cod ends together in the same way as the bellies. This work is usually carried out ashore in a net loft.

To put a trawl out. Side trawlers

First the bobbins must be rove to the skipper's instructions to form the ground rope and then the fishing lines seized on to the beckets on the spacer bobbins and the chains of the wing bobbins. The trawl is then roped out by fastening the lower wings and bosom to the fishing line by sittings, *ie* short lengths of twine. When this is completed the floats are made fast to the headline and the hides seized on to the underside of the cod end to prevent chafe; then the cod ends are tied up and the wing lines rove and made fast. Next the trawl is shackled to the headline and tow legs, which in turn are shackled to the butterfly of each dan leno. The trawl is then ready for paying away.

Preparing to shoot the gear

The skipper places the vessel on the proper tack, and with engines stopped the trawl doors are put outboard and hung in the gallows by reeving the sling chains through the brackets and placing the chain on to the hook provided. The ground cable is rove through the kelly's eye and shackled on to the swivel piece of the dan leño bobbin.

The kelly's eye is shackled into the back strops which are them-

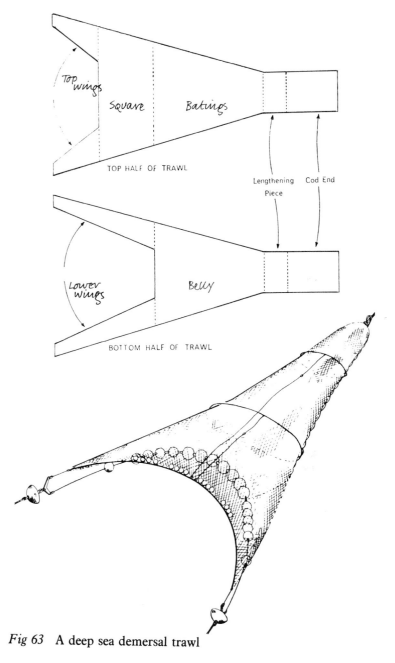

Top wings

Square   Batings

TOP HALF OF TRAWL

Lengthening Piece   Cod End

Lower wings   Belly

BOTTOM HALF OF TRAWL

Fig 63 A deep sea demersal trawl

41

selves shackled into the links provided at the back of the trawl doors. In the other end of the ground cable there is a stopper or cup which fits into the kelly's eye when the cables are paid out. To this stopper is shackled the independent wire which in turn is shackled to the flat link of the independent trawl warp.

The dan lenos are hung in the gallows by heaving on the ground cable. The dan lenos should be lifted off the deck by the gilson to enable them to be hove into the gallows easily.

The after wing and bunts are hoisted overboard and the slip wire secured in the after quarter rope strop. The cod ends and bellies are paid out next making sure that everything runs away clear. The fish tackle is put into the fore quarter rope strop and hove on until the bosom bobbins are in a position to be pushed overboard and hung by the fore quarter rope and after slip wire. The fish tackle can then be unhooked and carried clear. To enable the fore end to be put overboard the forward gilson is hooked on the wing bobbins and hove on until the fore bunt can be pushed overboard easily. The weight of the bosom, which is hanging overboard, pulls on the fore bunt and makes the operation easier and safer. When the fore gilson is unhooked and the after slip let go, the quarter ropes should be slipped only after making sure that no one is standing in the bight. The headline, which should be held up by a lashing in each quarter to make sure that the quarter ropes run clear, is then released and the trawl will be hanging in the gallows by the ground cables.

The skipper, having seen that all is clear, gives the order to lower away. The cable stopper will come to rest in the kelly's eye, the independent wire and warp will become slack and the whole weight of the gear will be on the trawl doors hanging by their chains. The independent wire should be disconnected from the warp, passed over the top of the door and secured to the brackets in such a way that it cannot get under the door when towing. The warp is connected to the door by means of the 'G' link, the weight of the door and gear is taken up by the warp so that the chains holding the doors may be released enabling the gear to be shot.

Shooting the gear

With the gear running clear from the ship, in reasonable weather conditions the engines may be put ahead with the starboard helm so that the doors may be lowered away quickly leading out to starboard.

This should be done after the vessel has gathered a little headway, with the engines stopped and swinging to starboard. The skipper, when sure that the doors and warps are clear, may then adjust his course and speed to be able to pay out the required length of warp. The warps are then put into the towing block by hooking the messenger over the fore warp, the messenger having previously been lead from the winch abaft the after gallows. When heaving, the hook will run down the fore warp, it will pick up the after warp and take both warps to the towing block. With the warps safely in the towing block the messenger may be unhooked and warps finally adjusted so that the gear is being towed evenly.

Towing the gear

When towing the gear, the skipper or officer of the watch will probably be occupied with keeping the ship on the plot and watching the compass, sounder, and the warps themselves. Nevertheless it should be remembered that the Regulations for Preventing Collisions at Sea must be strictly observed and a good look-out should be maintained at all times. Other vessels may be shooting, hauling or steaming and an adjustment to course or speed made in sufficient time may avert a collision or the fouling of one's own gear with that of another ship.

Should circumstances make it necessary to stop the vessel when towing, stern way will soon be gathered, and a hand should immediately be sent aft to report on the direction of the warps and if they are clear of the propeller before the engines are put ahead again.

A vessel towing her gear will experience no difficulty in altering course to starboard. Care should be taken when turning that the turn is not made too sharply, as the direction of the lead of the warps will become at too great an angle between the fore and aft line of the ship and the gear is likely to turn over. It will then be necessary to have it in and valuable fishing time will be lost.

When turning to port a vessel will begin the turn easily for about 30° but thereafter will turn more slowly because of the drag at the towing block on the starboard quarter.

Hauling the gear

When ready to haul the gear, speed is reduced according to weather and heading, the warps are knocked out from the towing block and the winchmen are ordered to heave in the warps simultaneously. Marks on the warps indicate when the doors are approaching the vessel and the skipper takes the necessary action as to speed and course, with regard to the weather. The trawl doors are brought up into the gallows hung off on the sling chains, the G links are unclipped and the cables hove in until the dan lenos come into the gallows, when the winch brakes are screwed down and clutches unshipped. On the longer side trawler where ground wires are commonly used, once the dan lenos are secured, the ends of the ground wires are connected to the warps fore and aft by clip links. As the warps are hove upon together, the ground wire and bobbins come up above the gunwhale and are dropped inboard.

The belly and baitings may be hauled aboard by becketting and the use of a running wire from the midship derrick or gilson block situated on the bridge. When the cod end is alongside, it is becketted and hauled aboard by using the fish tackle gear. The cod end is let go and the fish falls into the deck pounds ready for gutting and washing. The gear may now be prepared for shooting again.

The fish is properly gutted, cleaned and passed into the washer from where it is passed below to the fishroom. The mate is responsible for the proper stowage and efficient icing down of the catch.

German flying gear

German flying gear is designed to speed up the actions of hauling and shooting. Extra sheaves are fitted on top of the gallows, another on the foremast and one on the side casing. On longer side trawlers this gear is in common use.

The bunt bobbins are reduced from 20 ft to 10 ft and one $14\frac{1}{2}$ ft rubber ring piece is shackled into the 10 ft bunt. A 44 ft ground wire with a link and flat link in one end is passed through a kelly's eye, which is shackled into the lower leg of the butterfly. The ground wire is then shackled into the wing piece. The fishing line is left flying or may be made fast to a headline leg if desired. Quarter ropes are not used.

With this rig a 20 ft headline leg is required. If the headline leg length is altered, the ground wire must be adjusted accordingly. When hauling, a messenger wire with a G link in the end is passed through the sheaves on the foremast and fore gallows and another through the casing sheave and the sheave on the after gallows. When the dan lenos are hove up tight to the gallows, the G links are clipped on to the flat links on the ground wires and the messenger wires are hove on until a hook can be passed into the end of the after bunt and made fast on the after gallows. The forward messenger will then be able to heave the bobbins right inboard. The headline is brought in by the fore and aft gilsons and the trawl is hauled in the ordinary way by hand and becket.

When paying out the gear, the above procedure is followed in reverse and the gear is ready to shoot.

Coming fast

Should the gear foul an obstruction on the seabed, *ie* come fast, the wheel on a side trawler should immediately be put hard over towards the gear and the engines stopped if the ship has not lost headway and the warps are pulling out. When the warps are leading off the side, the engines may be put on dead slow ahead and the helm adjusted so that the ship does not fall on top of the gear. The fore clutch should be shipped as quickly as possible and the warps knocked out from the towing block, so that by heaving on the forward warp, both warps lead away from the ship forward of the beam. The after clutch may then be shipped, and by heaving on both warps and adjusting the helm and engines, the ship may be moved safely over the obstruction with the warps leading up and down. At no time should the warps be allowed to lead under the ship.

If the gear is not cleared when the ship is positioned above the obstruction the after warp should be unshipped and the fore warp hove on; the gear should then clear.

If, when heaving in on the fore warp, the ship's head does not come round it may be because the cable or some other part of the gear has been carried away. In such a case, great care must be taken not to foul the rudder or propeller with either of the warps. This may happen in the after gear parts when the outward pull of the door causes the after warp to lead across the ship's stern when being hove in.

Should the ship 'come fast' when towing before strong tides, heavy sea or swell, the above method of hauling should be strictly adhered to. Failure to bring the vessel's head to sea before shipping the after clutch could have disastrous results; with the ship beam on to the seas with warps fastened to the bottom the resultant loss of stability could be fatal. If in any doubt the ship should be helped round by heaving on the fore warp whilst paying out on the after warp.

Stern trawling

The basic fishing gear used in stern trawlers is similar to that used in side trawlers. The cod end, bosoms and bellies are paid out down the ramp when the vessel has a little headway. The doors are connected as in a side trawler and with a little more headway the warps are paid out simultaneously through the stern when the vessel has been brought on to her towing course. Towing blocks are not used. Hauling on a stern trawler is carried out by winching in the warps simultaneously. When the doors are hung up, the dan lenos are brought up to the gallows, messengers from the winch are made fast to the dan leno, swivels are set tight and, by heaving on the messengers and slacking the warps, the bobbins and bellies are brought inboard up the ramp. A strop placed around the bellies will serve to haul the cod end inboard into a suitable position to allow the fish to run down the hatch into the pounds on the deck below.

Demersal is the name given to those varieties of fish which live and feed close to the bottom of the sea. They may be caught by using a ground, bottom or demersal trawl and the species include cod, haddock, flatfish, berghylt, coalfish, *etc*.

Pelagic is the name given to those varieties of fish which live and feed in mid-water, *ie* herring, mackerel, sprats, *etc*. They cannot be caught by a ground trawl and therefore a pelagic or mid-water trawl has been developed. (See *Fig 64*)

'Delagic' trawls are basically mid-water trawls, the design of which incorporates features that allow the net to be fished demersally for those fish that are close to the bottom or pelagically for herring, mackerel, sprats, *etc*, without the need to change from one fishing mode to the other.

The assessment of a fishing situation may require a skipper to change over from one mode of fishing to another, that is, from bottom to mid-water or vice-versa. This would normally present the skipper and crew with some difficulties such as handling and stowing one set of gear and nets, substituting the other gear and nets, all having to be done in the confined space of a trawl deck. Many men are needed to perform this task and in the change over fishing time would be lost.

The 'Delagic' gear, (designed by the White Fish Authority to facilitate changing from demersal to pelagic fishing quickly) is aimed at a shoal of fish, so it may be raised quickly and it is for this reason that superkrub otter boards are used. These boards are $2 - 2\frac{1}{2}$ times as

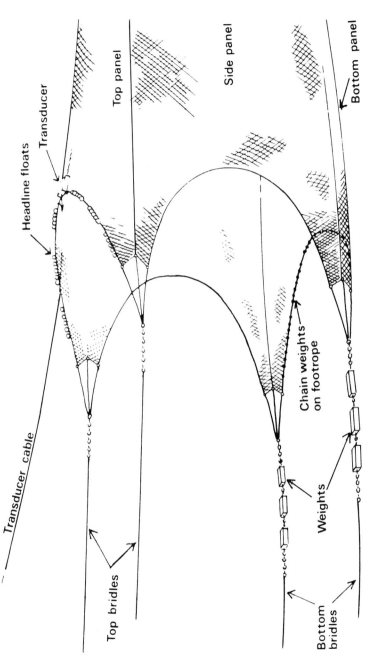

Headline floats

Transducer

Top panel

Side panel

Bottom panel

Transducer cable

Chain weights
on footrope

Weights

Top bridles

Bottom
bridles

Fig 64   Mouth of a pelagic trawl

47

high as they are wide and are cambered. They are rigged to tilt so that their spreading force has a relatively large lift component compared with bottom running boards. When speed is increased this lift component raises the gear more quickly. Because of their height to width ratio, they become very unstable if they touch the bottom and may be badly damaged. 'Delagic' gear is therefore rigged to keep the super-krub boards well clear of the bottom when the net is used demersally.

When using this type of gear it is important to know the vertical position of the net in the water. This information is vital when operating 'Delagic' gear close to or on the bottom, therefore reliable netsonde depth indicator equipment is essential.

Like most mid-water nets 'Delagic' trawls are very large compared with normal white fish nets and 'bang up' methods of hauling, as described at the beginning of this chapter, are not feasible. Usually a power block or net drum is required to handle the nets.

7 Seine net fishing

There are two forms of seine net fishing. In principle, the first type is similar to trawling or towing the fishing gear astern, except that it may be considered a more delicate and refined form of fishing compared to the normal stern or side trawling operation of the longer vessel. The second type, known as purse seining, is quite different to tow seining and does not involve the dragging of gear from the stern.

Seining by trawl

Seining by trawl may be carried out in several forms which differ by having various designs of net for use in catching different species of fish. Flat fish are either caught on the bottom or very close to it and a considerable spread of the wings is necessary. Normally the plaice seine does not use a ground rope but may have weights attached to the footrope.

The haddock gear has a greater height of net and may be regarded as the best type for all round seining, being capable of catching higher swimming species as well as flatfish. A ground rope when used has shorter wings and a very much wider mouth than the plaice seine and is a feature of the haddock seine net.

The deep seine gear, which is used mainly for catching cod, haddock or whiting, requires a greater head line height, which is gained by having a centre rope attached to and running along the middle of the wings and bag to the cod end. Apart from this modification, the deep seine is more or less the same as the haddock seine except that it has bridles or sweeps of 10 fathoms or more in length between the wing ends and the dan lenos.

The wing trawl, developed in recent years in order to catch cod, haddock or whiting, has become established as reliable and efficient gear. It is much lighter than the conventional otter trawl but heavier than a similar sized deep seine net. Like the deep seine, sweeps or bridles are used between the wing ends and spreader poles.

Purse seining

Purse seining is a completely different method of fish catching because it does not involve the towing of the fishing gear from astern.

As the name implies, purse seining requires that a net be put over the side in such a manner that it becomes a circular purse or bag to contain the fish.

A buoy is put out from aft to which is attached the head line and the bottom line. The net is mainly rectangular in shape, the upper edge rope floats and the bottom edge rope sinks as the net is paid out. Attached to the bottom edge line by beckets are metal rings through which the purse line is rove. The vessel steams ahead after setting down the buoy, in such a manner as to describe a circle, paying out the net until the circle is completed by the time the buoy has been reached. The result is a net hanging vertically downwards and forming a circular or cylindrical shape. The upper edge lines are brought on board and the purse lines are taken to the pursing gallow and are hove upon until a purse is formed. (See *Fig 65*)

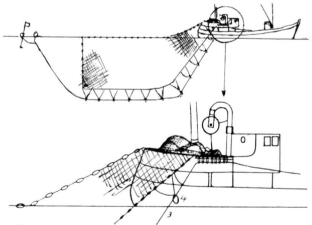

Fig 65 Shooting, pursing, hauling and brailing the purse seine.
(a) The shooting operation, showing (i) the buoy, (ii) the upper edge rope shackled to the buoy as well as the purse line, (iii) running through the rings and (iv) the net flowing off the upper dory deck.

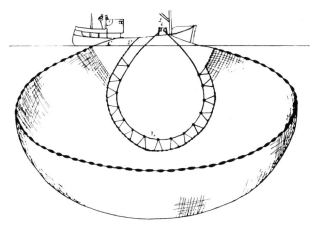

(b) The pursing operation showing (i) the retrieving ropes of the wing, (ii) the pursing gallow and (iii) the purse line.

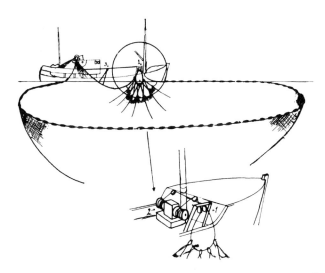

(c) The hauling operation, showing (i) the pursing gallow, (ii) the pursing winch and (iii) the rings unshackled from the purse line and reshackled on a leading line towards the powerblock.

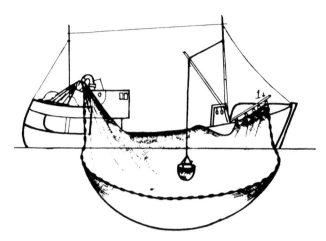

(d) The brailing operation, showing (i) the boom on which the breast is hooked and general arrangement of brailing. (*From Modern Fishing Gear of the World 2, published by Fishing News Books Ltd*).

When the purse has been formed and the bottom edge rope is alongside, the upper edge line and net are hauled in until a compact purse has been formed alongside the vessel, with the fish concentrated within. The illustration shows a power block being used for this operation. The fish may now be brought on board by using a derrick or boom and a basket which is dipped into the net until empty.

8   Care of the fish

Each one of the crew must endeavour to ensure that the fish is landed in the best condition. A glance at the voyage analysis will show the difference in price between fish of the best quality and poor fish. A big difference in price generally means that there has been a marked difference in quality. Much of this price difference can be avoided by taking proper care of the fish from the moment it comes on board.

When the ship is rolling heavily the deck boards should be shipped up two high across and down the middle of the fish pound to prevent the fish from sliding from one side of the pound to the other. If these boards are only one high, the roll sets the fish working or sliding to and fro. The result is that the fish looks five or six days old before it reaches the fishroom. Many a good haul of fish has been ruined because this precaution was not taken.

Another reason why the fish should be prevented from sliding about is that the crew have great difficulty in standing among fish on the move and this very much slows down the operation of gutting, thus giving the fish even more time in which to become chafed and soft and eventually unsaleable.

When gutting, only the stomach cavity is cut and not right down into the flesh. Knives should be kept sharp so that the fish is not torn. The flaps of the fish should not be broken, especially haddock, as mutilated fish are practically unsaleable.

The fish pound must be well hosed down before the cod end is emptied on to the deck. Fish dropped on deck among the guts and offal of the previous haul is immediately contaminated and has taken its first step to the fish meal factory.

The washing of fish is a most important feature. A plentiful supply of water entering the washer at considerable force is essential in order to avoid the entry of dirty fish to the fishroom. The boatswain must ensure that the water supply is sufficient at all times and that only well washed fish goes down the hatch.

Before taking any fish below, the fishroom pounds should be washed out again to ensure their thorough cleanliness. Care should be taken to remove all slime from any surface liable to come in contact with the fish, especially above and below the battens. The slush wells must be disinfected with chloride of lime or some other recommended disinfectant, the odour of which cannot be absorbed by the fish, and be thoroughly cleared of any small pieces of wood, brush bristles or any matter that may stop up the holes in the rose or strum boxes. The space under the fishroom floor must be kept sweet and clean by pouring some buckets of disinfectant, similar to that used in the slushwell, down the deck pumps on the outward passage and allowing the mixture to swill about under the floor helped by a certain amount of clean sea water. The whole area should be pumped dry before taking any fish below and kept dry until the cleansing operation on the following trip. Slush wells are also found in ships with double-bottom tanks.

Each fishroom pound is given a good 'bottom' of ice, at least one board, *ie* about nine inches deep, just before taking the fish into it. The ice will not then solidify. If the bottoms are made too soon they become very hard and the first layer of fish in the pound becomes badly squashed.

Plenty of ice must be distributed evenly among the fish and along the woodwork and against the ship's side to ensure that the fish does not come in contact with the wood, which must always be suspected of harbouring bacteria. Always look after the first caught fish, as if the trip was going to be of long duration no matter how promising the prospect of a short trip may appear.

Never go too far above the battens before putting the shelves on or squashed fish will be the result. Never miss a shelf no matter how hard pressed one appears to be for time.

Avoid having more than one fishroom hatch off at a time, especially during the summer months when the temperature of the outside air is considerably higher than that of the fishroom.

Plaice have a special tendency to slide about when they have been put down in the fishroom. This starts the formation of a frothy slime, which causes the plaice to slide even more and the whole pound of fish could be ruined. To prevent this the pound should be halved by shipping up the fore and aft boards dividing the 'front half' from the 'back half' and putting a good layer of ice on top of the fish. On top of this ice one or two fishroom boards should be laid flat fore and aft in each half and held firmly in position by wedging the ends. Stand on the boards when knocking in the wedges and give alternate knocks on the board and the wedge and so press the board down onto the fish and prevent any possibility of it working. The fishroom should never be left without taking this precaution when fishing on plaice.

Freezer trawlers

The freezing of fish is not a magical process that turns bad fish into good. The same care must be used in dealing with fish as is used in fresh fish trawlers, that is, they must be properly gutted and well washed. The fish should then be taken to the freezers as quickly as possible and be frozen. A general rule is that fish should be frozen for about three and a quarter hours, but this can vary a little depending on the type of freezer and the surrounding, or 'ambient', temperature.

Freezers commonly used for whole fish are called vertical plate freezers, as opposed to horizontal plate freezers which are used for fillets.

A very important aspect of freezing is that before the fish go into the plate freezers they should be sorted for size and type. Once the block of fish is frozen it is impossible to separate the fish from the block. If fish are mixed, the frozen block is an unsaleable product and causes loss.

Once frozen, the blocks of sized and typed fish must be carefully labelled with the labels supplied by the company. This assists in the proper sorting of the fish during the landing operation. Without correct labelling it is almost impossible for the people landing the fish to distinguish one type from another.

A second important aspect in a freezer trawler is that, when the blocks are put into the fish room, they should be properly stowed and boarded up. Failure to do this may allow the blocks to slide about, damaging the fish and parts of the fish room and fittings and possibly causing injury to personnel.

Part II Safety and survival at sea

9 Distress and rescue procedures

The International Regulations for Preventing Collisions at Sea, 1972, Annex IV states:

(1) The following signals, used or exhibited either together or separately, indicate distress and need of assistance:

(a) a gun or other explosive signal fired at intervals of about a minute;

(b) a continuous sounding with any fog-signalling apparatus;

(c) rockets or shells, throwing red stars fired one at a time at short intervals;

(d) a signal made by radiotelegraphy or by any other signalling method consisting of the group . . . — — — . . . (SOS) in the Morse Code;

(e) a signal made by radiotelephony consisting of the spoken word 'Mayday';

(f) the International Code Signal of distress indicated by N.C.;

(g) a signal consisting of a square flag having above or below it a ball or anything resembling a ball;

(h) flames on the vessel (as from a burning tar barrel, oil barrel, etc);

(i) a rocket parachute flare or a hand flare showing a red light;

(j) a smoke signal giving off orange-coloured smoke;

(k) slowly and repeatedly raising and lowering arms outstretched to each side;

(l) the radiotelegraph alarm signal;

(m)the radiotelephone alarm signal;

(n) signals transmitted by emergency position-indicating beacons.

(2) The use or exhibition of any of the foregoing signals except for the purpose of indicating distress and need of assistance and the use of other signals which may be confused with any of the above signals is prohibited.

(3) Attention is drawn to the relevant sections of the International Code of Signals, the Merchant Ship Search and Rescue Manual

and the following signals:

(*a*) a piece of orange-coloured canvas with either a black square and circle or other appropriate symbol (for identification from the air);

(*b*) a dye marker.

Obligations and responsibilities

The International Convention for the Safety of Life at Sea (1960) states that a master or skipper of a ship at sea receiving a signal from any source that a ship or aircraft is in distress is bound to proceed with all speed to the assistance of the persons in distress, informing them if possible that he is doing so. If he is unable or, in the special circumstances of the case, considers it unnecessary to proceed to their assistance, he must enter in the log book the reason for failing to proceed to the assistance of those in distress.

The master of a ship in distress, after consultation, so far as may be possible, with the masters of the ships which answer his call for assistance, has the right to requisition such one or more of those ships as he considers best able to render assistance. It shall be the duty of the master or masters of the ship or ships requisitioned to comply with the requisition by continuing to proceed with all speed to the assistance of those in distress.

The master or skipper shall be released from the obligation imposed in the first paragraph, when he learns that one or more ships other than his own have been requisitioned and are complying with the requisition.

These are briefly the obligations and duties imposed on those in charge of ships at sea by the International Convention for Safety of Life at Sea (1960). Skippers of fishing vessels on seeing or hearing any of the signals set out at the beginning of this chapter should take the appropriate action if it is possible to do so. A full description of search and rescue procedures is given in the IMCO publication *Merchant Ship Search and Rescue Manual*. (MERSAR)

General arrangements for search and rescue (SAR)

In general, distress incidents fall into two main categories:

(*1*) Coastal — in which some or all of the following may be available to assist: ships, aircraft, helicopters and shore-based life-saving facilities;

(2) Ocean — in which ships and long range aircraft may be available and in the more remote areas, only ships may be available.

To supplement the efforts of the ships in the area of a vessel in distress there is an extensive international SAR organisation. The SAR measures vary from country to country but most maritime nations have coast radio stations which always play an important part by guarding the international distress frequencies.

Distress frequencies and procedures

The radio watch on the international distress frequencies which ships must keep when at sea is one of the most important factors in the arrangements for the rescue of those in distress at sea. Since these arrangements must often fail unless it is possible for ships to alert each other or to alert or be alerted by shore stations for distress action, every ship should make its contribution to safety by keeping watch on one or other of these distress frequencies for as long as practicable whether or not required to do so by regulation.

Coast radio stations play an important part in rescue work by maintaining constant watch on the distress frequencies so that in the event of a distress signal being heard, they can not only alert other ships in the vicinity but also the proper shore authorities, who can bring the SAR services into action as required.

In the United Kingdom there are eleven coast radio stations, all of which keep watch on 500 kHz, 2182 kHz and Channel 16 VHF, except for Oban which watches on 2182 kHz only. Additionally, in Ireland there are two stations, Malin Head and Valentia, which watch on 500 kHz and 2182 kHz only. All of these stations keep a continuous watch, and all of the British coastal radio stations except Oban keep a continuous watch on VHF Channel 16.

All trawlers of 12 metres or more in length registered in the UK are required to carry radio telephony equipment and if they proceed outside of the area prescribed in Schedule 2 of the 1974 (Fishing Vessels) Radio Rules they have to carry radio telegraphy. It is also a requirement that a continuous watch be kept; this is usually carried out by having the receiver switched through to a loudspeaker in the wheelhouse, so that the watchkeeping officer and his men may listen on the distress frequency when the radio officer is off duty.

HM Coastguard maintains a continuous visual watch and also radio listening watch on 2182 kHz and VHF (Channel 16) at 52 stations, 28 of which are designated as rescue headquarters.

Procedure when sending a radio distress or urgency signal

All fishing vessels whether they are fitted with radio telegraphy or radio telephony are fitted with an automatic alarm signalling device.

The radio telegraph alarm signal, which consists of 12 dashes sent in one minute by an automatic keying device, activates auto-alarms on other ships within range and it should be followed by the radio telegraph distress signal which consists of: the distress signal, SOS, sent three times; then word DE followed by the call sign of the ship sent three times. If circumstances permit, an interval of two minutes should be allowed to elapse to enable operators to reach their apparatus and bring it into operation before sending the distress message.

The radio telephone alarm signal is also intended to give preliminary warning to other ships and coast stations either aurally or by activation of radio telephone auto-alarms. It consists of two tones transmitted alternately over a period of at least 30 seconds. The radio telephone distress signal consists of the word 'Mayday' spoken three times, followed by the words, 'This is', followed by the name of the ship, repeated three times.

On hearing either of these two distress signals being transmitted by W/T or R/T all stations must cease all transmissions capable of interfering with the distress call or associated messages, and must listen on the frequency used for the distress call.

Distress calls should not be addressed to a particular station but should be repeated with discretion until the distress message can be sent. The distress message consists of the distress call, followed by the name of the ship in distress and information concerning her position, the nature of the distress and the kind of assistance required. It is important that the position of the vessel be given in terms of latitude and longitude or if aground by giving a clear geographical indication, *ie* two miles north of Flamborough Head. All relevant information such as weather, abandonment, *etc,* should also be included in the distress message.

In radio telephone ships, a card of instructions giving a clear summary of radio telephone distress procedure must be displayed in full view of the R/T operating position. The distress signals described above indicate that a ship is threatened by grave and imminent danger and requests immediate assistance.

Urgency signals

The radio telegraphy urgency signal ($-$ . . $-$ / $-$ . . $-$ / $-$ . . $-$) repeated three times and the radio telephone urgency signal, which consists of the group of words 'Pan Pan', repeated three times, are provided for use in cases in which a ship making a call has a very urgent message to transmit concerning the safety of the ship or some person on board or within sight but it does not necessarily imply that the ship is in imminent danger or requires immediate assistance. The call has immediate priority over all other communications except distress calls and it should be used in all cases in which the sending out of an SOS and Mayday signal is not justified. The urgency signal and message must, where practicable, be addressed to a specific station, *ie* to the nearest coast radio station or to another ship known to be in the vicinity. The urgency signal may also be used when the master or skipper of a ship desires to issue a warning that circumstances are such that it may become necessary for him to send out a distress signal at a later stage but in such a case the signal need not be sent to a specific station. If precautionary action ceases to be necessary, the message should be cancelled at once.

Safety signal

The spoken word 'Securite' (pronounced say-cure-e-tay) repeated three times indicates that the station is about to transmit a message concerning the safety of navigation or giving important meteorological warnings.

A ship in distress should always transmit the appropriate alarm signal on 500 kHz or 2182 kHz followed by the distress message. It may be transmitted on any frequency available on which attention might be attracted, such as an inter-ship frequency which may be in use in local areas. Before changing frequency however, adequate time should be allowed for reply.

In certain cases, depending on location, it may be helpful to transmit the distress call and message on VHF Channel 16 (156.8 MHz), *eg* in estuaries, when close to coast radio stations, or when in company of other ships where it is known that VHF watch is kept.

Any message which you hear prefixed by one of the following words concerns safety:

Mayday   Pan Pan   Securite (pronounced *say-cure-e-tay*)

If you hear these words, pay attention to the message, call the skipper:

Mayday
(Distress)
Indicates that a ship or aircraft is threatened by immediate danger and requests immediate assistance.

Pan Pan
(Urgency)
indicates that the calling station has a very urgent message to transmit concerning the safety of a ship, aircraft or of a person.

Securite
(Safety)
indicates that the station is about to transmit a message concerning the safety of navigation or giving important meteorological warnings.

Silence periods

On the distress frequencies of 500 kHz, 2182 kHz and VHF channel 16 the following silence periods have been set aside during which times only distress, urgency and safety calls should be made. The silence periods leave the frequencies clear for emergency transmissions and vessels on passage and fishing should observe strict radio silence at these times. Ships in distress, survivors in liferafts, *etc* should, if possible, use these silence periods to transmit their calls and so make sure that they have been heard. Silence periods are of three minutes duration and begin:

Radio telegraphy silence period: At 15 mins and 45 mins past each hour, GMT

Radio telephony and *VHF silence period:* At each hour and half hour, GMT

Direction finding and homing

Subsequent to the transmission of the distress message sent on 500 kHz (W/T), two dashes of ten to fifteen seconds duration should be transmitted followed by the call sign to enable coast radio stations and other vessels to take D/F bearings. This transmission to be repeated at regular intervals.

In cases where 2182 kHz (R/T) is used, similar action should be taken, using a continued repetition of the call sign or name of ship or a long numerical count in place of the two long dashes mentioned in the previous paragraph.

Portable radio equipment which may be carried on fishing vessels for use in liferafts and capable of transmission and reception on 2182 kHz should be used by survivors in liferafts, preferably during the silence periods and so that SAR craft can home on the signal. If circumstances change and assistance is no longer required distress and urgency messages should always be cancelled as soon as possible.

Action by assisting ships

A ship may receive by radio an alarm and/or distress signal either directly or by relay from a ship or aircraft in distress, by a signal emitted by an emergency position indicator radio beacon (EPIRB), or by a visual or sound signal.

The immediate action to be taken on receipt of the message, whether received by radio, visually or by sound, would be to acknowledge receipt and if appropriate re-transmit the distress message. If the distressed vessel is seen or heard — proceed to the vessel. If the signal has been received by radio — try to take D/F bearings of the distress message, give your identity, position and ETA. Maintain a continuous watch on the distress frequency in use, operate the radar and, if in the vicinity of the distress, post extra lookouts and maintain VHF watch on channel 16. Repeat the distress call on both frequencies, 500 kHz and 2182 kHz, if you are able to for the benefit of other stations.

While proceeding to the area, plot the position course and speed of any other assisting vessels. If it appears that you may be one of the first ships on the scene, try to construct an accurate picture of the circumstances attending the casualty. The important information needed is weather, wind, sea, swell, visibility, *etc*, time of abandonment, number of crew on board, injuries, number of survival craft *etc*.

When on route to the distressed vessel prepare insofar as you are able some of the following which may be considered necessary: towing gear, line throwing apparatus, ships side lines, scramble nets, heaving lines, rope ladders, liferaft, derrick and runner, and any medical preparations which survivors may need.

Action by search and rescue (SAR)

HM Coastguard, a life saving service, is the authority responsible for initiating and co-ordinating all search and rescue measures for vessels or persons. As previously stated, there are coast radio stations strategically placed around the coast of the United Kingdom. These stations on receipt of a distress message will communicate the distress message to HM Coastguard. The Coastguard may itself receive a distress message but, no matter how it is received, it organises and co-ordinates SAR.

The Coastguard has facilities which include RNLI offshore and inshore boats, fixed wing aircraft and helicopters, civil helicopters and its own cliff rescue/breeches buoy equipment. Additionally, it may call on foreign SAR facilities.

Use of aircraft in assisting ships

RAF fixed wing aircraft used on SAR duties usually carry droppable survival equipment and pyrotechnics. These aircraft may be able to assist a ship in distress by:

(1) Locating her when her position is in doubt and informing the shore authorities so that ships in the vicinity going to her assistance may be given her precise position.

(2) Guiding surface craft to her position or, if the ship has been abandoned, to survivors in lifeboats, liferafts or in the sea.

(3) Keeping the casualty under observation.

(4) Marking a position by marine marker, smoke float, or flame float and illuminating an area to assist rescue operations.

(5) Dropping survival equipment.

The droppable survival equipment carried by RAF SAR aircraft is a sea-rescue apparatus consisting of three cylindrical containers connected in series by long orange coloured buoyant ropes to facilitate recovery. The longest container carries a liferaft which can take nine persons; it is designed to inflate automatically on striking the water. The other containers carry supplies. The overall length of the apparatus on the water is about 60 yards and the middle of the three containers is the liferaft. Additional liferafts may be dropped singly or in pairs.

The pilot always endeavours to drop the equipment down wind of survivors so that the equipment and survivors will drift together, but it may be necessary for survivors already in a liferaft or dinghy to trip the sea anchor or empty water ballast pockets to accelerate their drift towards the buoyant lines. On reaching the buoyant line survivors should haul in the rescue gear.

Outer containers should be discarded by sinking when emptied. The contents should be secured in case of loss in rough seas and should not be unpacked until required for use. Spare polythene containers are provided for storage purposes.

When a number of aircraft is engaged on a search for a casualty at sea, the procedure followed is to search an area which has been calculated to include the most probable position of the incident, allowing for any movement due to drift during the period of search.

Aircraft may be employed to search at night for shipping known to be overdue, or for survivors in liferafts or lifeboats. Unless distressed personnel are able and know how to indicate their position to the aircraft, the search may be valueless and could result in failure to locate survivors and transfer of the search to other areas. The aircraft will fly through the search area at between three and five thousand feet, or below cloud, firing a green Very cartridge approximately every five minutes. When a green flare is sighted it is most important that the following action is taken:

(*1*) Wait for the glare of the green flare to die out.

(*2*) Fire one *red* flare.

(*3*) Fire another red flare after about 20 seconds (this enables the aircraft to line up on your bearing).

(*4*) Fire a third red flare when the aircraft is overhead, or if it appears to be going badly off course.

Points to note:

(*1*) Each liferaft/lifeboat must carry at least three red flares.

(*2*) If the aircraft has been diverted to the search from another task it may fire flares of another colour (except red) — reply as above.

(*3*) If all else fails, use any means at your disposal to attract attention.

Use of helicopters in assisting ships

Helicopters based ashore in the United Kingdom and in HM ships at sea may operate from time to time with fishing vessels or merchant ships. These operations can be hazardous unless the following safety precautions are taken:

(1) The ship must be on a steady course giving minimum ship motion with the relative wind from about 30° on the port bow. If this is not possible the ship should remain stationary head to wind or follow the instructions from the helicopter crew.

(2) An indication of relative wind direction should be given. Flags or pennants are suitable for this purpose. Smoke from a galley funnel may also give an indication of the wind but in all cases where any funnel is making exhaust the wind must be at least two points on the bow.

(3) Clear as large an area of deck as possible and mark the area with a large letter H in white. Whip or wire aerials in and around the area should be removed if possible.

(4) All loose articles must be securely lashed down or removed from the transfer area. The downwash from the helicopter's rotor will easily lift unsecured covers, tarpaulins, hoses, rope, gash, *etc*, thereby presenting a severe flying hazard. Even small pieces of paper in a helicopter engine can cause a helicopter to crash.

(5) If a clear area cannot be provided, personnel can be lifted from a boat or liferaft towed astern on a long painter.

(6) On no account must the helicopter winch wire or load be allowed to foul any part of the ship or rigging. In the event of a load or the winch wire becoming snagged, the helicopter crew will cut the wire.

(7) The winch wire should be handled only by personnel wearing rubber gloves. A helicopter can build up a charge of static electricity which, if discharged through a person handling the winch wire, can kill or cause severe injury. The helicopter crew will normally discharge the static electricity by dipping the winch wire into the sea, or by allowing the hook to touch the ship's deck, prior to beginning the operation.

(8) The helicopter will approach the ship from astern heading into the relative wind and can lower on to or lift from the clear area (or boat towed astern). The maximum length of winch wire is about 50 ft (Sea King's 240 ft). The helicopter must keep clear of any obstruction such as masts since any contact with them by either the main or tail rotor would be disastrous for the helicopter.

(9) When being landed from the helicopter the instructions given by the helicopter crew must be obeyed as there is a risk of fatal injury from the tail rotor which, due to its high speed of rotation, is difficult to see.

Use of helicopters, rescue, medical evacuation

Whenever possible, and if time allows, all the preceding safety precautions should be taken. However, in a distress situation it may not be possible to meet all the requirements. Under such circumstances the operation may necessarily be slower, but it should be borne in mind that helicopters have operational limitations and should not be delayed at the scene of the rescue. Cases have arisen where the rescue has been hampered by survivors trying to take personal belongings with them. In distress situations, transfers are limited to personnel only.

The types of helicopters used for SAR duties in the United Kingdom are usually either Whirlwind and Wessex. The Whirlwind can carry up to three survivors and the Wessex up to seven. Helicopter rescue is not normally undertaken over the sea at night, or when the wind speed exceeds 45 knots. However, Sea King helicopters could be used over longer ranges up to about 200 miles and at night. They have a capacity for carrying 12 survivors, but both range and capacity can be increased under certain circumstances at the discretion of the operator. When a distress message is received either visually or by radio from a ship in distress, steps taken by the rescue authorities may include the despatching of a helicopter to assist in the rescue.

Once the helicopter has become airborne, the speed with which it locates the ship and the effectiveness of its work depends to a large extent on the co-operation of the ship itself. From the air, especially if there is a lot of shipping in the area, it is very difficult for a helicopter pilot to find the particular ship he is looking for, unless that ship uses a distinctive distress signal which can be clearly seen. The orange coloured smoke signal carried in liferafts, a well-trained Aldis lamp and the use of the heliograph in bright sunlight could be used. The use of these signals will save valuable time in locating the casualty.

It is essential that the ship's position be given accurately if the original distress call has been made by radio, along with information on type of ship and colour of hull, if time allows.

Helicopters are well practised in rescuing survivors from either the deck or the sea and two methods are employed:

(1) The survivor, whether on deck or in the water, is rescued by means of a strop. Whenever possible a crewman is lowered from the helicopter, together with a strop which is secured around the survivor's back and chest, and both are winched up. On occasions

it may be necessary for the survivor to position the strop himself and give the thumbs up sign when ready to be hoisted.

(2) If a survivor is injured to the extent that a strop cannot be used a crewman is lowered with a stretcher from the helicopter. The injured man can be secured in the stretcher and hoisted up. If he is already in a Neil Robertson type stretcher, this can be lifted into the helicopter or placed in the rigid framed stretcher belonging to the helicopter.

The helicopter pilot and crewmen are professionals in these methods of rescue and well intentioned assistance from either the survivor himself or third parties in securing survivors invariably results in delays. The deck party should therefore remain stationary and allow the helicopter to move to them.

Designated SAR helicopters can communicate with lifeboats on VHF on the marine distress band 156.8 MHz (Channel 16). They normally have no MF communication equipment.

Lifeboats

The RNLI, a voluntary organisation which is organised for the sole purpose of saving life at sea, has 135 offshore lifeboat stations strategically situated around the coasts of the United Kingdom and the Republic of Ireland. Each of these lifeboats can reach a casualty up to 30 miles offshore within four hours of being launched. In addition they have a minimum search capability of four hours. Crews and boats are normally available at all times (day and night) throughout the year. Additionally the RNLI have about 120 inshore lifeboats, which are small, fast, inshore rescue craft. The lifeboat is another facility which is made available to HM Coastguard, who is responsible for initiating and co-ordinating SAR operations.

All lifeboats are fitted with VHF radio and MF R/T (medium frequency directional finding) equipment. Radar is installed in about 100 lifeboats, with D/F equipment covering 2182 kHz in nearly all offshore lifeboats. It is imperative to give an accurate position when sending a distress or urgency message. Not only will the lifeboat reach the distress scene more quickly, but the steaming range will be reduced if extra ground is covered by having to look for a casualty which has been given an inaccurate position.

Wave-quelling oils

There is little doubt that oils, when properly used, are very effective wave quelling agents. However, when survivors are likely to be in the water, the pumping of oil should only be carried out when absolutely necessary and then the greatest of care should be taken.

Experience has shown that vegetable and animal oils, including fish oils, are the most suitable oils to use as quelling agents and are the least harmful to men in the water. If none of the former oils are available, lubricating oils should be used. Fuel oil should never be used unless absolutely unavoidable and then only in small quantities. Tests have shown that 200 litres of lubricating oil discharged slowly to leeward, through a rubber hose with an outlet just above the sea, while the ship proceeds at slow speed can be an effective agent for quelling seas over an area of at least 4,500 square metres.

Position reporting

All that has been written so far concerning distress situations, has relied on a vessel requiring assistance being able to send a distress message by means of a visual or radio signal. Because of the international watch kept on radio distress frequencies by ship and shore stations there is a high probability that distress signals would be heard and relayed. Positive and accurate information in the form of a distress call from a ship should therefore be precise and reliable.

However there have been occasions where a sudden disaster onboard a ship at sea has prevented the sending of a distress message. In such cases a long time may elapse before the alarm is raised because no one is aware of the incident, and no action is taken. In order to reduce the time lag in such situations a position reporting system has been evolved.

All British owned fishing vessels of 80 ft length and over, and many smaller vessels, are required by their owners to operate a daily reporting system. The skippers report their daily position at an arranged time via an appropriate UK or foreign radio station. The purpose of the procedure is to enable search and rescue authorities to be alerted as soon as possible should a regular contact fail to be made and to give them an approximate initial datum position if a search and rescue operation has to be initiated.

It cannot be stressed too strongly that the operation of the scheme depends on the fishing vessels regularly reporting their positions, and the owners or their representatives ashore promptly informing HM Coastguard when they do not receive a report. The system undoubtedly involves a risk of unnecessary searches being made because of radio equipment failure; delay due to atmospheric conditions in a particular area from where a ship is transmitting; long delays at busy radio stations, and occasionally by the responsible person on the fishing vessel omitting to send the routine daily report.

In the case of radio failure, it is vitally important that the vessel concerned:

(1) If fishing in company, requests another vessel to report, and continues to do so. Uses any other means possible to send in a report.

(2) If unable to act as above, and radio repairs cannot be effected on board, proceed to the nearest port for repairs and report from ashore.

Failure to send in a daily report can cause worry and distress to the family of crew members and search and rescue operations may be initiated unnecessarily. Position reporting is an instrument for search and rescue, therefore, skippers should make full use of position reporting facilities wherever they exist. They should set up a daily routine system of position reporting, subject to checking, for all occasions when at sea, whether fishing or steaming to or from fishing grounds.

'Open line' for fishing vessels – UK code of operations

The Code of Operations introduced by the UK Board of Trade on April 1st 1979 provides a listening-watch/communications service for fishing vessels that would otherwise have no organized reporting procedure.

The scheme is designed to provide greater safety for small boats and to reduce the number that simply 'disappear' each year.

1 Objective. To provide a special listening watch and communications in the interests of fishing vessel safety.

NB Distress (MAYDAY) and urgency (PAN) calls requiring immediate assistance should continue to be made on 2182 kHz.

2 Frequencies: calling and answering instructions. (a) Vessel should listen on 1792 kHz before calling. (b) Call Coast Radio Station on 2381 kHz, giving name of vessel and call sign or number if there are other vessels with a similar name. (c) Coast Radio Station will reply on 1792 kHz.

Note: During distress operations other ships may be using 2381 kHz but this does not change these arrangements.

3 Starting date. The open line will be available between 1700–0900 hours every night, commencing on the night of 1/2 April 1979.

4 Coast Radio Stations (CRS). Wick, Stonehaven, and Oban will operate the scheme in Scotland.

5 Method of Operation. Each CRS taking part in the scheme will provide one radio officer during the overnight period to listen for calls from fishing vessels. This listening watch, together with any necessary action arising from the calls received, will be his only task, except for the Oban officer who will also be listening on 2182 kHz.

(A) Safety calls. One of the two major objectives of the channel is to facilitate the transmission of messages to the shore, which, although *not* calling for *immediate assistance* to the vessel, are concerned, for example, with the need to obtain early advice on particular problems or to warn the shore of possible difficulties developing at sea.

The types of call that may be made under this heading are those that fall under the broad heading of 'safety'. The following examples are illustrative:

(i) Mechanical problems. A skipper might wish to seek advice from the shore about problems with engine or steering gear. In this case the CRS would put the skipper in contact with the appropriate person ashore and would log the incident as well as reporting the matter to the Coastguard for information.

(ii) Bad weather. Skippers may wish to report to the CRS when their vessels are experiencing conditions of force 8 or more. Again this information would be logged and reported to the Coastguard.

(iii) 'Good neighbour call'. Skippers should report to the CRS if a fellow-skipper fishing in the same area fails to be sighted or to make radio contact when this could be expected. In these circumstances, the CRS would take steps to make contact with the vessel and would notify the Coastguard.

It is *most important* that skippers making calls as in the examples above should arrange with the CRS to call again at a pre-arranged time or times in order to confirm that the reported difficulties have been satisfactorily resolved, or that the bad weather has abated. If these calls fall due outside the overnight watch period they should continue to be made on 2381 kHz at pre-arranged times. This continuing liaison is necessary to enable the CRS and the Coastguard to know when the vessel concerned no longer needs a 'watchful eye' being kept on it. Ideally vessels should listen on 2182 kHz until all is well.

(iv) Radio breakdown. If a vessel has a radio failure it should seek to inform a nearby vessel or offshore installation of the fact. (Offshore installations keep watch on 2182 kHz and Channel 16. The oil companies have agreed to relay messages concerned with safety.) The contacted vessel or installation should then call the CRS which will note the circumstances and report them to the Coastguard and, if requested, to others ashore.

(B) Location calls. It is hoped that the availability of the 'openline' will encourage skippers to be in touch with the shore more frequently in order to establish the whereabouts of their vessels. This is something that may well take time to develop as the scheme gets under way. The Department of Trade, the Post Office and the Coastguard will assist where possible attempts made to make full use of this facility. There are a number of ways in which the vessel's whereabouts might be made known to the shore:

(i) Regular contact. Skippers and fishermen who regularly contact their wives or relatives at a specified time could as an alternative call the CRS on 2381 kHz. Contacts ashore who remained unaware that a particular call has been made could ring the CRS for confirmation.

(ii) Reporting-in. Individual skippers wishing to make regular reports of position while at sea should when leaving harbour notify the CRS of their intended reporting-in schedule. In the event of vessels failing to report in on schedule the CRS would, of course, take steps to raise the vessel and notify the Coastguard accordingly. In the event of larger scale position reporting schemes developing, say on a port basis, other arrangements would be made.

(iii) Group reports. Vessels fishing together might wish to nominate one of their number to report in on behalf of them all to the CRS along the lines of the example above.

6 *VHF*   Vessels operating within VHF range of the shore already have safety calling arrangements similar to the new scheme using channel 16 to call the Coastguard. These arrangements will continue unchanged.

7 *Reception.*   Because there will be some variation in reception during hours of darkness, particularly for vessels well out to sea, it may not always be possible to contact a particular Coast Radio Station although more distant ones may be clearly heard. In these circumstances skippers should be prepared to make contact with another CRS in the scheme which will arrange to re-transmit as necessary.

8 *2226 kHz.*   The Post Office are exploring the possibility of using channel 2226 kHz to alert vessels at sea as part of these safety arrangements. This would provide a useful additional frequency to back up the 'open-line' scheme.

Icelandic shelters

In addition to the normal emergency services offered by most countries, *ie* coastguard, aircraft and seaborne rescue craft. The Iceland National Life-Saving Association has set up shelters around the coast of Iceland where the shipwrecked fishermen may seek refuge. These shelters, which are either purpose built or converted farmhouses, contain either R/T or telephone, flares, signal rockets, food, clothing, medical supplies, heating equipment and fuel. On the roads and tracks surrounding the island are direction boards which are spaced at varying distances within 1,000 metres. The survivor who has got ashore by his own efforts in an uninhabited part of the inhospitable Icelandic coast in winter time, should look for notice boards and shelters in order to raise the alarm and use the shelter until help arrives.

Tankers — use of rockets

In the event of a trawler having to assist a tanker in a distress situation, it may be found necessary to pass a line between the two ships in order to make up a tow or in order to haul boats or rafts from one vessel to the other.

It may be dangerous to establish communication by means of a rocket-throwing apparatus with an oil tanker should that vessel be carrying petroleum spirit or other inflammables. The assisting vessel should lie to windward of the tanker and ascertain whether it is safe to fire a rocket in her direction before doing so.

When a vessel in distress is carrying petroleum spirit or other inflammable liquids and is leaking, the following signals should be exhibited to show that it is dangerous to fire a line carrying rocket because of fire risk.

By day: Flag B of the International Code of Signals
By night: A red light hoisted at the mast head

When visibility is bad the above signals may be supplemented by the use of the following International Code Signal made in sound: GU (— — . .. —) 'It is not safe to fire a rocket'.

The technique of passing lines from ship to ship by floating lines down from windward with a buoyant container is well known.

Emergency position indicating radio beacons

An Emergency Position Indicating Radio Beacon (EPIRB) is a device which is designed to float off automatically from a vessel which has sunk or capsized. The beacon will then transmit on the distress frequency 2182 kHz and may also transmit on 121.5 mHz/243 mHz (for SAR aircraft) and 500 kHz. It is housed in a free floating buoy and will enable ships and aircraft to home onto the distress signal using D/F, thus reducing the area of search in which survivors may be expected to be found. EPIRBs will be of particular value when a vessel has been overwhelmed suddenly and when there has been no time to transmit a distress message. There is also a type of EPIRB housed in a tethered buoy which remains secured to the sunken vessel.

EPIRBs are not as yet carried in British fishing vessels to any extent but their use may become more widespread in the future. This equipment is mandatory in some foreign fishing fleets.

Signals transmitted by EPIRBs are distress signals and vessels intercepting such signals should take the appropriate action.

10   Visual signals, ships in distress and shore stations, United Kingdom

In the event of a ship being in distress off, or stranded on, the coast of the United Kingdom, the following signals should be used by life saving stations when communicating with the life saving personnel ashore.

(1) Replies from life saving stations or maritime rescue units to distress signals made by ship or person:

Signals	*Signification*
By day – Orange smoke signal or combined light and sound signal (thunderlight) consisting of three single signals which are fired at intervals of approximately one minute. *By night* – White star rocket consisting of three single signals which are fired at intervals of approximately one minute.	'You are seen, assistance will be given as soon as possible.' (Repetition of such signals shall have the same meaning.)

If necessary the day signals may be given at night or the night signals by day.

(2) Landing signals for the guidance of small boats with crews or persons in distress:

Signals	*Signification*

By day – Vertical motion of a white flag or the arms or firing of a green star signal or the code letter 'K' (— . —) given by light or sound signal apparatus.

By night – Vertical motion of a white light or flare or firing of a green star signal or the code letter 'K' (— . —) given by light or sound signal apparatus. A range (indication of direction) may be given by placing a steady white light or flare at a lower level and in line with the observer.

'This is the best place to land.'

By day – Horizontal motion of a white flag or arms extended horizontally or firing of a red star signal or the code letter 'S' (. . .) given by light or sound signal apparatus.

By night – Horizontal motion of a white light or flare or firing of a red star signal or the code letter 'S' (. . .) given by light or sound signalling apparatus.

'Landing here highly dangerous.'

By day – Horizontal motion of a white flag, followed by the placing of the white flag in the ground and the carrying of another white flag in the direction to be indicated or firing of a red star signal vertically and a white star signal in the direction towards the better landing place or signalling the code letter 'S' (. . .) followed by the code letter 'R' (. — .) if a better landing place for the craft in distress is located more to the right in the direction of approach or signalling the code letter 'L' (. — . .) if a better landing place for the craft in distress is located more to the left in the direction of approach.

'Landing here highly dangerous. A more favourable location for landing is in the direction indicated.'

By night – Horizontal motion of a white light or flare, followed by the placing of the white light or flare on the ground and the carrying of another white light or flare in the direction to be indicated. The use of a red star signal and visual/sound signals as described above to be used as appropriate.

Breeches buoy

Co-operation between a ship's crew and HM Coastguard in the use of rocket rescue equipment

Should lives be in danger and the endangered vessel is in a position where rescue by rocket equipment is possible, a rocket with line attached will be fired from the shore above the vessel. Take hold of this line as soon as possible and, having done so, signal to the shore as indicated in A(*1*) below.

Alternatively, should the vessel carry a line-throwing appliance and this is first used to fire a line ashore, this line will not be of sufficient strength to haul out the heavier line and those on shore will, therefore, secure it to a stouter line. When this is done, they will signal as indicated in A(*1*) below. On their signal, the line should be hauled in until the stouter line is on board. The rocket line is a very light line and should be hand hauled back on board; the winch should not be used because any sort of check or snag could part the line and time would be lost.

If a rocket line is received from ashore, make the appropriate signal to the shore when it is held and proceed as follows:

(*1*) When the appropriate signal, *ie* 'haul away', is seen from the shore, haul on the rocket line until the tail block with an endless fall rove through it (called the 'whip') is aboard.

(*2*) Make the tail block fast close up to the mast or other convenient position, bearing in mind that the fall should be kept clear from chafing any part of the vessel and that space must be left above the block for the hawser. Unbend the rocket line from the whip. When the tail block is made fast and the rocket line unbent from the whip, signal to the shore again as below A(*1*).

(*3*) As soon as this signal is seen on the shore a hawser will be bent on to the whip and will be hauled off to the ship by those on shore. Except when there are rocks, piles or other obstructions between ship and shore, a bowline will have been made with the end of the hawser round the hauling part of the whip.

(*4*) When the hawser is on board, the bowline should be cast off. Then having seen that the end of the hawser is clear of the whip, the end should be brought up between the two parts of the whip and made fast to the same part of the ship as the tail block, but just above it and with the tally board, close up to the position to which the end of the hawser is secured (this will allow the breeches buoy to come right out and will facilitate entry to the buoy.

(5) When the hawser has been made fast on board, unbend the whip from the hawser and see that the bight of the whip has not been hitched to any part of the vessel and that it runs free in the block. Then signal to the shore as A(*1*) below.

(6) Those on shore will then tighten the hawser and, by means of the whip, haul the breeches buoy out to the ship. The person to be rescued should get into the breeches buoy and sit well down. When secure he should signal again to the shore as indicated below in A(*1*) and those ashore will haul him to land.

(7) During the course of the operation, should it be necessary to signal either from the ship to the shore or from shore to ship to 'Slack away' or 'Avast hauling', this should be done as in paragraph A(*2*).

It may sometimes happen that the state of the weather and the condition of the ship will not allow a hawser to be set up; in such circumstances a breeches buoy will be hauled off by the whip, which will be used without a hawser.

The system of signalling must be strictly followed. It should, however, be noted that the rescue operations as a whole will be greatly facilitated if signal communication (by flashing lamp or VHF) is established between the ship and shore or lifeboat. Coastguard rescue companies very often have trained signalmen.

A. Signals to be employed in connection with the use of shore life-saving equipment.

Signals	*Signification*
(*1*) *By day* – Vertical motion of a white flag or the arms	In general 'Affirmative'. Specifically 'Rocket line is held'.
By night – Vertical motion of a white light or flare or a green star.	'Tail block is made fast' 'Hawser is made fast' 'Man is in breeches buoy' 'Haul away'

(2) *By day* – Horizontal motion
of a white flag or arms
extended horizontally.

By night – Horizontal motion
of a white light or flare or
a red star.

In general 'Negative'.
Specifically 'Back away'.
'Avast Hauling'

B. Signals to be used to warn a ship which is running into danger.

Signals

Signification

The International Code
Signals 'U' or 'NF'. The letter
U (. . —) flashed by lamp or
made by fog horn, whistle, *etc.*

'You are running into
danger'

If it should prove necessary, the attention of the vessel is drawn to
these signals by a white flare, a rocket showing white stars on bursting
or an explosive sound signal.

11 Inflatable rafts

The inflatable raft is now widely used on board all types of ships as a life saving facility. They are provided on most British fishing vessels and at the present time it is a requirement that induction courses for pre-sea trainees include a short course on the use of the inflatable raft. These courses provide the prospective seafarer with a knowledge of action to take prior to abandonment of a ship, abandonment, and basic survival technique.

In the event that a fishing vessel has to be abandoned and the distress message has been sent as described in Chapter 9, the order to abandon can only be given by the skipper by word of mouth, supplemented by a continuous ringing of the alarm bells and/or the sounding of the ship's whistle. The reason for this is that everyone should be made aware of the abandonment.

When joining a ship for the first time, the student will be unfamiliar with many aspects of the vessel's facilities. The first and most important step for anyone to take after joining a ship is to find out from the Emergency Station Card: the station allocated to him for liferaft, fire and emergency; the places where the liferafts and fire fighting equipment are kept; and his duties and responsibilities at these stations.

Liferafts are usually stowed and kept either in fibre glass containers fitted into cradles on the deck (*Fig 66*), packed in canvas valises (*Fig 67*) in cut away recesses, *ie* in funnel or deckhouse casing, or in collapsible wooden boxes fitted to the deck (*Fig 68*). The rafts kept in the wooden boxes are the canvas valise type. Whenever possible, rafts are sited so that they are sheltered from the effects of icing but as close as practicable to the ship's side to facilitate easy launching. The fibre glass raft in the cradle and the valise raft in the wooden box are secured by means of strapping with quick release slip of the Senhouse type.

Before abandoning ship, a fisherman should insofar as circumstances allow, put on as much warm clothing as possible and wear a lifejacket. He should also take the emergency portable radio transmitter as it is an important aid in search and rescue. If circumstances permit, blankets should also be taken.

To launch an inflatable raft, the painter, which runs out from the valise or container, must be properly secured to the ship. The raft is then put over the side, and when the painter comes tight the CO_2 release mechanism will inflate the raft. If this does not happen, a hard pull on the painter will inflate the raft.

If the raft inflates upside down, which is unlikely, it can be inverted. Two straps are situated on the bottom of the raft along with a CO_2 cylinder. If someone stands on the cylinder, holding the straps one in each hand and throws his weight backwards, the raft should come to rest the right way up. If the raft is manoeuvred so that the topside or tube arch is facing the wind, the job will be much easier to do. The raft will of course fall on the man but because the bottom is soft and pliable he should not come to any harm.

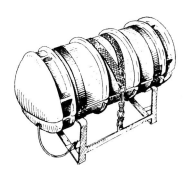

Fig 66 Fibre glass container, raft stowage

Fig 67 A canvas liferaft valise

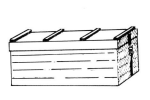

Fig 68 Collapsible wooden box, raft stowage

81

The raft should then be brought alongside the ship by adjusting the painter to a proper length. It can then be boarded directly from the ship by means of a rope ladder, rope, or scramble net. Entering the water should be avoided. On side trawlers and smaller fishing boats it may be possible to board directly from the deck. From high freeboards, *ie* freezer trawlers, one should not jump directly onto the raft since the raft might be damaged or someone injured. If jumping is the only alternative, the fisherman should jump into the water directly alongside the raft and then board the raft as quickly as possible.

When the raft is full, the painter should be cut with the knife provided and the raft should be moved away from the ship's side. The drogue or sea anchor attached to the buoyancy tubes near the entrance should then be put out so that drift is reduced. When the raft is first inflated, excess pressure in the buoyancy tubes escapes through a pressure release valve. It may sound (to the uninitiated) as if the raft is punctured, but it is not cause for alarm; the screeching noise will stop when the correct pressure is reached.

When the skipper has given the order to abandon ship, the rafts should be launched according to the procedures as practised at liferaft drills. There will almost certainly be time to get clear of a ship — it only takes a very short time to launch and inflate a liferaft — but panic and hysteria will impede an efficient abandonment.

Associated equipment

Inflationary pressure breaks open the raft from inside the container in which it is stowed; the buoyancy tubes which run around the raft are inflated as are the arch tubes which support the canopy.

The following items of equipment are normally fitted to all liferafts. The particular type of items and their form and manner of attachment to the raft depends upon the type of raft involved.

Lifeline. Fitted outside and inside the buoyancy chambers.

Righting strap. Provides the means of righting the raft in the unlikely event of it inflating upside down.

Hauling in lines. At the entrances to the raft as boarding aids, webbing in the form of rungs, or hand holds.

Boarding ladders. At each entrance.

Sea light. Mounted on top of the raft to assist location in darkness. Internal light fitted to arch tube.

Rescue line and quoit. Stowed at one entrance attached to a lifeline loop. For use as a heaving line to be thrown to survivors in the water.

Drogue and line. A sea anchor in the form of a drogue and line, provided to reduce rate of drift. Folded and stowed adjacent to one entrance, outside on a loop patch on the buoyancy chamber. The free end of the line is attached to a loop patch situated at 90° to the entrances so that when the drogue is deployed, the liferaft will drift with the entrances at right angles to the prevailing wind and sea.

Paddles and sponges. Tied to an anchorage patch on the floor.

Floating sheath knife. Fitted with a buoyant handle mounted on the arch tube or canopy strut. Use for cutting the painter.

Equipment bag

Contains: Leak stoppers (*Fig 69*), torch and batteries, repair kit, baler, spare sea anchor, topping up pump, rubber plugs, instructions on life saving signals and marine liferafts.

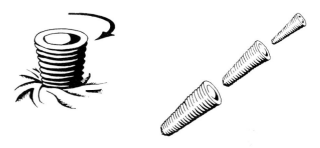

Fig 69 Leak stopper

Emergency pack. See separate list.

Valves. Non return pressure relief valves fitted to each chamber and floor for topping up with pump.

Radio aerial. A fabric sleeve type tube being assembled to the canopy fitted to mount a radio aerial.

Liferaft instruction leaflet. Headed 'Immediate Action' on booklet secured and folded inside the canopy of the raft adjacent to the water catchment.

The above items conform to the Merchant Shipping (LSA) Rules No 35 and the Fishing Vessels (Safety Provisions) Rules 1975.

Immediate action

Once the liferaft is launched and away from the ship and the drogue is streamed, there are certain immediate actions which must be taken. A responsible officer or person should take charge of the raft. If it is known that the position has been reported, the chances of being rescued quickly will be good. If uncertain as to whether the position has been reported, assume that it has not and be prepared for a long waiting period of several days. There are no rules in rescue.

If there are other rafts in the vicinity, try to keep together. This can be done by throwing the drogue in their direction and hauling the liferafts together. Repeat as necessary. Make the liferafts fast to each other on a lazy line to accommodate any sea which might be running. When doing this, look out for any survivors who may be in the water and use the quoit to bring them in. Rafts in company are easier to see visually by radar or from aircraft.

If there is no officer on board a raft, elect a leader and abide by his decisions. In cold climates, pump up the floor of the raft, which will provide insulation from the cold sea water. Close the entrance flaps so that body heat is kept within the canopies. If a seaman has been in the water try to dry him and keep him warm. On some trawlers there are insulated bags known as SAM suits, which can be pulled on by a man and drawn to around the neck in order to preserve body heat. Use one of these if a man has been in the water and is suffering from exposure (hypothermia). Dry out the bottom of the raft by using sponge and bailer and issue everyone with sea-sickness tablets.

Do not issue any water ration during the first 24 hours in the raft to normally healthy men. Thereafter issue one pint per day but not a whole pint at once. It should be given out in three or four equal issues at fixed intervals during the day. Do not drink salt water. Food rations should be issued in a similar manner.

The officer in charge should try to keep up morale. Being actively employed is good for morale. Watches and duties should be allocated as soon as possible. The raft not only keeps survivors afloat, it protects and preserves life. Because the canopy is double skinned, the buoyancy chambers and the inflated floor surrounds the survivors with a layer of gas and still air. Keep it this way by having regular inspections and effect repairs according to the instructions in the booklet. Examine the raft for flabbiness and correct by using the topping up pump. Set lookouts and attend to the water catchment bag. Use the portable radio on silence periods if possible.

If ships or aircraft are searching for liferafts their attention may be drawn by the use of the pyrotechnics provided in the emergency pack. However, these parachute rocket signals and hand flares are in limited supply and should be used sensibly. Never ignite them in the hope that they may happen to be seen when the presence of ships or aircraft is not apparent. Wait until an approaching ship is as close as it is thought likely to get. In the case of an aircraft, wait until it is actually in sight and heading approximately in your direction. The heliograph by day and the signalling torch by night will be useful supplements. The empty water tins if hung high in the raft on the canopy will not only improve the range but will help to make a better target for radar searches.

In addition to the equipment bag previously described, there is another emergency pack which contains: Safety tin opener, first aid kit, drinking vessel, heliograph and whistle, parachute distress signals, hand held signals, fishing kit, ration packs and water, sea-sickness tablets, liferaft instructions, SAM suits (where supplied), and bailer.

If a liferaft and survivors make it to shore, the raft should also be brought ashore if possible. The conditions ashore may be such that the raft will still need to be used as a shelter, *eg* in uninhabited, remote areas with extremely cold conditions when immediate aid unlikely. The raft should be lashed down in a sheltered place.

12   Fire prevention and fire fighting

Fire prevention

Serious fires at sea are best prevented by good ship husbandry, by attention to the correct maintenance of fire fighting appliances and regular fire drills. The crew should be fully aware of their fire stations as set out on the Emergency Station Card which must be displayed on all vessels of 24.4 metres length and over. Every fisherman should ensure that he is familiar with the operation and stowage of the fire fighting equipment.

The fire alarm signal:– Continuous sounding of alarm bells and/or ship's whistle.

Accommodation

In fishing vessels bad personal habits, such as smoking when turned in and the careless disposal of cigarette ends, have often caused fires resulting in injuries and loss of life. Everyone should be concerned with keeping the living quarters clean and tidy to reduce the risk of fire.

The following is a list of some precautions which should be taken to avoid fires and fire spread.

DO NOT use cardboard boxes as waste bins, lidded metal boxes are the answer.

DO NOT tie washing lines to electric cables, fire detector or sprinkler heads.

DO NOT use electric light bulbs of more than 60 watts in bunk lights. (Strip lights are safest). Use only correct wattage bulbs throughout the accommodation.

DO NOT rig unauthorised lighting on wandering leads.

Galleys on board ships always present a fire hazard. The cook and his assistant must be fully conversant with the fuel controls and valve settings on oil fired cooking stoves. Other crew members who are likely to use the galley should be instructed in the correct operation of controls and valves.

Pans containing hot cooking fats and oils must be watched carefully.

Engine room

One of the most common causes of engine room fire is an oil leak or spillage. Oil, especially under pressure, leaking on to a hot exhaust, electric motor or generator can ignite and spread very rapidly.

Every precaution should be taken to avoid overflows and spillages when transferring oil or filling tanks.

Oil leaks and spillages should not be tolerated. Leaks should be rectified and spillages mopped up immediately whenever they occur. Oily rags, waste etc. should be disposed of at once; drip trays emptied regularly; tank tops and bilges should be kept clean and oil free.

Working spaces

Working spaces should be kept tidy. Rubbish, rags, rope yarns, *etc*, should not be allowed to accumulate and become a fire hazard. Fish meal holds should be considered as fire risk areas due to the susceptibility of fish meal to spontaneous combustion.

Fire equipment

All fire fighting equipment should be checked for proper stowage and condition by the Mate and Chief Engineer at the start of each trip and at each fire drill. Any faults should be rectified or reported as appropriate. Ventilator flaps and emergency fuel oil 'shut-off' valves should be checked at the same time. Compressed air breathing apparatus sets and spare cylinders, fire detection and sprinkler systems should be tested every week. The emergency fire pump should be tested by being operated at every fire drill. All such tests should be recorded.

Fire drills

The Fishing Vessels (Safety Provisions) Rules 1975 set out the number, type and positioning of fire fighting equipment to be provided for fishing vessels of varying lengths.

It is also mandatory that a fire drill be carried out, in vessels of over 24.4 metres, at the beginning of each voyage and at intervals of not more than 14 days thereafter. Should more than 25% of the crew be replaced in any port a muster must be held within 48 hours of leaving that port to ensure that the crew understand and are drilled in their assigned duties. The opportunity should be taken at each drill to give instruction to the crew on the operation and use of fire equipment.

In vessels under 24.4 metres the crew must be made familiar with all fire and life saving appliances and trained in their use at intervals of not more than one month.

When drills are carried out, the fact must be entered in the log book. If for any reason fire or lifeboat drills are not carried out, this fact should also be recorded, stating the reason.

Where appropriate Emergency Station Cards should be made out and displayed before sailing.

For the purpose of this drill an outbreak of fire should be assumed to have taken place in a part of the vessel chosen by the skipper. When the alarm is sounded the crew should muster as detailed on the station card.

The fire and emergency fire pumps should be started and the main fire pump charged with water. Hoses should be run out and have water passed through them. Fire extinguishers should be unshipped and one used. Compressed air breathing apparatus and smoke mask should be broken out and worn.

When the drill is completed any extinguisher which was used must be recharged; a full cylinder must be fitted to the breathing apparatus set; hose must be drained and air dried before being coiled from the middle and restowed and controlled jet/spray branches checked, lightly greased, placed in a light plastic bag and restowed.

It is essential that each drill should be treated as a dress rehearsal for a real fire.

Fire fighting

In the event of a fire being discovered the alarm must be raised at once and the Bridge alerted.

The person discovering the fire, after raising the alarm and sending someone to alert the Bridge, should, if it is safe to do so, tackle the fire using the appropriate extinguisher. A determined and skilful attack in the early stages of a fire will, in most cases, prove successful.

When the general alarm of fire is sounded personnel will muster at assembly points detailed previously (*eg* that specified in the Emergency Station Card). From those points, they will be directed to attack the fire or engage in related duties as necessary. The number and position of assembly or muster points will depend on the size of vessel and the number of crew carried.

If the fire is not successfully attacked by the use of extinguishers, or is beyond the capabilities of extinguishers when discovered, a controlled attack will have to be made by the vessel's fire parties using hoses and nozzles or by the operation of fixed installations (*eg* CO_2 flooding in engine rooms).

At a very early stage in any fire an effort must be made to confine and reduce it by closing all adjacent doors, port holes, ventilators and other openings, so that the air flow is reduced.

All fires require *fuel, oxygen and heat*. Remove any one of these elements and a fire will be extinguished. By stopping the air flow the supply of oxygen will be reduced and by the correct use of extinguishers the heat will be reduced and the fire extinguished either by cooling or smothering depending on the agent used.

Recommended colour code and use for fire extinguishers:–

Extinguisher	Colour	Use
Water	*Red*	Solid/dry fires, timber, rags, paper, clothing *only*.
Foam	*Cream*	Oils and fats (liquid fires).
Carbon dioxide (CO_2)	*Black*	Oils, fats and electrical equipment.
Dry powder	*Blue*	Electrical equipment, oils, fats, solids.

Each extinguisher should be positioned to cover the potential fire risk for which it is intended.

When a small fire has been discovered, the alarm raised and an initial attack made, other extinguishers should at once be brought to the scene. Adjacent combustible material should be kept wet by using a spray to prevent the fire from spreading and if possible removed. Fire and Emergency fire pumps started, hoses laid out and charged with water and breathing apparatus broken out and worn.

Do not wait to see if the main fire equipment is required. (*Fig 70*)

Fig 70 Use of fire extinguisher

Solid/dry fires

These fires occur mostly in accommodation spaces and if caught in their early stages can be easily controlled and extinguished by the use of one extinguisher. However, never rely on one extinguisher putting out a fire completely; several extinguishers of the appropriate type should be brought to the fire area. Always make absolutely sure a fire is completely extinguished by thoroughly soaking the burning and surrounding material.

If a fire has a good hold, a line or lines of hose will have to be used. Heat and smoke rise — therefore, by crawling along the deck the fire fighters will be in the air stream feeding the fire and will find conditions at deck level cooler. Visibility is better at this level and enables the fire fighter to see the fire and so direct the water jet from either an extinguisher or line of hose into the heart of the fire. (See *Fig 71*)

When, because of heat and smoke, it is impossible to get into a cabin or compartment, it should be sealed and all adjacent bulkheads and decks kept thoroughly cooled by water sprays. A watch must be kept on ventilation trunking, false deckheads and panelling in compartments next to the fire area for hidden spread of fire.

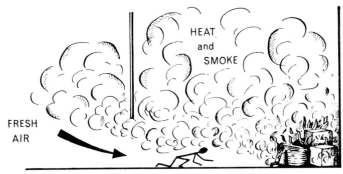

Fig 71 Air supporting combustion drawn in at low level

When it is thought that the fire has gone out in a sealed compartment great care must be taken when opening up. Heat and fuel (either solid or gaseous) will still be present in the area — only oxygen and/or additional heat is required to cause an explosion or flash over fire.

ALWAYS HAVE A CHARGED LINE OF HOSE READY WHEN OPENING UP.

Make sure all electrical power is off and ventilate carefully and progressively.

Fires in combustible liquids

Fires involving fuel, diesel and lubricating oils, hydraulic oil, paraffin, petroleum spirit and cooking fats and oils, unlike fires in solids which build up relatively slowly, occur almost instantaneously, sometimes with explosive violence, and spread very rapidly.

The reader will note from the extinguisher chart that it is inadvisable to use water on fires involving combustible liquids. Water, if used, must be in the form of a spray and used with expertise. Water in the form of jets must never be used as these scatter the burning fuel and increase the size and intensity of the fire.

Fires in combustible liquids usually occur in engine rooms and galleys and it is an important first step, apart from attacking the fire, to shut off the fuel supply and prevent air reaching the fire. All skylights, deck hatches, doors and ventilation systems servicing these spaces should be closed and shut off.

In the event of the engine room being evacuated the space should be sealed and the CO_2 or steam smothering system actuated by the use of controls and valves sited outside the space. Re-entry should only be

91

made by men wearing breathing apparatus and equipped with a line of hose. Care must be taken when opening up. Entry should be made at as low a level as possible preferably by the tunnel escape if one is provided. Skylights should be partially opened to allow air to be drawn through the tunnel and upwards towards the skylights thus clearing smoke and fumes and increasing visibility.

Small liquid fires

These may be effectively dealt with by spreading sand over the area using a scoop or shovel, by foam, CO_2 or dry powder.

Foam extinguishers

When used on burning liquids direct the stream of foam over the surface to strike a vertical or near vertical surface at the rear of the fire so that the foam builds up and flows back across the fire to form a thick blanket. Do not direct the foam into the burning liquid. (See *Fig 72*)

Fire in a pan of fat or oil may be effectively tackled by covering with a damp towel or sack and turning off the source of heat.

CO_2 extinguishers

These should be used in a figure eight or sweeping motion across the surface of the fire. If directed straight at the fire the velocity of the gas will cause the fire to flare and spread.

Dry powder extinguishers

These may be directed onto the burning liquid as the powder leaves the spreader at a low velocity in the form of a falling cloud. It has the advantage over foam that it extinguishes the fire nearest the fire fighter first but there is no cooling affect and lays only a thin layer of powder over the surface as against the thick blanket provided by foam.

There is still found on many fishing vessels the pistol type of D.P. extinguisher. This is operated by cocking a hammer and pulling the trigger. The pistol must be aimed low at the base of the fire to ensure the powder spreads. (See *Fig 73*)

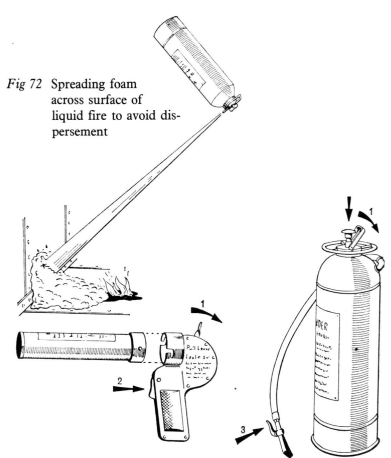

Fig 72 Spreading foam
across surface of
liquid fire to avoid dis-
persement

Fig 73 Small and large powder extinguishers

Electrical fires

All fires of electrical origin should be dealt with by using CO_2 or dry powder extinguishers. Even though it is known that the power is switched off high voltage electrical equipment, such as W/T or radar circuits, water should still not be used. Use only CO_2 or dry powder extinguishers.

It is good fire fighting practice in all cases of fire to remove panelling to ensure that a fire is not spreading unseen behind wooden bulkheads and false deckheads.

Automatic fire detection system

There are two types of systems fitted in trawlers designed to actuate either when smoke or combustion products are present, or when there is an unusually rapid rise of temperature which is excessively high.

When the detection system is actuated, the fire alarm will sound and a zone light will appear on the detector panel showing from what part of the ship the alarm has originated. The detector panel is usually sited on the ship's bridge. This system also operates the closing of fire doors and smoke doors, and it switches off the ventilator system. Even when alarm systems are fitted, the normal hourly fire and integrity rounds must be made.

Sprinkler systems

Some vessels are fitted with these systems in accommodation spaces. The system consists of a pressure tank containing one ton of water, control valves, a pump and pipe work terminating with a sprinkler head in each unit of accommodation.

In the sprinkler head is a quartzoid bulb containing a liquid which expands when heated. Also within the bulb is an air bubble, which governs the temperature at which the head operates.

When a fire occurs, the liquid expands, the bubble bursts and a glass valve is released. A jet of water then flows, strikes a plate and forms a spray which helps to control or extinguish the fire. When the head operates, the pressure in the system falls and micro switches operate the alarm signal, activate the sprinkler pump, close fire/smoke doors and stop the ventilator fans.

The sprinkler system should never be stopped until the fire is under the control of the fire party and then only on the orders of a ship's officer.

Both of these automatic systems should be tested weekly and the tests should be recorded.

Stability and handling of vessel

There is no reason why a shallow skim of water cannot be used on a deck to keep it cool, but in the case of a serious fire where large volumes of water are used, skippers must see that the water is not allowed to accumulate in large quantities, and as far as possible pumps

94

should be used to clear excess water. Free surface water (which is explained in the Chapter 22) can be extremely dangerous. Regardless of whether the compartment containing the slack water is high or low within the ship, at sea or in harbour, large volumes of free surface water may prove to be disastrous. In the past, large ships in dock have been capsized because of the indiscriminate flooding of hold spaces which have caught fire. (See *Fig 74*).

When at sea with a fire on board skippers will be able to assist the fire fighting party by reducing speed to dead slow in order to minimise the relative wind. The skipper may also be able to alter course to put the fire area on the leeside so that smoke, sparks and gases will blow clear of the ship. It will be apparent that a fire under the whaleback would require the wind to be put astern, but any decisions would be made with regard to circumstances, *ie* sea room, adjacent navigational hazards, *etc*.

Skippers are also reminded that a distress or emergency message may be sent depending on the circumstances of the fire and the ability to cope. Other vessels might assist in many ways.

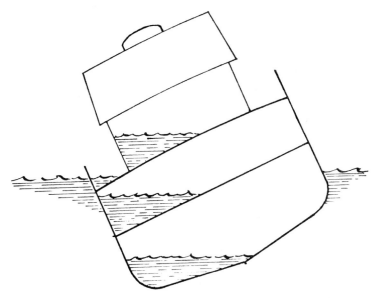

Fig 74 Loss of stability from use of water when fire fighting

13 Emergencies at sea

An emergency at sea may best be described as a situation which has arisen with little or no warning, putting a ship or persons on board in grave or imminent danger, when only the immediate and correct action taken will be likely to resolve or reduce the gravity of the situation.

Fire and abandonment emergencies have already been dealt with in previous chapters, where it was stressed that an officer should know the position of all liferafts and fire equipment and how such equipment may best be used. An officer who knows his own ship, its capabilities and limitations in bad weather, will avoid many emergencies by taking action in sufficient time to prevent serious damage.

The seaman who knows his ship and is familiar with and understands the pumping arrangements for fuel, water tanks, deck line connections, *etc*, has an immediate advantage in emergencies such as fire, collision, grounding and loss of stability because of an intake of water. If the trawler officer knows the amount and type of gear in the ship, such as blocks, tackles, wires, ropes, sand, cement, boards, tarpaulins, *etc*, then no time will be lost when an urgent situation arises which has to be dealt with quickly.

Explosives

A rare but extreme hazard to trawlermen is mines, torpedos, depth charges, bombs or other explosive missiles which are sometimes picked up in trawls. The following guidance is given for dealing with them:

(*1*) A suspected explosive weapon should not be landed on deck if it has been observed before the cod end has been opened. In side trawlers, the trawl should be lowered back into the sea and where possible towed clear of regular fishing grounds before cutting away the net as necessary. The position and depth of water where the explosive weapon was cut away, should be passed to the Naval

Authorities via the Coastguard, ship's agent or owners, or fishery officer, and, if possible, marked by a dan buoy.

(2) In the event of the weapon not being detected until the contents of the trawl have been discharged on deck, or in the case of a stern trawler, when the cod end has been hauled up the ramp, the skipper must decide whether to rid his ship of the weapon by passing it over the side or to make for the nearest port, informing the Naval Authority by radio without delay. His decision will depend on circumstances, but he should be guided by the following points:

(a) Great care should be taken to avoid bumping.

(b) If retained on board it should be stowed on deck, away from heat and vibration, firmly chocked and lashed to prevent movement.

(c) It should be kept covered up and damped down properly by wet sacking and the use of a spray nozzle hose. (This is important because any explosive which may have become exposed to the atmosphere is liable to become very sensitive to shock if allowed to dry out).

(d) The weapon should be kept onboard for as short a time as possible.

(e) If within two or three hours steaming of the UK coastline, the safest measure will generally be to run towards the nearest port and lie a safe distance off shore to await the arrival of Naval Explosive Disposal Unit. Under no circumstances should the vessel bring the mine or weapon into harbour.

(f) No attempt should be made to clean the weapon for identification purposes, open it or tamper with it in any way.

(g) A ship with an explosive on board, or in her gear, should warn other ships in the vicinity, giving her position and, if applicable, intended position of jettisoning.

Drifting mines may occasionally be sighted. They should be reported immediately to the Naval Authorities via the Coastguard and coast station giving the time of sighting and an accurate position, so that an appropriate warning to shipping may be broadcast.

Man overboard

Much has been written in seamanship books on this subject and how best to turn a ship round and return to the position where the man may expected to be picked up. If we take a realistic view of what happens when a man falls overboard, it will be seen that an officer of the watch has very little time in which to take immediate action to avoid the man being drawn into the propeller race.

A trawler steaming at 12 knots will pass a man overboard at a speed of 21.6 feet per second. If the man has fallen overboard, let us say from amidships about 100 feet from the stern of a trawler at a speed of 13 knots, then he will have been passed in less than five seconds. If the vessel is trawling with a speed of about five knots, he will then have been passed in about 12 seconds.

If the officer of the watch actually sees the man fall overboard, the chances of him being able to stop the engines in a few seconds are remote. The wheel should be put hard over towards the side where the man has fallen so that the stern may be thrust away from him. Experience shows that a man overboard will float clear of the ship, even if no action is taken, by reason of the bow wave and displacement effect. Bearing in mind that fishing vessels operate between the UK and into the Arctic Circle in cold climates, it is important that the man's position be marked and that he be picked up as soon as possible. Loss of body heat is as great a danger as drowning. It is vitally important that the bridge lifebuoys be released as soon as possible. The man in the water may be able to reach the lifebuoy for support, but just as important is the fact that the light and smoke signal attached to the float will act as a marker to which the ship may return.

Immediate action

(*1*) As soon as the message or call 'Man overboard' is received, release the bridge lifebuoy, with the self-igniting light/flare.
(*2*) If safe (navigationally) put the wheel hard over towards the side from which the man has fallen.
(*3*) Set lookouts to keep the man and lifebuoy in sight at all times. Call the Skipper.
(*4*) Sound the emergency signal and/or the 'Man overboard' signal.
(*5*) Turn the ship round (see remarks below).
(*6*) Have the boat or liferaft made ready.
(*7*) Inform any ships in the vicinity of the incident.

The best action to take if the man and/or the lifebuoy is in sight is to let the trawler come right round on full rudder, reducing speed towards the end of the turning circle so that the man in the water is brought to leeward for the boat or liferaft to pick up. If the lifebuoy was not released as soon as the man fell overboard, skippers should steam slowly back on a reverse course from the lifebuoy's position. The self-igniting light will burn for a period of not less than 40 minutes, which should give a good departure position from which to search.

Should it become necessary to steam back down the track to search for a man who has been reported as missing and there is no knowledge of when he fell overboard, the following method of reversing course may be used. Put the wheel hard over to port or starboard until the ship's head comes round to but not past 60° from the original course. Now put the wheel hard over in the opposite direction until the ship's head has swung 240° and on to a reciprocal course. It will be found that most single screw ships will now be on or close to the original track. Lookouts should be posted to search for the man.

Grounding and refloating of vessels

No two stranding of vessels are likely to be identical and it is not possible, therefore, to produce a set of rules on how to refloat a stranded vessel. The advice given below covers some general principles but the success (or otherwise) of any particular salvage operation will depend upon the degree of planning and skill used in its execution.

Serious damage and possible loss of a vessel may result in attempting to refloat a grounded vessel unless the operation is conducted with proper forethought. The following advice is offered to skippers who may require assistance or who may be asked to assist another vessel.

Action after grounding

When a vessel goes aground, the engines should be stopped immediately and should not be moved again until the skipper is satisfied that:
(1) His vessel is in a fit condition to be refloated and not making water which cannot be controlled.
(2) Refloating his vessel will not cause further damage to the propeller, rudder or hull.

The skipper's first actions on grounding should be to:
(1) Sound the general alarm.
(2) Make ready liferafts and lifeboats if carried.
(3) Transmit the appropriate distress signal.
(4) Send the mate and chief engineer to check for damage.

(5) Alert his owners and the nearest local insurance company agent.

Refloating

Before attempting to refloat, the skipper should take into consideration the nature of the bottom and the state of the tide. If the vessel is
lying on a rocky bottom she may be holed and by working the engines
or taking a tow from another vessel the damage may be aggravated.

If the vessel is lying on sand, shingle or mud, it may be possible to
refloat immediately. In such circumstances the engines should be
worked astern for short periods only and the engineers should report
at once if sand or silt is being drawn into the intakes. On a falling tide,
unless refloating is almost immediate, it will be necessary to wait for
the following tide. If the vessel cannot be refloated immediately,
soundings should be taken all round her with forward and aft
draughts noted.

Jettisoning of gear

Skippers should consider ways of lightening the vessel as a way of
refloating her. Jettisoning of ice, catch and fresh water may make an
appreciable difference to the draught and jettisoning of fishing gear
and anchors, cables, *etc* may also help; particularly if the vessel is
aground forward. When jettisoning ship's gear, it should be buoyed
for subsequent recovery.

Use of assisting vessel

When seeking the assistance of another vessel, skippers should give
careful thought to the procedure to be adopted before making any
attempt to refloat. Generally speaking, a vessel aground will refloat
most easily if she is taken off in the reverse direction to which she has
gone on. This means towing her off astern. Pulling her round by the
head should not be attempted as this may cause serious underwater
damage.

Skippers of vessels rendering assistance must exercise great care
when approaching a vessel which has run aground in order to avoid
damage to their own vessel. If they are in any doubt about the depth of
water in the vicinity of the stranded vessel they should anchor in a safe
position and pass the tow by boat, rocket line or other means.

Use of anchors when aground (See also *Chapter 5*)

It is possible, in good holding ground, to get a better purchase from the use of ground tackle and the winch than from a tug or another trawler. Skippers should, therefore, consider the use of their bower anchors for this purpose if there is a suitable vessel available to lay them out. If there is no suitable boat available, see the following paragraph, which describes how best to use anchors from another ship. The anchors and a length or more of cable on each bow should be laid out in a narrow V in the direction in which it is desired to refloat and warps shackled on. Anchors and cables must be buoyed before being laid. The lead for the warp should be kept as low as practicable in the stranded vessel to avoid forcing the stern lower into the water.

If it is not possible for the stranded vessel to get her own anchors away, it may be advantageous for the skipper of the assisting vessel to put his own anchors down and shackle them to the warps of the stranded vessel. The assisting vessel can then tow independently while the skipper of the stranded vessel attempts to heave the boat off

If circumstances allow, the assisting vessel may be able to drop her anchor in an appropriate line with the stranded vessel, paying out several lengths of cable before connecting up to the grounded vessel. By towing on the warp and heaving on the anchor simultaneously a strong and continuous bollard pull will be exerted on the vessel aground. Experience shows that by keeping the towing warp tight throughout the operation, immediate advantage is taken of any tidal range or surge from ground swell which may take place.

If a skipper is in any doubt as to the best course to be followed after grounding, he should seek the advice of the insurance company either directly or through his owners or the nearest agent. In certain circumstances it may be better to wait for professional salvors to arrive than to make a hasty and ill-judged attempt to get off quickly. On such occasions, the skipper should ensure that all openings are made watertight and if there is a danger of the vessel working on the bottom, it may be necessary to take ballast on board either in the tanks or by flooding compartments to keep the vessel firmly on the bottom.

Beaching a damaged ship

If a ship is so badly damaged that the ingress of water cannot be brought under control, it may be possible to beach her in time to save the ship. The optimum conditions for beaching would be, at or about high water, a sheltered bay with a soft and shelving bottom.

In tidal waters and if there is any choice, it is better to ground the vessel on a falling tide, rather than to force her on to the beach. However, there are many factors which may govern a beaching situation, the main one being how quickly the ship is taking water and the rate at which she is settling in the water.

In an extreme case, such as severe damage following a collision, with a fast intake of water into a large compartment (such as the fish or engine room), the vessel would have to be beached regardless of tidal conditions.

In less urgent cases where time allows, circumstances such as tidal range or whether it is necessary for the damaged area to be uncovered at low water will have to be considered. Vessels should not, if possible, be beached too high up on a spring tide. This may make refloating unnecessarily difficult.

Vessel immobilised at sea

A ship immobilised at sea because of engine or steering gear trouble requiring a tow to a safe port should follow the advice given in *Chapter 5* under the headings 'Use of anchor cable when towed' and 'Sea anchors'.

A skipper of a disabled vessel which requires towing to a place of safety should:
(1) Inform his owners and the nearest insurance company's agent.
(2) Wherever possible arrange to be towed by a vessel which is insured with the same company as that of his own vessel.
(3) Under circumstances whereby there is no insured vessel available (as in (2) above) and the need for assistance is immediate, skippers should agree terms with the salvage vessel under Lloyd's Standard Form of Salvage and Agreement, commonly known as Lloyd's Open Form.

Approach to a vessel requiring a tow

In the open sea, the assisting vessel should not attempt to go alongside the ship which is to be towed. A line should be passed either by floating pellets downwind towards the disabled vessel, by firing a rocket line or by towing a line from leeward around the stern of the disabled vessel.

If the disabled vessel is at anchor, going alongside in fine weather in a single screw ship is not a similar operation to that of going alongside a quay, for two reasons. A quay or jetty is a fixed object and cannot move. A skipper going alongside a jetty may make allowances for wind and tide as they affect his ship. A vessel at anchor in a moderate wind will pivot round her stem, to a degree varying with the strength of the wind, tide and swell. (See *Fig 75*)

Even in calm weather, an anchored vessel will pivot if a fine approach is made by the vessel which is to go alongside. The water pressure or displacement effect from the bows of the assisting ship will push the stern of the anchored vessel away and her bows will swing across or towards the line of approach. This interaction will take place even if the disabled ship is being steered, is at anchor, or is using a sea anchor. Therefore the passing of a line by any means is a safer method of making a connection than by going alongside.

If a successful tow is nearing completion and a harbour or estuary is being approached, the towing vessel should reduce speed in plenty of time and shorten the tow. The ship being towed will not sheer too

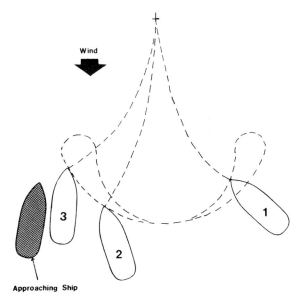

Wind

3

2

1

Approaching Ship

Fig 75 Approaching a ship at anchor

103

much on a short towing bridle and will be conducted more safely in narrowing waters where other shipping may be encountered. Correct towing signals should always be exhibited by day or night when towing or being towed.

Wherever possible the towing vessel should hand over the towed vessel to harbour tugs for berthing before entering a harbour or a narrow tidal estuary. If, however, there are no harbour tugs available and the assisting vessel has to go alongside the towed vessel, great care should be exercised in the mooring together of the two vessels because of the reasons given previously.

Having taken the way off and slipped the tow, the towing vessel should turn round and approach the tow from astern with very little headway in such a manner that when abeam of the tow the distance between the two vessels will be about 40 feet in parallel. Heaving lines should be passed, then breast ropes, so that the vessels may be gently brought flat alongside of each other's fenders. If, when this operation is being carried out, the disabled vessel sheers because of wind or tide, the assisting vessel will, because of her distance off, be able to act appropriately or steam away altogether. In any case the bringing together of two vessels in any sort of sea or swell should be avoided, and the operation should be carried out in reasonably calm conditions. Vessels of different lengths, period of pitch and/or roll, because of different stability conditions, will cause damage in spite of fenders when there is any sea or swell running.

Anchor cable use when towed

If a trawler becomes immobilised to the extent that she needs to be towed to port, the anchor cable should be used for towing.

If there is no immediate danger, the towed vessel should bring the anchor and cable under the flare of the bow and onto the foredeck in order to unship the anchor. This will leave the unstudded or open link and the joining shackle free to connect to the eye of the towing vessel's warp.

If time or conditions do not permit the anchor to be unshipped then a successful tow can still be accomplished with the anchor still connected to the cable. In this event neither the crown shackle on the anchor stock, nor the cable joining shackle, must be used for the connection. If this is done, a sideways pull will be made on whichever shackle is used and they will distort under the stress, loosen the pin, the anchor will be lost and the tow will part. Connection of the towing vessel's warps must be made by a suitable shackle to the first unstudded or open link. The shackle selected must be of a suitable size and strength and should be properly seized when shackled up. (See *Fig 76*) If it is not possible to shackle to the first open link, then the shackle should be passed around the cable and secured to it's own standing part. A trawl door bracket shackle would probably be suitable. Smaller shackles should not be used as they will readily part under stress and the tow will be lost.

When the connection has been made, the disabled vessel should pay out two or three lengths of cable, screw up the windlass and put a preventer on the cable. This preventer should be of wire rope and equal in strength to that of the towing warp. A good method of doing this is to arrange the length of cable paid out so that (let us assume) the

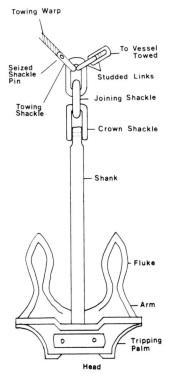

Fig 76 Connecting a tow when anchor and cable are to be used

third cable shackle is on deck near to the inboard end of the hawse-pipe. Set up a threefold wire purchase at the outer open link of the third shackle, with the standing part of the purchase on the bitts or bollards behind the windlass. The hauling part of the purchase may then be passed via the bitts to the winch and set tight before being stopped off and secured. The brake, compressor or other holding device may also be used but the preventer should bear the weight of the tow.

Connecting and getting the tow under way

When proceeding towards a disabled vessel, the assisting vessel should make ready all the gear necessary for towing. Rocket line throwing apparatus should be prepared in a clear area free from obstructions. Messenger lines should be flaked out so that they may be run away freely, with a few lengths of warps similarly disposed. Skippers are aware that the modern polypropolene ropes are buoyant so that if floating pellets are attached a quick and efficient connection can be made by floating the line downwind either from the assisting vessel or the disabled vessel. Recently a disabled vessel, in a force nine, ESE gale in the North Atlantic used up all her rockets unsuccessfully attempting to establish a connection with an assisting vessel. Polypropolene messengers with pellets were then floated to leeward, were picked up immediately by the assisting vessel, and a successful connection and tow ensued.

On coming up to the disabled vessel, time will probably be saved in the long run if the skipper of the towing ship makes a careful and deliberate assessment of the attitude and drift both of the disabled vessel and of his own when stopped. It is therefore a good practice to circle a disabled vessel at close range before attempting to pass a line. If uncertain as to how his own ship will lie and drift, he should stop her clear of the disabled ship and note her behaviour before attempting to pass a line. If it is obvious that the rates of drift are going to be very different, *eg* a side trawler intending to tow a deeper laden freezer trawler, then it is essential that the tow is passed as quickly as possible and that everything is prepared before passing the line, as described above.

It is stressed, however, that the state of the weather, condition of the disabled vessel, and above all the need to connect up quickly because of the situation which a disabled vessel may be in, *eg* the proximity of a lee shore, must be taken into account when the skipper is planning the operation.

When the messenger line has been passed between the two vessels, the towing warp should be hauled across by the disabled vessel. The assisting ship should bend the messenger on to her towing warp above and clear of the eye; this will enable those on the disabled ship to make a quick connection to the anchor cable. When passing the messenger line and warp, the assisting vessel should try to maintain a steady heading and distance off, so as to avoid making the transfer unnecessarily difficult. When the warp has been connected to the towed vessel's anchor cable, about three lengths of cable should be paid out and the cable secured, as described in the section headed *Anchor cable use when towed* on page 104.

The towing vessel at this stage should exercise great care and patience on going ahead, by intermittent bursts of ahead movement at slow speeds while paying out the towing warp as necessary until about 10 to 12 lengths (250-300 fathoms) of warp have been veered. The greatest stresses on the gear will be made when the inertia of the towed vessel is overcome. The towing vessel will be forewarned of the stress to come by watching the towing warp which will slowly alter its angle between the towing block and the sea, possibly from the vertical upwards towards the horizontal. Engines should be stopped, and, if there is only a little way on the vessel, the catenary (or bight of the towing warp) will become shallow and might even come out of the water. If it appears that the towing warp is to become horizontal, be prepared to pay out more warp from the towing winch so as to avoid a heavy strain on the gear. The length and weight of the warp and anchor cable should overcome the inertia of the towed vessel, the catenary should fall below the surface of the sea, and, if the engines are put ahead again at minimum revolutions and gradually increased, the bight of the towing warp should remain immersed at all times. An aid to overcoming the towed vessel's inertia is for the towing vessel to begin the tow heading down wind at an angle of about 45° to that of the direction in which the towed trawler is laid. Once the tow is moving, speed should be gradually increased until the maximum towing speed is attained.

After the tow is under way, any alteration of course should be made gradually a few degrees at a time until the required heading is reached. If it is possible, the vessel being towed should steer, and the propeller should be allowed to trail by disconnecting the shaft between engines and thrust block. The fixed propeller offers high resistance underwater and reduces the speed of the tow considerably as well as adding stress to the towing gear.

During a long tow in good weather there are no particular problems as long as the towed vessel rides comfortably astern and is not subject to yawing. The length and weight of the towing gear is all important and the bight should remain well immersed at all times. If the bight of the tow rope appears in good weather, then it is not long enough and the warp should be veered, if there is a sufficient depth of water. If the weather deteriorates and the catenary shows a tendency to appear then speed should be reduced and/or the tow lengthened.

During the tow, the condition of the gear should be kept under constant observation in both ships for any signs of weakness, so that appropriate action can be taken if necessary. The towing warp should be parcelled by hides or sacking where nipped, and freshened every few hours by veering with an appropriate reduction of speed.

Towing a ship stern first

In the case of a disabled vessel being damaged forward and remaining afloat only because of her collision bulkhead, it may be thought wiser to tow her stern first, in order to avoid further weakening forward.

If the disabled vessel is down by the head, the actual towing of the vessel may not necessarily be more difficult, but the connection may be more complicated from the stern of a disabled side trawler. If possible the disabled vessel should connect to the towing warp by means of a bridle consisting of two lengths of cable or warp of equal length, one from each quarter. The rudder should be set in the midships position and secured.

If the disabled vessel is deeper aft than forward, the use of a second vessel connected astern of the tow may be necessary in order to maintain a course and prevent excessive yawing.

Hull damage

Small holes such as a rivet hole may be plugged by knocking a tapered broom handle into the hole. When this has been done a cement box should be fitted around the hole and left to harden. If a small hole has been caused by corrosion, great care should be taken when plugging, a split or fracture might result if the plug is hammered in too heavily. A more permanent repair may be made as follows.

To act as a float use a cane or stick, as long as is convenient, of a diameter allowing it to pass freely through the hole and attach to it the end of a ball of twine. Push the stick through the hole and pay out the twine until the float reaches the surface of the water. Pick up the float and send down a length of marline or light line by hauling in on the twine. Have a threaded bolt with a good head on it, a large washer and a gasket made of rubber or other suitable jointing fitted on to the shank of the bolt. Make the head of the bolt fast and by using marline hitches on the bolt shank pass it down to the hole where it may be pulled inboard. Have a suitably threaded nut, washer and gasket ready to fit once the bolt is inboard and the marline is clear. Put on plenty of red lead and tallow and screw up tight. It should be unnecessary to make a cement box on this type of repair if the gaskets and washers cover the hole.

Small cracks which are not too wide may be covered from the outside of the ship by cowhides, blankets or tarpaulins. Firmly secure the material to be used between two lengths of lines. By passing the bights over the bow and moving aft, the cowhide, blankets or tarpaulin may be manoeuvred until over the crack in the hull. By spreading the lines carefully and setting them tight; the crack will be covered and the water pressure will help to seal the fracture by pushing the material into the hole. Under reasonably dry conditions a cement box can then be made.

Cement boxes may be used after leakages have been reduced as much as possible by use of plugs, wedges, oakum, bedding and tallow. If the leak is stopped completely by these methods, a cement box may be applied immediately. It is always advisable to use the ship's frames when making a cement box. Pound boards may be cut to size so that they fit tightly and wedged between frames above and below the damaged part. If the damage extends across a frame, then two sets of boards above and below the damage can be fitted. Allow a good overlap over the damage and fill with mortar. Cover the mortar by nailing boards over the surface of the mortar to the wooden framework.

When mixing sand and cement use two parts of sand to one of cement. Gradually add water into which soda has been dissolved until a stiff but workable mix has been made. All the surfaces to which the mortar is to adhere should be clean and free from grease and running water. If running water from the plugged damage is still present, a channel, tunnel or piping should be laid so that the cement box can be made. When the cement box has set, the channel or piping may then be plugged. Ship's husbands and skippers should always make sure that quick-drying cement is shipped when stores are taken.

Collision damage

In most cases of collision, except that suffered by a bulbous bow, the fracture begins above the waterline and extends downwards in a 'V' shape with localised fractures and indentations. When the damage has taken place in smaller compartments such as a fuel tank fore peak, after peak, *etc*, it is vitally important to seal off the damaged compartment by closing all openings such as doors, hatches and pipe lines which might cause flooding in another area. Having isolated the compartment, use of a collision mat as described previously may allow the pumping out of the damaged area. Sound judgment with quickly taken action may avoid flooding and subsequent abandonment in cases where damage is adjacent to or just below the water line. The transfer of fuel and water, *etc*, may be sufficient to list or trim the vessel and so incline the vessel in order that the damaged area clears the water line to permit plugging. The transfer of fuel or water will not in itself reduce the reserve buoyancy of the ship, except for the effect of the free surface when the transfer is taking place. The flooding of a side tank from the sea carried out to list the vessel will reduce stability by increasing the draught and lowering the reserve buoyancy. Transfer of fuel and water must always be regarded as the safer method of creating a list in a vessel which has been damaged and is already subject to an ingress of water. In all cases of leakage, engine room and portable pumps should be brought into use immediately and if necessary baling by buckets hand-to-hand should be organised.

Extensive damage to hull

A vessel which has suffered extensive damage to a large compartment may well find that the resources on board are inadequate to effectively deal with the situation. The ship which remains afloat after such damage to a large compartment should make for the nearest port or anchorage either by her own power or by being towed. Do not try to reach a more distant port where full repair facilities are available for the following reasons. Because of flooding, the ship's stability will have been reduced considerably by loss of buoyancy due to the extra weight of water on board and free surface effect. The deeper the ship sinks in the water, the greater will become the pressures on the bulkheads within the ship and risk of rupture. If conditions deteriorate, the possibilities of beaching will be more likely if approach is being made towards the nearest port or anchorage. Temporary repairs may be effected at the nearest port which will allow the vessel to proceed to a port with good repair facilities.

Shoring of bulkheads

If resources on board permit, bulkheads may be stiffened by shoring with timber. If for example the bows of a ship are extensively damaged to such an extent that the forepeak chain locker, *etc*, are flooded and the ship is down by the head, it may be considered necessary to stiffen the collision bulkhead which separates the next compartment from the flooded area. This will allow the ship to steam towards the nearest port with the collision bulkhead strengthened against the pressures to which it will be subjected to when underway.

By setting up vertical timber pillars between a conveniently placed deckhead thwartship beam and the deck, horizontal shores may be set up against the bulkhead to act as stiffeners. The vertical pillars should be chocked off and braced at the deck and the horizontal stiffeners to the bulkhead should be wedged and set up against horizontally placed planking spread athwart the collision bulkhead. Two or three sets of stiffeners should be set up across the width of the bulkhead in order to strengthen the bulkhead evenly. Any improvised timber buffer work, well set up, chocked and stiffened evenly will strengthen a bulkhead against pressures from outside. Progress to the nearest port should be made at a moderate speed having due regard to the damage.

Part III   Navigation

14   Buoyage systems: combined lateral and cardinal

Around the coasts of the United Kingdom a lateral type of buoyage system known as the International Uniform System of Buoyage was in use but is in process of being replaced. The lateral system incorporates a wreck marking system and other special buoys marking outfalls, spoilgrounds, danger areas, *etc.* This system, however, has many variations in different countries.

Some countries adopted, as an alternative to the lateral system, a cardinal system whereby the compass was divided into four quadrants by diagonals running NE to SW and from NW to SE respectively. Buoys used in this system were can or conical and indicated the general direction of a danger, and the safe side on which to pass. Wrecks were marked cardinally, but were only marked by green wreck buoys being set down in either the east or west quadrants. Transition buoys are used to indicate the transition from lateral system to the cardinal system or vice versa.

The reader will acknowledge that unless the mariner had a full and complete knowledge of the various systems, passing from neighbouring countries' coastal and river waters which used different systems could be hazardous and confusing. It became clear to all mariners that agreement on standardisation on buoyage would be sensible.

The International Association of Lighthouse Authorities decided to harmonise buoyage, hopefully for world-wide use, and as a result of this decision, on the 1st April 1977 a new system began to be progressively introduced in NW European waters, which is expected to take approximately 3-4 years to complete.

The change-over in the English Channel and the new system will be known as the Combined Cardinal and Lateral (Red to Port) System 'A'. (See front endpaper)

The Uniform System will be phased out as System 'A' is introduced.

The Combined Cardinal and Lateral System (Red to Port) — System 'A'

In connection with the harmonisation of maritime buoyage systems the International Association of Lighthouse Authorities has now approved one of the two systems for world-wide use. This system known as System 'A' — the Combined Cardinal and Lateral System (Red to Port) will be applied as follows:

(1) It was intended that System 'A' should be progressively introduced over a period of three years, commencing 1st April 1977.

(2) Work began in the English Channel area and the system is being progressively implemented along the coasts of the countries bordering the whole of the North Sea and the Baltic.

(3) This system applies to all fixed and floating marks (other than lighthouses, sector lights, leading lights and large navigation buoys) and the system will indicate to the mariner the lateral limits of navigable channels; natural dangers such as obstructions, wrecks, etc; other areas or features of importance to the mariner; and new dangers.

There are five types of marks in the system which may be used in any combination, each of the five types of marks have significant characteristics which depend on the following features:

By night: colour and rhythm of light
By day: colour, shape and topmark

The following should be read in conjunction with *Fig 77*.

Lateral marks define the conventional direction of buoyage in one of two ways, *ie* the general direction taken by the mariner when approaching a harbour, river estuary, or waterway from seaward, or in other areas as determined by the appropriate authority. In principle the buoyage should follow a clockwise direction around continental land masses.

In all cases the conventional direction will, if necessary, be indicated in nautical documents, charts, *etc*.

Port hand
Colour and shape: Red, can or spar
Topmark (if any): Single red can
Light (when fitted): Red, any rhythm

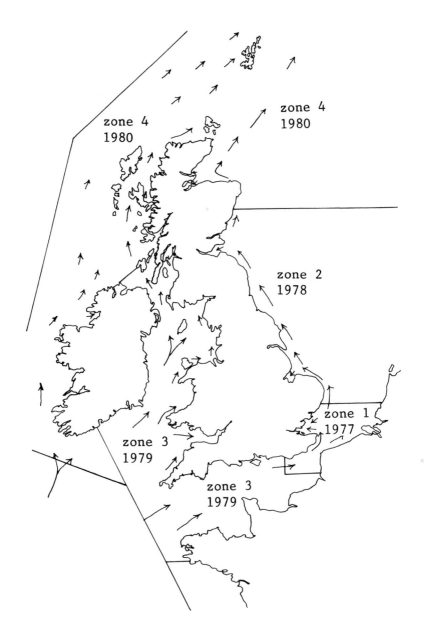

Fig 77 Conventional buoyage direction

114

Starboard hand
Colour and shape: Green (black may be used), conical or spar
Topmark (if any): Single green (black) cone, point up
Light (when fitted): Green, any rhythm

Where for exceptional circumstances an authority does not consider green (starboard hand) a suitable colour, black may be used.

Where marks do not rely upon can or conical buoy shapes, they should carry the appropriate topmark (*eg* River Humber where boat-shaped floats are used).

Where marks are numbered or lettered, the sequence should follow the conventional direction of buoyage.

Cardinal marks   Indicate the four quadrants (north, east, south, west) and are bounded by the true bearings NW — NE, NE — SE, SE — SW, SW — NW, taken from the point of interest at the centre of which may be a wreck, obstruction, *etc*. The cardinal mark is named after the quadrant in which it is placed. The name of the cardinal mark indicates that it should be passed on the named side of the mark.

The cardinal mark indicates the safe side on which to pass a danger, it indicates the deepest water in any area or it may draw attention to a feature in a channel such as a bend, junction, bifurcation or the end of a shoal.

North mark	*Topmark:*	Two black cones one above the other, points up
	Colour and shape:	Black above yellow, pillar or spar
	Light:	White. Rhythm – very quick flash or quick flash.
East mark	*Topmark:*	Two black cones, one above the other, base to base
	Colour and shape:	Black with a single broad yellow band, pillar or spar
	Light:	White. Rhythm – very quick flash (3) every 5 seconds or quick flash (3) every 10 seconds.
South mark	*Topmark:*	Two black cones, one above the other, points down
	Colour and shape:	Yellow above black, pillar or spar

	Light:	White. Rhythm – very quick flash (6) + a long flash every 10 seconds or quick flash (6) + a long flash every 15 seconds.
West mark	*Topmark:*	Two black cones, one above the other, point to point
	Colour and shape:	Yellow with a single broad black band, pillar or spar
	Light:	White. Rhythm – very quick flash (9) every 10 seconds or quick flash (9) every 15 seconds.

* A long flash = light appearance of not less than two seconds duration.

* A very quick flashing light emits 100 or 120 flashes per minute.

* A quick flashing light emits 50 or 60 flashes per minute.

The double cone topmark is the most important feature of the cardinal marks by day.

Isolated danger marks   are erected on or moored on or above an isolated danger which has navigable water all around it. The double sphere topmark by day is its most important feature.

Topmark:	Two black spheres one above the other
Colour and shape:	Black with one or more broad horizontal red bands, pillar or spar
Light:	White, group flash (2)

Safe water marks   serve to indicate that there is navigable water all round the mark; these include centre line marks and mid-channel marks. Such a mark may also be used as an alternative to a cardinal or lateral mark to indicate a landfall.

Colour and shape:	Red and white vertical stripes, spherical, pillar with spherical topmark, spar
Topmark (if any):	Single red sphere
Light (when fitted):	White, Rhythm — isophase, occulting or one long flash every 10 seconds

Special marks   are those not intended to assist navigation but which indicate a special area or feature referred to in nautical documents. For example:

116

Ocean data acquisition Systems (ODAS) marks
Cable or pipe line marks
Traffic separation schemes, where use of conventional channel marks may cause confusion

Military exercise zones
Recreation zone marks
Spoil ground marks

Colour and shape: Yellow, shape optional but not conflicting with navigational marks

Topmark (if any): Single yellow X shape

Light (when fitted): Yellow. Rhythm — any, but not those described above, *ie* cardinal, isolated danger, safe water marks

New dangers are newly discovered hazards not yet indicated in nautical documents. New dangers include naturally occurring obstructions such as sandbanks or rocks, or man made dangers such as wrecks. New dangers shall be marked in accordance with these rules. If the appropriate authority considers the danger to be especially grave at least one of the marks shall be duplicated as soon as practicable.

Any lighted mark used for this purpose shall have an appropriate cardinal or lateral VQF or QF light character.

Any duplicate mark shall be identical to its partner in all respects.

A duplicate mark may carry a racon coded 'W' showing a signal length of one nautical mile on the radar display.

The duplicate mark may be removed when the appropriate authority is satisfied that information concerning the new danger has been sufficiently well promulgated.

General. The above system has simplified many aspects of navigation for the mariner. In conventional channels the lights and colour of buoys to port are red, and to starboard the buoys are normally green with a green light. Topmarks are red can or green conical to match.

By day black and yellow pillar or spar buoys with two cones will indicate a cardinal buoy. Some memory aids for cardinal buoys are:

By day the cardinal buoys will carry two black cones and by assuming the top of the chart is north, the bottom south and the right is east, *etc*, then by following the cones in a clockwise direction starting at north:

117

North mark:	Cones point up, to the north, pass to the **north**.
East mark:	The bottom cone has been inverted, they are now base to base, pass to the **east**.
South mark:	The top cone has now been inverted, both cones point down to the south, pass to the **south**.
West mark:	There is now only one position left for the two cones to take, and that is point to point, pass to the **west**.

By night the cardinal buoys all show a quick or very quick flashing light. This should alert the mariner immediately to some form of hazard. On this occasion think of the face on the chartroom clock and relate it to the illustrated figure showing the four quadrants. If we start at the north mark or quadrant, thinking of it as midnight or noon, and follow the compass and clock around in sequence:

North mark:	A continuous very quick flashing light which will flash white between 50 and 120 times per minute and is easily recognisable. Pass to the north.
East mark:	3 o'clock on the clock face, showing Group (3) quick flashes every 5 or 10 seconds. Pass to the east.
South mark:	6 o'clock on the clock face, showing Group (6) quick flashes plus a long flash every 10 or 15 seconds. Pass to the south.
West mark:	9 o'clock on the clock face, showing Group (9) quick flashes every 10 or 15 seconds. Pass to the west.

The isolated danger mark by day is, like the cardinal mark, a pillar or spar, with its predominant colour black. The secondary colour, unlike the cardinal marks (yellow), is red. It has two distinctive black balls and generally it can be related to the cardinal (hazard) mark. By night it shows a group flash (2) white light. It can be passed on either side by giving it a wide berth.

The safe water mark may be spherical, pillar or spar, and can be easily remembered because it is different to any other buoys in that its colouring is white and red vertical stripes. Its top mark is a single red ball and its light is distinctive in that it is a single long flash, isophase or occulting white light as opposed to other hazard lights which are either grouped and/or very quick flashing.

Characteristics and chart abbreviations

On Admiralty charts the position of a buoy, beacon, light vessel, *etc*, is shown by a small circle drawn at the centre of the base line. Large scale charts showing more detail of soundings and lights give buoys, beacons, *etc* drawn properly to shape; the colour or colours of the buoy are shown below the buoy's position — the small circle. A buoy painted black and white would be shown BW. The abbreviations for the colour of buoy's beacons are shown in capital letters and those in use are as follows:

B — Black; G — Green; R — Red; W — White; Y — Yellow. BW — Black and white; RW — Red and white; BY — Black and yellow; BYB — Black, yellow and black.

When buoys, *etc*, are lighted they will have a magenta flare below the buoy to indicate a light. The characteristics of the light, in abbreviated form, are painted to one side of the light as is its name or number, if any.

Light characteristics

There are five main types of light characteristics for floating and shore lights; namely fixed, flashing, occulting, alternating and isophase.

Fixed (F): a continuously showing light.

Flashing (Fl): periods of darkness which are longer than the period of light.

Occulting (Occ): appears as a fixed light, which is eclipsed at regular intervals by periods of darkness. The dark periods are shorter than the light periods.

Isophase (Iso): a light where the periods of light and darkness are of the same duration.

Alternating (Alt): when viewed from any one bearing over which it shows, exhibits two or more colours (Not part of System 'A', but may be shown by a lighthouse or lightship)

Quick flash (QkFl): when the rate of flash is 50 or 60 flashes per minute.

Very quick flash (VQkFl): where the rate of flash is 100 or 120 flashes per minute.

Long flash (LFl): a long flash of not less than 2 seconds duration. Some of the above symbols may be seen together. For example:

GpFl (3)10S. Group flash 3 every 10 seconds. 3 light flashes show every 10 seconds, the interval of 10 seconds begins with the first flash and ends at the first flash of the succeeding group.

GpOcc. Group occulting. A continuous light broken at regular intervals by short eclipses.

GPF (4)Y. Group flash, 4, yellow.

System 'A' applies to all fixed and floating marks so that jetties, minor points of land, *etc* will be marked accordingly. Where the lateral colours are used to mark pierheads, jetties, *etc*, in British waters, to avoid confusion with ships' navigation lights, fixed shore lights shall be shown in pairs disposed vertically. Alternatively a single red or green light may be used but it must be flashing or occulting.

In order to distinguish spar buoys from fixed beacons on Admiralty charts, spar buoy symbols will be sloped, in accordance with standard practice. Beacons will be shown in the vertical.

Lights not in System 'A' will be those of lighthouses, leading lights and sector lights. A lighthouse may show an alternating light as previously described or it may show a sector light or lights. Sector lights usually show a red light over a danger area or approach, and a white light over a safe area or approach. Trawler skippers should consult the chart and Admiralty Light List when approaching sector lights.

If lighthouses, lightships and buoys emit signals other than light signals, this will also be shown on charts using one of the following: diaphone, horn, whistle, bell, siren, racon, *etc*. The use of the radar reflector symbol shown below will be discontinued.

Lightships and lighthouses may indicate the height of the light above sea level, (MHWS) and the luminous range of the light.

The abbreviation, Mo, when shown, indicates a fog signal which consists of one or more characters in the morse code, *eg* Horn Mo (WA).

Large scale charts give more detail of lights and signals than a small scale chart and should always be used in conjunction with the volume of the Admiralty List of Lights.

15   Tides and tidal streams

Gravitational attractions of the sun and moon create fluctuations in the mean level of the sea and the resultant effects are known as tides.

The moon is approximately 400 times nearer to the earth than the sun and it exerts a force of attraction which is about $2\frac{1}{4}$ times greater than that of the sun.

Spring tides occur, however, when the sun and moon are on the same meridian, their combined attractions create a maximum tide which is known as a spring tide. If we take a practical example, say London which lies on the Greenwich meridian in latitude 51°28′30″ N, then when the sun and moon are in conjunction above the Greenwich meridian they will create a spring tide. Because of gravitational forces, a spring tide will also occur at the same time, in a position diametrically opposite to that of London on the earth's surface, in 51°28′30″ S, on the 180° meridian of longitude.

When the sun and moon are on opposite meridians, *ie* the sun over the Greenwich meridian and the moon over the 180° meridian, we will again experience spring tides, along with a full moon. Because the lunar day and the solar day vary, the moon moves away from the sun each day by $12\frac{1}{2}$° of right ascension and after a little more than 14 days we have the recurring spring tides. In theory we have spring tides at approximately fortnightly intervals when the sun and moon are either in conjunction or opposite on the celestial sphere. The student may now ask, why then do spring tides not occur at noon and midnight when the sun and moon are in conjunction or opposite? This would happen if the seas were frictionless and the world smooth with the same depths and no land masses and no wind. This is not the case so there is a time lag in the creation of the tides. To summarise, spring tides will occur when the moon is new (in conjunction) and when it is full (in opposition).

Neap tides

From what has already been explained it will be seen that the moon is largely responsible for creating a tidal effect, with the sun's power of attraction assisting to a lesser degree when both bodies are above the same meridian. We know that the moon moves on past the sun each day by $12\frac{1}{2}°$, so that after a little more than seven days the sun and moon are separated by 90° of right ascension.

The sun with its weaker attraction is trying to make a tide on a meridian, the moon is making a tide at a longitude meridian which is 90° away. The forces are acting against each other and the result is that we have a high water neap tide on the meridian below the moon and a low water neap tide on the meridian below the sun.

During the intervening period of about seven days, from the position of conjunction to the position described above for neap tides, there will be intermediate tides, progressively reducing from springs to neaps. When the moon is in the position described above it is said to be in the first quarter.

The movement of the moon in relation to the movement of the sun continues so that after a little more than 14 days they are in the opposite position, when once again we have spring tides and a full moon.

The movement continues until the third quarter is reached, when the moon is in quadrature with neap tides occurring. This celestial movement continues until we get back to the position of conjunction, with the tides progressively increasing from neaps to springs.

In order that the reader may find it easier to understand the effect of the sun and moon upon the earth's tides, the following explanation of terms, *etc*, will help when examining *Figs 78a* and *b*.

The celestial sphere, or concave, is the heavens or space which surrounds the earth. For practical purposes, we assume that it is a hollow sphere, with all the heavenly bodies being on its surface and the earth at its centre.

The First Point of Aries is the point from which right ascension is measured. It is the point where the sun's centre crosses the celestial equator when changing from south to north declination. When this occurs on March 21st each year, it is known as the vernal or spring equinox.

Right ascension is the angular distance measured eastwards from the First Point of Aries to the point where the great circle through the

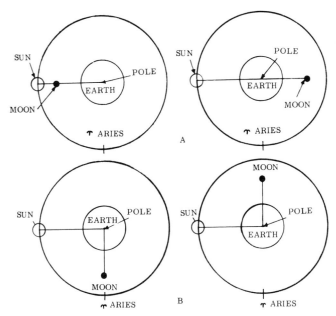

Fig 78 Influence of moon and sun on tides (a) springs (b) neaps

pole and the body cuts the equinoctical (celestial equator). Right ascension is always measured in hours from zero to 24.

Meridian is an imaginary great circle which passes through the north and south poles. All longitude lines are meridians. A heavenly body when reaching the highest point of its arc is said to be on the observer's meridian, *ie* the sun at noon.

To sum up, it will be seen that spring tides will occur when the sun and moon are either in conjunction or opposition. Neap tides occur when the sun and moon are in quadrature, with intermediate tides between these positions. A tide being raised in any place on the earth's surface will have another such tide raised diametrically opposite to it on the other side of the earth.

Because the earth revolves around its own axis, one revolution per solar day, any given meridian will pass through two areas of attraction giving high water and consequently two areas of low water.

Variations in the time of high water from day to day may be explained if we suppose that the sun and moon are in conjunction over the same meridian. When the earth revolves for twelve hours over 180° we might expect to reach the second high water. However, during this interval the moon has moved away from the sun by a little more than 6° of arc. The influence of the moon on the sea level has changed away from that of the sun by this distance and the second high water has moved on to a diametrically opposite position to that of the moon. It will therefore take the meridian 12 hours 25 minutes to reach the second high water position. It will take a similar time to get back under the moon again, so that a lunar day in this tidal context is 24 hours 50 minutes, equalling a tidal day.

Before passing on to the more practical aspects and application of tides as they affect the mariner, a list of tidal definitions is set out below:

Tides. The twice daily rise and fall of the mean sea level.

High water. The highest level reached by a particular tide to which reference is made.

Low water. The lowest level reached by a particular tide to which reference is made.

Slack water. The period when a tide has ceased to ebb or flow, at high or low water, preceding a change of direction of the tide. The slack water period is usually of longer duration on neap tides and shorter on springs.

Chart datum. Is a fixed level of the sea, below which nearly all soundings are given on Admiralty charts, usually in fathoms or metres. It is the mean level of the sea above the ground, at low water ordinary spring tides (MLWOS). The advantage in using MLWOS as a datum is that the mariner can nearly always be sure that the depth shown on a chart is the minimum.

Drying heights. When shown on a chart are heights of features which are uncovered by the sea at MLWOS tides. The height to which they are uncovered is distinguished from normal depths of water by being underlined. Drying heights are always given in feet or metres, never in fathoms.

Lowest astronomical tide. (LAT) is the lowest level which can be predicted to occur under any combination of astronomical conditions and under normal weather conditions. LAT levels are only reached occasionally and not necessarily every year. The amount of water shown on a chart using LAT as the datum will be less than that shown on a chart which has MLWOS as the datum.

Height of tide. Is the vertical distance at any moment between the level of the sea and the chart datum. The height of tide does not include the amount of water which may be below chart datum, and

cept gives 11.3 ft, the amount to be subtracted from the cast depth before plotting on the chart. (See *Fig 80* (left))

Depth from cast	30 ft	(5 fms)
Reduction	11.3ft	
Corrected depth	18.7ft	Look for about 3 fathoms on the chart.

The following is a shorter method and one which is sufficiently accurate for all practical purposes. (See *Fig 80* (right))

Describe a semi-circle as before on one side of a vertical scale, placing LW at the bottom and HW at the top of the scale which should be divided into feet. Divide the semi-circle into six or twelve equal parts. On the semi-circle mark off the time after HW (2h.16m) on the time scale and draw a horizontal line across until it intercepts the vertical line — at 10.5 ft.

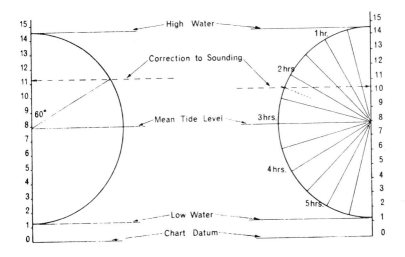

Fig 80 Correcting a sounding

This correction of 10.5 ft is not quite accurate when compared to the calculated method which gives 11.3 ft but it is a quick rough guide. The inaccuracy occurs because a time scale of six hours between high and low water was used on the semi-circle. Nevertheless a permanent scale should be made by the prudent mariner. The diagram would be permanent except for the rise of tide scale which could be marked in appropriately when a cast is taken.

Skippers and mates who pilot their ships into their home ports, ie Hull, Grimsby, Fleetwood, etc, should have a proper understanding of tides to assist the estuarial navigation. We have seen that there are 'phase inequality of tides' in that spring tides reach a maximum height at high water and neap tides reach a minimum height at high water. Likewise the spring tide rises to a maximum, and neaps fall to a minimum, below the mean tide level. Intermediate tides between springs and neaps range progressively from the spring heights to neap heights, or vice versa depending on which phase they are in.

A proper understanding of what is meant by mean tide level is essential for the mariner who is to navigate in tidal waters with minimum under keel clearance. In ports where the tide is semi-diurnal and regular, an understanding of what takes place around the mean tide level is invaluable. The mean tide level is the same for all tides whether they be springs, neaps or intermediate tides, when the port is semi-diurnal and regular. Local knowledge and examination of tide table predictions for a port will show whether the tide is regular or not. If there is a mean tide level of 16 ft on neaps there will be a mean tide level of 16 ft on springs or any other tide. The reason for this is that the tide falls below its mean level by the same amount as it rose above it. If we now look at our tidal diagram (*Fig 81*) with a mean tide level of 16 ft and a time scale of six hours, by drawing lines from each hour horizontally to the vertical scale we find that the regular tide follows a pattern. On the flood tide it will be seen that in the hour preceding the mean tide level the tide rises as much as it did in the first and second hours combined. In the hour following the mean tide level, the rise is roughly equal to the rise of tide during the two hours before high water.

From this it will be seen that the greatest rise of tide taking place on the flood will be between four hours and two hours before high water. The velocity of the flood will be greater during these two hours so that allowance for tidal effect in fog or when manoeuvring will have to be taken into account to a different degree at different times when on passage in the estuary.

If we assume that we are at Albert Dock, Hull and the mean tide level at three hours before high water is 16 ft, by watching the rise of tide on the dock cill gauge move from 16 ft to 20 ft in one hour, a rise of 4ft, we know that the remainder of the flood will produce about four feet more during the last two hours, giving a total height of 24 ft. This simple calculation may be made at other ports, *ie* Grimsby or Fleetwood, so it is possible to estimate the rise of an actual tide.

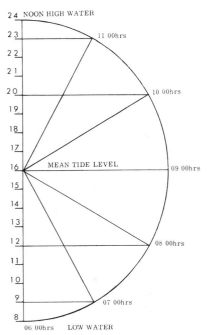

Fig 81 Mean tide level, regular/semi diurnal tide

Again if we take a mean tide level for Fleetwood as being 17.5 ft, watch the rise of tide for one hour from the time the 17.5 foot mark is reached and this proves to be 5ft, then we know roughly that HW would make 27.5 ft because the rise in the last two hours will approximately equal the rise in the preceding hour. By applying the drying heights in the Dock channel against 27.5 ft the skipper can determine the depth of water in which he may sail at high water.

We now move on to charts and the soundings given on them. Whilst the mariner knows that because they are chart datum, based either on mean low water springs or LAT and are minimum depths, the chart itself may be the result of an old survey, made many years ago. The soundings may not be accurate, and a prudent mariner will always allow for navigational uncertainties by preserving adequate clearance both horizontally and vertically.

Tidal streams

The influence of the sun and moon which create the tides as already described give rise to the horizontal movement of the sea from one place to another, where a tide is to be made. This movement is known as a tidal stream. These tidal streams, which are directly related to the time of high water, follow a fairly regular pattern and direction depending on the tide, *ie* a spring or a neap.

The Admiralty and other nautical publications show tidal streams for different parts of the world. If we examine the Admiralty publications for the British Isles we find that there are 14 atlases which cover the United Kingdom. Each atlas shows the speed and direction of the tidal stream for each hour, beginning six hours before HW at Dover and finishing six hours after HW.

The direction of the tide is shown by arrows, a lightly drawn short arrow indicates a weak stream, and an emphasised long black arrow indicates a strong stream. The mean strength of the stream is indicated between arrows, thus 20,35 indicates a 2.0 knot stream on neaps and a 3.5 knot stream on springs. The comma shows the approximate position of observation of streams.

Meteorological conditions will affect both the time and height of tides. Gale force winds, depending on direction, may reduce or hold back a tide, particularly a neap tide. A gale or hurricane force wind blowing in the same general direction as a flood tide, will create a tidal surge of exceptional height and velocity if the tide is a spring. In estuaries and ports fed by rivers, the effect of heavy rains and melting snow creates a higher tide than predicted but because it runs towards the sea, it will reduce the speed of a flood tide and increase the speed of the ebb. The actual time of high water may well be earlier than predicted, with no slack water period at all and an early running ebb. Because of the fresh water, the predicted height of low water will be less than the actual low water, but prudent mariners will not rely on this.

16 Navigational instruments and appliances

The handlead and line

This means of sounding, in common use before the advent of electronic navigational aids used for sounding and position fixing, is rarely used by the present-day mariner. Nevertheless it still remains an important piece of equipment which is reliable in shoal waters. Mariners should be familiar with the markings on the leadline and should use the line for no other purpose than sounding.

The hand lead, weighing between 10-14 lbs, is fitted with a wire grommet which is parcelled and served. The line, which has been stretched, has an eye splice in one end which is big enough to be passed through the grommet of the lead, over and under the lead, and set tight. The line is marked accurately as follows:

2 fathoms,	a piece of leather with two tails
3 fathoms,	a piece of leather with three tails
5 fathoms,	white linen
7 fathoms,	red bunting
10 fathoms,	a piece of leather with a hole in it
13 fathoms,	blue serge
15 fathoms,	white linen
17 fathoms,	red bunting
20 fathoms,	a cord with two knots

Different materials are used in order that the leadsman may tell by feel which marks he has in hand in the dark. The fathoms marked as above are called 'marks'. The fathoms not marked are called 'deeps' and are called out by the leadsman, *ie* 'by the mark 5', 'deep 6'. Fractions over fathoms are called 'and a quarter five', 'and a half five', but three quarters is always called as 'a quarter less six' or whatever the next highest mark or deep may be.

The lead may be used to check the echo sounder for accuracy when the ship is stopped or when at anchor.

Arming the lead

The bottom of the lead has a cavity not unlike that of the bottom of a wine bottle which is filled with tallow to which sand, gravel, and shells become embedded. These specimens with the corrected sounding help to fix the ship's position by reference to soundings on the chart and the abbreviations indicating the nature of the bottom.

Logs

Patent or taffrail logs   With the advent of impeller and pressure logs built into ships the old patent log is not in such common use nowadays. The use of Decca navigator and other position fixing systems has also caused a reduction in its use. The patent log is streamed from the stern of a ship and consists of a rotator, a fish, a long line, a governor wheel and a clock, with a shoe fitting into a plate screwed into the taffrail. (See *Fig 82*)

The rotator, with a balanced bronze body and four curved fins, is so constructed that it will turn freely and smoothly when towed. From the nose or cone there runs a plaited line which is clipped on to a 'fish' which is at the end of the log line. The fish, which is ovoid in shape,

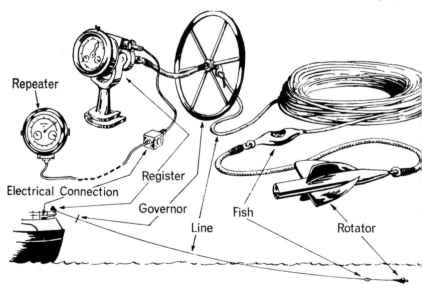

Fig 82   Patent log

132

has a hole at one end through which the log line will just pass. The end of the line is then pulled through the side of the fish through a larger access and secured by using a figure-of-eight knot, which tightens when pulled. The interior of the fish is grooved to provide purchase for the knot. The log line runs towards the stern of the vessel and is slipped on to a governor, which reduces any whip which may take place when the ship is under weigh at full speed. The governor is now connected to the clock, which is slid into a U-shaped plate. The clock, as its name implies, has clockwork mechanism geared to register a nautical mile for a given number of revolutions of the rotator. By reading the log at fixed intervals, say every hour, an approximate idea of speed and distance covered may be assessed.

Two errors must be allowed for when using this type of log. The log in itself may have an inherent error, *ie* if the vessel steamed 100 miles in still water and the log showed 98 or 102 miles then it would be 2% slow or fast. Only by use and trial will this error be found either by checking the log when abeam of shore marks where the actual distance run is known or by checking against two known positions.

The second error may be caused when the ship is steaming against or with a strong tide. The positive or negative slip of the tide on the rotator fins will create a small error.

Impeller and pressure logs   These logs are fitted into the bottom of a ship via a tube which projects through the hull into the sea. The impeller log, as its name implies, is rotated by passing through the sea when the ship is steaming and the revolutions are converted into distances and speed registers in the wheelhouse or chartroom.

The pressure log is similarly projected into the sea from the ship's bottom. The principle that pressure on the tube varies directly with the speed of the ship enables speed and distance to be recorded as it is with the impeller log.

Electro-magnetic log   A probe projecting through the ship's bottom from which a magnetic field is generated. The speed of the water passing through this field, when the ship is steaming, is measured and recorded as speed and distance.

NB In all these types of logs it must be noted that it is speed and distance through the water which is being measured and *not* speed and distance over the ground. Tides and currents must be taken into account when using logs which are motivated by the action of water passing the ship.

The magnetic compass

The magnetic compass is made up of needles, a compass card (*Fig 83*), a pivot and a compass bowl. The needles which point to the magnetic north are fitted into the card so that the north end of the needles coincide with the north mark on the card. The float of the card, which is sapphire, sits on an iridium pivot in order to reduce friction to a minimum. The card, if not of the dry card type, is suspended in the bowl in either white spirit or alcohol and distilled water which will not freeze. The bowl is suspended on gymbals so that the card will remain horizontal regardless of the movement of the ship. The bowl is made of non-magnetic material, with a glass top, and the gymbals are carried in a binnacle, or fitted on some ships into a deckhead. If a binnacle is used it would be made of non-magnetic material, wood and brass or man-made glass resinated plastic.

The compass will, in theory, point to the magnetic north and this would be so if it was fitted on board a non-magnetic ship which was

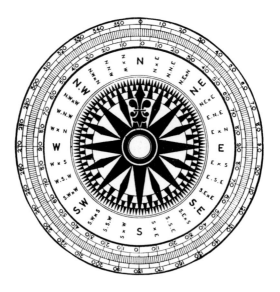

Fig 83 Graduated magnetic compass card

made and fitted out entirely in wood or plastic. But this is unlikely, so the compass on each individual ship has to be corrected for all the magnetic influences which will be exerted upon it by the inherent magnetism contained in the ship itself. These local influences are known as deviation. The compass adjuster, by using permanent magnets and soft iron, adjusts the compass so that it will point to the magnetic north. However, whenever a ship alters course and the ship's head points in a different direction the various magnetic influences alter the direction of the field relative to the compass which is still trying to point to the magnetic north. The compass adjuster will adjust the compass as near as possible for all the headings around a compass and if there are any small deviations of 1° or 2°, he will leave a deviation card on board which shows the residual deviation on each point of the compass. The navigator will have to use this card, before setting a course to steer, or after taking a bearing which he intends to lay off on a chart.

We have determined that the compass, apart from the deviation, points to the magnetic north. But the north which we use for navigation, chartwork, *etc* is the true north or geographical north where all the longitudinal meridians converge. The magnetic north lies in a different position to that of the true north. The difference between magnetic north and true north is known as variation. It is found by looking at the chart in use where it is shown on the compass rose. Variation in any one place does not remain static but will increase or decrease from one year to another by a small part of a degree, expressed in minutes. Variation varies from place to place and will of course change as a ship moves along the surface of the earth. For the fisherman it will be of interest to note that on approaching Halifax, Nova Scotia from Newfoundland the variation alters by 10° in less than 500 miles but it varies in the English Channel by about 5° in 400 miles. Variation charts are available and should be consulted on these changes.

Rules for correction of courses and bearings

Before giving the helmsman a course to steer, the navigator will have to take the true course from his chart and correct it for variation and deviation. The combined effect of variation and deviation is known as compass error. Deviation and variation may be expressed as being either east or west. If they are of the same name, both east or both

135

west, they are added together to make the error. If not, the difference becomes the error and takes the name of the larger.

Example

Variation	10° E	Variation	10° W	Variation	10° E
Deviation	2° E	Deviation	2° E	Deviation	2° W
Error	12° E	Error	8° W	Error	8° E

Before steering a course by compass the navigator must change the true course to a compass course by applying the error. When a compass bearing has been taken it must have the compass error applied to it so as to convert it to a true bearing for use on the chart. The compass card and true compass rose on a chart, the two points of interest, are marked from north which is zero to 360°, in a clockwise direction. Apply the error as follows:

From compass to true	*From true to compass*
Westerly error minus	Westerly error plus
Easterly error plus	Easterly error minus

If, however, the navigator wishes to use the magnetic compass on a chart, which of course differs from the true compass rose by the local variation, then only the deviation should be applied as follows:

From compass to magnetic	*From magnetic to compass*
Westerly deviation minus	Westerly deviation plus
Easterly deviation plus	Easterly deviation minus

Always remember that when applying deviation to a course or bearing that the deviation used should be that which applies for the deviation of the ship's head when the bearing was taken, or for the course which is to be steered.

Marks on a compass card

The 32 points of a compass have for many years been used as the principle marks on a compass. Each point of $11\frac{1}{4}°$ ($\times 32$) made up the 360°. By looking at the figure it will be seen how a particular direction could be given in points, as follows. (See *Fig 83*)

North	East	South	West
N×E	E×S	S×W	W×N
NNE	ESE	SSW	WNW
NE×N	SE×E	SW×S	NW×W
NE	SE	SW	NW
NE×E	SE×S	SW×W	NW×N
ENE	SSE	WSW	NNW
E×N	S×E	W×S	N×W
East	South	West	North

Half and quarter points between the whole points can be used but references to courses and bearings are only accurate to about $2\frac{1}{2}°$. This type of compass work and reference prevailed for many years and has been handed down to us by our forebears. It is simpler and more accurate to use the 360° compass when giving courses and bearings, particularly when passing information by radio. Always make sure that the bearing or course when used either by word of mouth or written is given its proper annotation (T) true, or (M) magnetic.

Gyro compass

Gyro compasses are mechanical and as a result are not affected by either the magnetism of the ship or that of the earth and are therefore not subject to variation or deviation. The gyro compass readings are always related to true north and the card is marked in the three figure notation only, ie 0°–360°, in a clockwise direction. Thus NE by a gyro when written would be 045°T, when spoken, 'zero four five degrees true'.

The directive force of a gyroscope is provided by the rotation of the earth. It works on the principle that the axis of a perfectly balanced wheel suspended in gymbals, in such a manner that it is free to tilt or turn, will continue to point in a fixed direction as long as the wheel is spinning at a very high speed. By rotating the wheel mechanically and at high speeds, the axis of the wheel will point to the true or geographical north pole. A compass card is fitted to the mounting of the gyroscope, so that the north and south shown on the card, is parallel to the line of the wheel's axis. Whatever way the ship turns, the north on the card will point to the true north pole.

The gyroscope is, whenever possible, positioned on the centre line of the ship at the roll and pitch centre, so that the movement of the vessel affects it as little as possible. The gyroscope is powered by electricity and should be run up for a period of five hours before use, so that it will be settled and reliable. From the gyroscope, repeater compass cards may be run off by electrical transmission to other parts of the ship — usually the wheelhouse or bridge wings for steering and the taking of bearings. Repeaters for use by the helmsman may take the shape of a roller tape, showing 30° – 40° of tape through the small window and will be lit for the helmsman to steer by. The lubber line is a marker or pointer which is in line with the fore and aft line of the direction of the ship's head.

Repeater compasses which are for use in taking bearings will be slung in gymbals and will be provided with either an azimuth mirror or bar sight. The azimuth mirror is a prism fitted on top of a compass bowl so that it can be turned through 360° around the compass card. A shore bearing or heavenly body by means of the reflective prism can be brought down on to the edge of the compass card so that an accurate bearing between the observer's eye, the centre of the compass, and the edge of the compass card can be taken.

As long as the gyroscope is in good order and there is a steady input of electrical power, the repeaters will give satisfactory service, but the navigator must be aware of a small error which may have to be applied to the gyro. This error will be fairly constant and is due to course, speed and latitude. The axis of the gyroscope takes up a north-south position and it is, of course, at right angles to the earth's direction of rotation. When a ship is steaming east or west there is no steaming error, but when a ship steams due north, there is a slight deflection of the axis and the compass north, to the west of the true meridian. When steaming south there is a similar deflection of the compass north, to the east of the true meridian. The deflection is greater in high latitudes. The error may be found in tables or may be found:

$$\text{Tangent course} = \frac{\text{Ship's speed} \times \text{Cosine course} \times \text{Secant latitude}}{900}$$

The gyro-compass is marked numerically from 0°–360° clockwise, so that if it is found that there is an error and the gyro-compass indicates a direction which is numerically greater than the true course then it is called *high*. Conversely a numerically smaller reading of the gyro-compass than the true is known as *low*.

138

The simple rules for applying gyro error are as follows:–

When converting direction from *compass* to *true, subtract* the gyro error if *high* and *add* the gyro error if *low*.

When converting from *true* direction to *compass* direction, *add* the gyro error if *high* and *subtract* the gyro error if *low*.

Example:

(1) A vessel is steering 045° by gyro compass and there is a gyro error of 2° high. What is the ship's true course?

Ship's head compass	045°	
Gyro error	2°	High (subtract) compass to true
Ship's true course	043°	

(2) A vessel has to make a true course of 130° but there is a gyro error of 2° high. What course must she steer on the gyro compass?

True course to make	130°	
Gyro error	2°	High (add) true to compass
Compass course to steer	132°	

(3) Flamboro Head bears 270° by gyro compass, gyro error 2° high. What is the true bearing?

Gyro compass bearing	270°	
Gyro error	2°	High (subtract) compass to true
True bearing	268°	

Aneroid barometer

The aneroid barometer (*Fig 84*) is a dry barometer which contains a metallic chamber, partially exhausted of air and hermetically sealed. Variations in pressure of the earth's atmosphere allows the volume of air within the box to expand or contract. This change in volume is passed by means of levers to the hand on the face of the barometer so that an increase of pressure makes the hand rise and a decrease causes it to fall. There is no correction to be applied to an aneroid barometer except for the height above sea level and index error. An aneroid

139

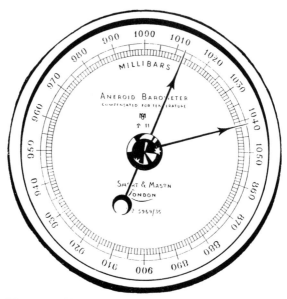

Fig 84 The aneroid barometer

barometer should be checked fairly regularly against the corrected reading of a mercury barometer.

Mercury barometer

The mercury barometer is a more reliable barometer than the aneroid, but more expensive and more difficult to fit into the confined space of a trawler's wheelhouse. The mercury barometer consists of a long metal case which holds the tube and cistern containing the mercury. The barometer is fitted to a bulkhead on a base plate and is slung in gymbals so that it remains upright, regardless of the movement of the ship. The mercury within the tube has above it a space which is exhausted of gases and the atmospheric pressure on the mercury in the cistern at the bottom of the tube balances the column of mercury. The fluctuations in pressure are shown as movements in the length of the column of mercury, against which a scale in millibars has been accurately set. The scale is graduated in millibars and marked at intervals of 10 MB. The scale may be read to an accuracy of 0.1 MB by means of a vernier scale.

When reading the mercury barometer the observer's eye should be exactly on a level with the upper edge of the mercury column so as to

140

eliminate parallax. The surface of the mercury will be convex in shape and the reading should be taken by turning the vernier screw so that the lower edge of the vernier just touches the uppermost part of the domed surface of the mercury.

Corrections to the mercury barometer have to be made for height, latitude and temperature. There may well be an index error on the instrument which will be given on the maker's certificate issued with the barometer, as will be the standard temperature for the barometer. The principles of correction are as follows:

(1) The mercury in the barometer falls 1 MB for every 30 ft of height. Always add.

(2) The correction for latitude is made for the changing effect of gravity, greater at the pole than at the equator. Consequently the barometer reads lower than standard when the latitude is more than 45° when the correction is plus. Latitude less than 45° correction is minus.

(3) The mercury rises 1 MB for every 6°C so that the difference in the temperature taken from the thermometer attached to the barometer and the standard temperature on the certificate for the barometer must be applied. If the temperature is greater than the standard, apply minus correction, if temperature is less, apply plus correction.

Correction tables may be found in all good nautical almanacs.

Barograph

The barograph is a type of aneroid barometer which transmits expansion and contraction in the box with a partial vacuum to a roll of paper via a lever and pen (as opposed to a dial). The roll of paper is turned by clockwork so that the roll completes one revolution in seven days enabling a complete pressure record to be kept. The vertical lines on the barograph roll represent time and the horizontal lines represent pressure.

Thermometers

There are three main types of thermometer used by seamen, *ie* Fahrenheit (F), Centigrade (C), and Absolute or Kelvin (A). The scales used for these three:

141

	F°	C°	A°
Boiling point	212°	100°	373°
Freezing point	32°	0°	273°
Scale	180°	100°	100°

From the above scales it can be seen that C and A have the same scale and that 1° of Centigrade is equal to 1° of Absolute. The latter has, however, a range from 0° to 373° so that all temperatures below freezing point are positive. In the case of Centigrade, however, any temperature below freezing will be shown as negative.

In the case of Fahrenheit, the range is 212° with a scale of 180° so that basically we have a comparative value of 1.8°F = 1°C or A and consequently a closer division of temperature values.

Fahrenheit chose 32° as his freezing point because it is said, he believed that 0°, *ie* 32° below his freezing point, was the extreme of cold. To be able to convert one temperature reading to another is a fairly simple matter if one remembers the scales as set out above.

When converting from F° to Centigrade, deduct 32° and multiply by 5/9.

When converting to F° from Centigrade, multiply by 9/5 and add 32°.

When converting from C° to A° add 273°, from A° to C° subtract 273°.

Formulae for conversion are:

$$F = \frac{9C}{5} + 32. \qquad C = \frac{5(F-32)}{9}$$

Examples

(1) Convert 212°F to Centigrade:

$$C = \frac{5(212-32)}{9} = \frac{5 \times 180}{9} = 100°C$$

(2) Convert 100°C to Farenheit:

$$F = \frac{9 \times 100}{5} + 32 = \frac{900}{5} + 32 = 212°F$$

The maximum thermometer

It is designed to record the highest temperature during a given period. The tube of the thermometer is reduced in bore close to the bulb. The thermometer in the horizontal position, with the temperature rising, allows the mercury to expand and force its way past the constriction so that when there is subsequently a fall in temperature, the mercury contracts below the constriction, leaving the mercury in the upper tube to remain as a record of the highest temperature reached.

Minimum thermometer

Designed to record the lowest temperature during a given period. Spirit is normally used and there is a small index, shaped so that when the temperature falls the index sinks down the stem towards the bulb. When subsequently the temperature rises the spirit passes the index and leaves it to register the lowest temperature.

Hygrometer

Consists of two ordinary thermometers, placed side by side, one of which is known as the wet bulb. The dry bulb records the temperature of the surrounding air. The wet bulb is wrapped in muslin with a wick leading to a canister of water which keeps the bulb damp. When the air is dry and has little water content, evaporation takes place on the surface of the wet bulb and because heat is extracted, the temperature will fall. The difference between readings on the two thermometers is of significant value.

A consistent difference of reading of say 10° is a sign of good weather, but any significant reduction in the difference may indicate the approach of a depression. At the other extreme, we may have a situation whereby the temperatures are similar and there is little or no depression on the wet bulb. This happens when the air is so saturated that evaporation cannot take place and mist/fog is forming.

The sextant

The sextant is an optical instrument used for measuring the angles subtended between any two points. Angles up to 120° may be measured even though the sextant's arc is only 60° or a sixth of a circle,

143

hence the name sextant. (See *Fig 85*) Any type of angle may be measured but the navigator is mainly concerned with those on either the horizontal plane or the vertical plane.

In coastal navigation the sextant can be used to obtain two horizontal angles between any three chosen points and so obtain a fix either by station pointer or drawing (see section on *Station pointer*). A distance off a known point of land or lighthouse may be found by using the vertical angle between the top of the object, the observer's eye and the base of the object. The navigator must know the height of the shore object from the summit to the base and the vertical angle, and by use of distance-off tables and a bearing, a position can be obtained. When out of sight of land the vertical angle between a heavenly body and the horizon is a basic necessity for working out one's position line.

By looking at *Fig 85*, it can be seen that the index arm is pivoted at the top of the sextant where an index mirror is fitted. The bottom of the index arm is able to slide along the arc which is graduated in degrees with a more accurate reading to a minute or part of a minute obtained from the micrometer. The index arm is clamped to the arc, but by a simple finger press may be released for movement.

In line with the telescopic sight, fitted to the frame of the sextant is a fixed glass, half mirror, half plain, which is called the horizon glass.

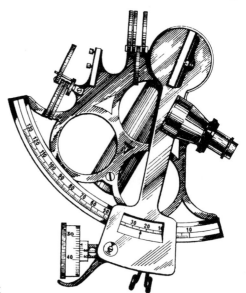

Fig 85 The sextant

When the zero on the arm is at zero on the arc the index mirror should reflect an image alongside the true image seen on the horizon glass. Shades are fitted at both the index and horizon glasses for use in bright weather and to darken the glare of the sun when it is being used.

Adjustments and sextant errors

The first adjustment of the sextant is to set the index mirror perpendicular to the plane of the instrument. Place the index near the middle of the arc. Hold the instrument face up and arc away from the eye. Look into the index mirror so that the true and reflected arc can be seen. If the arcs are in line the index mirror is perpendicular but if not adjustment can be made by moving the screw at the back of the index mirror until they are in line.

The second adjustment is to set the horizon mirror perpendicular to the plane of the instrument. With the index exactly at zero hold the instrument so that the plane is nearly horizontal. Look through the horizon mirror and see if the true and reflected horizons are in line, if not they may be brought into line by slowly moving the adjusting screw at the side of the mirror.

The third adjustment is to set the horizon mirror parallel to the index mirror when zero on the arc coincides with zero on the arm. Set the arm as described at zero on the arc. Hold the sextant vertically and look through the horizon mirror to see if the true horizon and reflected horizon are in line. If they are there is no error, if not, move the adjusting screw at the top of the horizon mirror until the horizons coincide.

If, however, this third adjustment seems to be small, one may find the index error by moving the micrometer until the horizons coincide. The reading on the micrometer will be an index error which may be applied to all future sights or angles taken. Note should be taken as to whether the error is 'on' or 'off' the arc.

NB When the reading is on the arc, the index error is subtracted from future readings.

When the reading is off the arc the index error is added to future readings.

Because four minutes of arc is equivalent to one nautical mile, when working out astronomical sights it is not good policy to have more than two minutes of index error. It is too easy to forget the error: if it is possible to adjust the horizon glass, it should be done.

Use of sextant

To observe a vertical angle, clamp the index at zero on the arc and look at the object through the telescope and horizon glass. The reflected image will appear in the horizon mirror. With the left hand unclamp the index arm. With the right hand move the sextant downwards in such a manner that the reflected image remains in the mirror, and until the horizon or lower object has been reached. Release the clamp with the left hand and make the final adjustment with the micrometer wheel. Remember that the left hand keeps the index mirror at the top of the sextant arm pointing at the object and that the right arm moves the sextant, its arc and reflection down until the reflected object has reached and is co-incident with the second object. Several practice shots will soon make the student proficient.

To observe an horizontal angle hold the sextant in the right hand, arc up and with the index arm at zero. Look through the telescope and horizon glass at the right hand object which will be seen co-incident in the glass and mirror. With the sextant held in the horizontal plane by the right hand, unclamp the index arm with the left hand. Keep the index mirror pointing at the object with the left hand and swing the sextant slowly left with the right hand until the second object is reached and is seen by the eye in the horizon glass. Release the clamp and adjust the micrometer with the left hand until the objects are finally coincident in the horizon mirror.

Reading the sextant

The arc of the sextant is marked in degrees only, from 0° to 130° on the arc, and from 0° to 5° off the arc. The scale is numbered at every 10° of arc and each 10° section is marked in single degrees with a longer mark on each intermediate 5°. The micrometer indicates the number of minutes on the wheel of the drum (see *Fig 85*) indicated by an arrow. To find the number of seconds we must now look to the vernier scale to the right of the micrometer wheel. There we will see one minute broken down into fractions, *ie* six graduations, each of which equals ten seconds. The arrow is zero, and six lines indicate the seconds. Where any one of these fixed lines comes into true conjunction with a line on the chronometer wheel, then that is the number of seconds to be used with the previously noted degrees and minutes. (On the illustrated sextant the reading is 23°-33'-20".) Some sextants have the minutes shown on the vernier as being in five parts, *ie* twelve second intervals. The student must understand the sextant and its readings, and only by practice will confidence in its use be attained.

The station pointer

This instrument consists of a circular frame which is marked off in degrees. From the centre of the circle running outward past the circular frame there are three legs. The middle of these three legs is fixed to the frame at zero degrees. The outside legs are movable at the centre circle pivot and are clamped on to the outer circle. They may be swung around the circle by releasing the pressure on the clamps by use of the knurled finger screws. By finding two angles subtended by three shore objects, the legs may be set to subtend these angles. By placing the station pointer on the chart so that the legs run through the positions of the objects, the position of the ship is fixed as being the centre of the circle. (*Fig 86*)

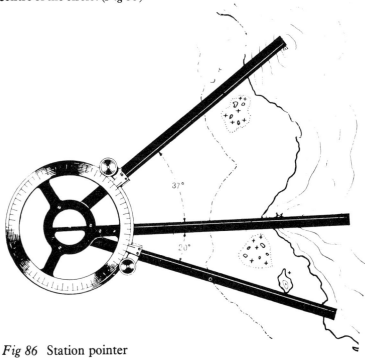

Fig 86 Station pointer

The angles may be determined either by sextant or by taking three bearings on the compass. If no station pointer is available tracing paper may be used. Mark a spot on the tracing paper and from it draw a base line. Use this base line as the middle of the three bearings or angles taken by sextant. Measure the angles subtended by the other two shore objects from this base line, and use the tracing paper over the chart as the station pointer would be used. *Note:* when bearings are used it does not matter whether they be true, magnetic or compass as long as they are all the same and taken simultaneously. It is the difference between the bearings which gives the required angles.

Automatic steering gear

The use of automatic steering gear has become widespread during the last decade, in both merchant and fishing fleets. It is said that it is more economical on fuel because it steers a ship on a straighter course and saves time.

There are many different types of automatic steering gear, too numerous to mention in this book, but they work on similar principles. One of the original types still in use consists of a brass ring fitted on to the top of the compass bowl. This ring is marked from 0°-360° so that the compass card direction and that on the steering ring are the same. When a new course has to be steered the ring is moved so that the new course coincides with the lubber line. The automatic steering gear alters the course until compass card heading and that on top of the bowl coincide.

A second type is that of a black box, fitted to a bulkhead, marked with an illuminated ring from 0°-360°. From the middle there is an arrow pointing to the degrees on the ring from the middle of the circle, which indicates the course being steered. The arrowed indicator is fitted to a centre knob, which can be used to select a fresh course by simply turning the knob and arrow to the new course required. The compass card heading should always match the black box heading once the course has been set. In both the above types of automatic steering there is usually a limit to the amount by which the navigator can alter course. Because the system is controlled by sensors, which put helm on according to the amount of the alteration, the alteration at any one time is usually restricted to a maximum of 30°. When the ship's head has moved towards this maximum alteration then the navigator may apply a second maximum and so on. The danger in altering course by let us say 90° is that the sensors would seek the new course by putting the steering gear hard over and would continue to try and put more helm on. The ship would take on a violent swing and the sensors may well lose control. It is always advisable to make successive alterations limited to less than 30° with this type of steering. Manufacturers' instructions should be read and fully understood. Combined with automatic steering there is usually a steering tiller to which one may switch over. There may be more than one tiller, possibly one in the wheelhouse and one on each bridge wing.

The third type of automatic steering is that whereby the ship may be steered by the tiller mode as described above. The tiller is usually a small polished round bar about six inches in length with a knob at the end. It is usually horizontal and is housed in a box fitted on to the fore part of the wheelhouse in such a position that the helmsman can see not only the fore part of the ship but the compass and helm indicator. By moving the tiller to port or starboard the rudder is moved in that direction. When released the tiller handle comes back to the midship position. To take off the helm which has been put on, the tiller bar has to be moved across to the other side. On this third type of steering, course is altered by using the tiller until the ship is steady on the new course. The change-over to automatic steering may then be accomplished by pushing the hand tiller down into a groove marked automatic. The compass course is then maintained by the automatic sensors which use the rudder to keep the course.

The advantages of automatic steering gear is that it allows a vessel to maintain a good straight course and a check on the course can quickly be made simply by looking at the compass occasionally. Unfortunately, this very useful equipment has led to some lack of bridge discipline in that a bridge may not be manned for short, and on occasions, long periods. The need to maintain a continuous and efficient lookout is now more important than ever it has been. Because an officer of the watch knows that a good course is being steered by automatic means is no excuse for him to neglect to keep a proper lookout. There have been many cases whereby ships have been proceeding on automatic steering when they have run into another vessel or gone aground, because the officer of the watch felt it safe to go into the chartroom for a lengthy period, or the lookout felt it safe to leave the bridge for some reason. The automatic steering may steer very efficiently, but it cannot keep a lookout.

When in congested waters, estuaries and rivers, the hand mode of steering should *always* be used. In such areas any malfunction of the automatic gear can lead to collision or grounding almost immediately.

Pelorus

This instrument is constructed to be used in conjunction with a compass under circumstances whereby the subject of a bearing cannot be seen from the compass position.

In many trawlers the compass or gyro repeater may be in the wheelhouse or sometimes in the deckhead of the wheelhouse, where it is either difficult or impossible to take an accurate bearing of a landmark, seamark, *etc*.

The pelorus, a circular brass plate marked 0°-360°, is mounted on a pedestal, which fits into a shoe mounting available on each bridge wing. From the centre of the pelorus compass rose there will be an alidade bar sight by which the observer may take a visual bearing. The bar sights may be moved in the horizontal plane around the compass rose. With zero on the pelorus set in the fore and aft line of the ship, a bearing which is relative to the ship's heading may now be taken. Great care must be taken to ensure that the bearing is taken when the ship is exactly on course or that the ship's heading is noted exactly at the time the bearing is taken. Station pointer bearings may be taken by pelorus without recourse to the compass if two or more landmarks are visible.

17   Coastal navigation

Navigation is the science and art of conducting a ship safely from one place to another. Generally we may consider modern navigation as falling into three categories — coastal, astronomical and electronic. This is a convenient method for separating the three types of navigation for discussion or reading, but it is important to remember that the different types of navigation may be used together. We may have, for example, a single bearing taken by compass of a distant point of land, which when used with a radio bearing or an astronomical position line will give a good positional fix.

When it is necessary to go from place A to place B, the *course to be made good* is the line joining the two places. This will not necessarily be the *course to steer* which will have to be found by allowing for the effects of tide, current, wind and compass error.

A single bearing, an astronomical intercept, a single radio bearing, or a radar bearing will always give the navigator a line which can be put on the chart, and on which the navigator knows he stands. This single line is known as a position line and if the navigator can obtain a second position line, where the two lines cross will give a position. Coastal navigation largely consists of the use of position lines, referred to as bearings. These bearings may be put down on a chart to provide a position or fix. To make sure that a correct course is being made good, intermediate position lines must be taken whenever possible so that a check is made on the true direction. If we suppose that a prominent point of land lies in a direction by compass 180° from the observer, then the *bearing* of the land is 180° If we reverse the bearing and draw a line on the chart 360° from the point of land we then have a position line on which the observer stands. If we are able to take a second bearing simultaneously, let us suppose of yet another point of land bearing 090°, reverse it to 270° and lay it off from the point of land, we have a second position line on which the observer stands. Where the first and second line cross each other on the chart is the observer's position, known as a fix. Two bearings may not always be necessary.

By looking at the chart two convenient and conspicuous objects may be marked; a chimney or church may be seen and if the observer waits until either the church or chimney is in line with let us say a small island, then a line drawn through both will provide a transit bearing. By taking a single compass bearing and laying it off on the chart as a position line, where it crosses the transit bearing will be the fix.

The best positions are always obtained from bearings which have a large angular distance between them, the ideal being 90°. It will be obvious that two shore objects which, when looked at by an observer, are so close together that the angle subtended at the observer's eye is about 20°, will not be very reliable because 20° is the angle of convergence and they run together slowly. Therefore an error of 1° in the bearing will separate the lines by some considerable distance. Do not use angles of less than 40°.

The primary method of fixing should, whenever possible, be by means of visual bearings. In trawlers this may entail the use of the pelorus on which a relative bearing is taken and applied to the ship's head. (See *Chapter 16, Pelorus*)

A quickly taken range and bearing obtained from a radar picture of a mark not positively identified is no substitute for the fix by compass.

Fix by cross bearing

Fig 87 illustrates an observer who took two simultaneous bearings of points A and B, bearing 310° and 030° respectively. When drawn on the chart the position lines cut clearly with an angular separation of 80°.

On the same figure the course to be made good (100°T) is already on the chart but the observed position is at C. It is clear that relative to the land, the true position by observation is on the landward side of the course line and that the ship may have to be pulled out or, if no danger exists, a new course line will have to be drawn from C with an allowance for the northward set which has been experienced.

Fix by vertical angles and a bearing

At small distances a position line may not necessarily be straight because it forms part of a circle. If we look at *Fig 88* we will see a lighthouse. The height of the focal plan of the lighthouse is known to be 120 ft above sea level (MHWS) and is taken from the charts. Let us

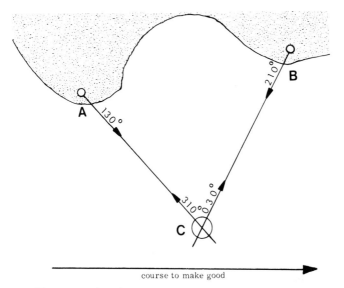

Fig 87 Two cross bearings

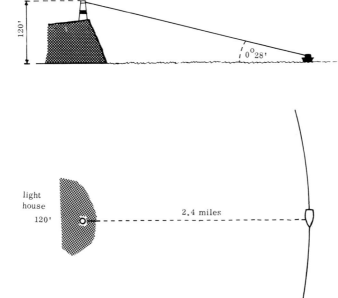

Fig 88 Vertical sextant angle

suppose that we use a sextant to find the vertical angle between the top of the lighthouse, the ship, and the base of the lighthouse. (Refer to *Chapter 16, Use of sextant*) If we find that the vertical angle is 0°-28°′ then with the height of the lighthouse we may now find from the 'distance-off' tables in Burton's or Norie's that the ship is 2.4 nautical miles distant from the lighthouse. *Fig 88* illustrates the procedure, the top drawing shows in elevation the sextant angle and the bottom drawing the plan view and the position line as an arc of a circle drawn with the point of the compasses at the lighthouse as the centre of the circle. A bearing taken with the sextant angle, when the ship is abeam, will provide a fix.

If the observer needs to pass the lighthouse at a given distance off for any reason, let us say five miles away from a lighthouse of 150 ft in height, look up the height and distance in the 'distance-off' tables to find the angle to set on the sextant. By looking through the telescope of the sextant when abeam of the lighthouse, the reflected image should be on the waterline at the base of the lighthouse. If it is, the distance off is five miles. If the reflected image is below the waterline the distance off is more than five miles. If the reflected image is above the waterline, the distance off is less than five miles and it will be necessary to pull out by altering course.

Fix by station pointer and horizontal angles

By taking simultaneous compass bearings well spread out on one side of the ship a good fix will be obtained. As described in *Chapter 16, Station pointer*, three bearings of suitably spaced points of land will provide two horizontal angles subtended from the middle bearing. By examining the bearings taken and illustrated in *Fig 89,* the station pointer can be set with the angles 50°-60° from the middle leg and by placing the station pointer on the chart so that the three legs pass over the three shore marks the position is fixed at the centre of the station pointer.

By using a horizontal angle set on a sextant, an off-shore danger can be cleared as illustrated in *Fig 90*. Place the point of the compass on the off-shore danger D, draw the circle with the safe distance off as a radius. Now draw the course to be made good so that it just touches this small circle to seaward. This point should now be joined by straight lines to the two fixed identifiable objects ashore, A and B, one on each side of the danger. The angle of 53° subtended between A and

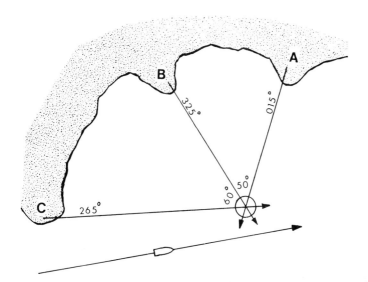

Fig 89 Fix by station pointer

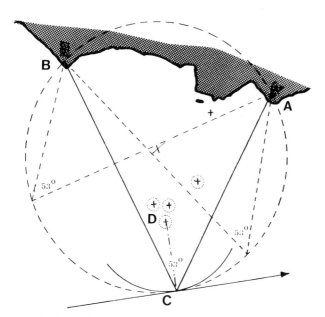

Fig 90 Horizontal safety angle

B at position C, is the largest that can be allowed to occur between the fixed objects ashore. When set on the sextant it will indicate to the navigator whether he is passing clear of the danger or not.

If, through the sextant's telescope, the right hand object A is reflected to the left of B which is seen directly, the ship is outside the danger circle. If however the reflected object appears to the right of the directly visual object B, the ship is inside the danger area and should be pulled out, in this case to starboard, until the objects appear together on the horizon glass of the sextant. (See *Chapter 16, Use of sextant*)

Running fixes

A running fix is used to find a position when only one identifiable object ashore can be used. It is the least reliable type of coastal fix because its accuracy depends on the estimated run of the ship between two bearings of the same object. However, the running fix demonstrates that once having obtained a single position line which the navigator knows the ship is on, it can be transferred to cut with a second position line. The fix, however, is only as good as the estimated course and distance made good. To obtain a good running fix, the navigator must have a reasonably angled bearing with a fair idea of the course and distance run.

In *Fig 91* at 1050 GMT a ship steering 070°T at a speed of 12 knots sighted a lighthouse bearing 040°T. Half an hour later at 1120 GMT the same lighthouse bore 356°T.

The course will already be laid off on the chart. The first bearing 040° taken at 1050 GMT should be laid off from the lighthouse as a position line. Where it cuts the course line will be an estimated position.

From the lighthouse lay off the second bearing taken at 1120 GMT so that it crosses the course line. The distance steamed by a 12 knot ship in half an hour would be six miles. From the first estimated position (1050 hours) measure off six miles along the course line. If this measured distance places the ship on the second bearing at the second estimated position then the ship has made good a course of 070°T and has run six miles. The estimated course and distance has been accurate and no set or drift has been experienced.

If, however, the distance run of six miles, as *Fig 91* illustrates, takes the ship past the second bearing, then with the aid of the parallel

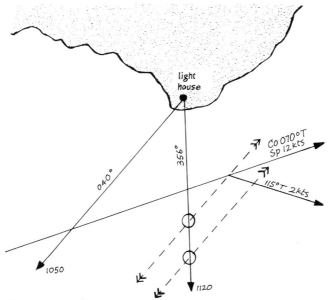

Fig 91 Running fix

rulers the first bearing should be transferred and drawn through the course line, at the position where the distance run ended. Where the first bearing cuts the second bearing is the ship's position. Measure the distance back and reverse the course to prove the geometry of this method.

If the navigator knows from his Admiralty Tidal Stream Atlas that a tidal stream of 115°, two knots was effective in this area, then after measuring off six miles for half an hour's steaming along the course line, a further allowance should now be made of one mile (half hour of tide) 115°T. The original bearing taken at 1050 GMT of 040°T must now be transferred through this last position and where it cuts the second bearing is the ship's 1120 GMT position.

Three cross bearings

So far we have dealt with fixes which have included the use of two bearings or a bearing and a sextant angle. It is much more satisfactory and accurate, however, to use three bearings and to find that they cross together or nearly together at one place. If the three position lines do not quite cross together the navigator will find that he has a

157

small triangle on the chart, which is called a 'cocked hat'. The middle of the 'cocked hat' may be used as the position if it is small. If however the 'cocked hat' is large, the bearings should be re-taken and/or a check made to see if a mistake has been made in applying the compass error. (See *Chapter 16, Application of compass errors*)

If the navigator is in doubt about the identity of shore marks, three bearings will prove the accuracy of identity, or otherwise. By looking at *Fig 92*, it can be seen that two bearings of a lighthouse and beacon were taken about 90° apart, and a fix at position A was established. By taking a third bearing from a position marked Flag Staff, a new position B was fixed and it was found that the wrong beacon had been used in the first plot.

Two sextant angles

The use of a single vertical sextant angle and a bearing has been illustrated. By using two vertical sextant angles of different shore objects and following the procedure prescribed earlier, we will have two ranges or distances from two points. By looking at *Fig 93*, it can be seen that the distances off positions A and D will provide a fix, if the distances off are used as radii of circles.

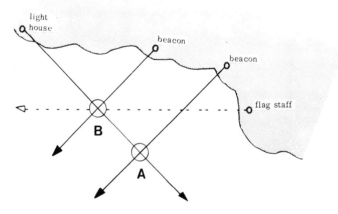

Fig 92 Three cross bearings

158

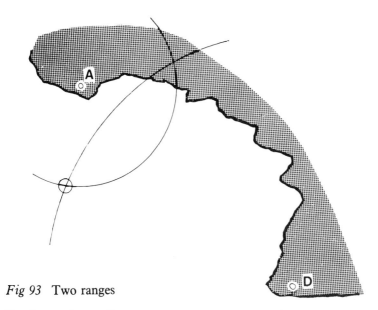

Fig 93 Two ranges

Bearing and sounding

When there is little difference in the heights of high and low water and where the soundings have a definite character and line, an approximate position may be found by using a single bearing and sounding. The sounding must have been corrected as described in *Chapter 15* and should lie along the position line. If, however, the soundings are uniform in depth, the chart in use has not been surveyed for many years, or the soundings are widely separated and not in lines, then this method of position fixing is not of value and may well be dangerous.

Angles on the bow

By doubling the angle on the bow, the navigator may fix his position by using the simple principles of geometry in the isosceles and right-angled triangle. Triangles all have three sides and three angles, the sum of which is 180°. We know that in an isosceles triangle two sides are of the same length. It follows that if we have two sides of the same length then the opposing angles are of the same size in degrees. *Fig 94* illustrates that there is a ship at A steaming due east and there is a point of land two points ($22\frac{1}{2}°$) on the port bow. With the ship continuing to steam along the course line, we wait until the first angle at A has doubled and is now 45° on the port bow and note the distance

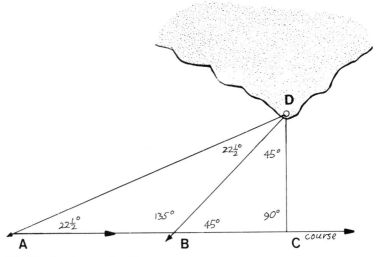

Fig 94 Angles on the Bow

steamed. If we look at the figure again we see that at position B, by taking 45° away from 180° we have angle ABD = 135°. Therefore the angle at D must equal 22½° and by doubling the angle of 22½° on the bow we now have an isosceles triangle. The sides opposite are equal and because we know how far we have steamed from A to B we now know the distance B to D is the same, which is the distance off.

We now come to the 'four point bearing' an angle made at position B of 45° between the course line and point D. This is really a continuation of the isosceles triangle except that by doubling the angle of 45°, we know in advance that our second angle will be the ship's position when we are abeam. The ship's position when abeam of a point of land is always of importance to the navigator, he now has an exact time and position of departure to his next point of interest and it is a good position to alter course. By taking the time and distance run from B to C we have formed a right-angled triangle BCD with the right angle at C. Angle D must be 45° and because sides BC and CD are equal, we have a beam bearing and distance off.

Tidal effect on courses

By looking back to the section on 'Running fixes' it will be seen how a tidal stream affects the run of a ship when steaming. For the purposes of illustration and examination, the laying off of a tidal effect or current at the end of a run is acceptable. It is also reasonable to

160

compare an expected position with a fix and name the difference as being due to speed and direction of current and wind. A navigator who knows the speed and direction of a tidal stream or current should allow for it before giving a course to steer so that the proper course can be made good.

If we look at *Fig 95* and suppose that a 15 knot ship wishing to make good a course of 090° is about to pass two islands, from between which there runs a current of 2½ knots in a direction 180°. From the departure point A, lay off the 090°T course which would be made good if the vessel steamed 15 miles in one hour and was unaffected by current to point B. Now lay off from A the departure point, the current's speed and direction expected over one hour, 180° — 2½ knots, to position C. Join C to B and the resultant course of 080°T is the course to steer in order to make good a course of 090°. *Note*: Always equate the ship's speed in knots to that of the current. The student may be told that a 15 knot ship is expected to be affected by a current running south at 2½ knots, over a distance of 90 miles when steaming east, and asked what course to steer to maintain an east course. The common factor is the 15 miles the ship covers in one hour and the 2½ miles the current runs in one hour.

Charts

It will now be evident from reading and studying position fixing in this chapter that it is of the utmost importance to use the largest scale chart available for coastal navigation. Charts vary in scale and as east

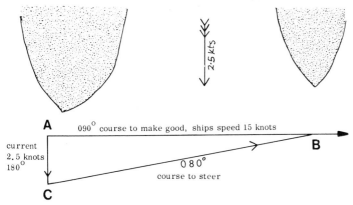

Fig 95 Effect and allowance for tide on course

coast fishermen know a single chart from the Humber to well up the Norwegian Coast is available. West coast fishermen are also aware that there is a chart which covers an area from Scotland to Norway. These small scale charts may be used to run off a long course, for measuring overall distance and general observation of likely impediments. But large scale charts, giving more space per mile and greater detail of lights, shore marks and soundings should be used for navigational purposes. Official charts issued by the Admiralty, local authorities and foreign governmental charts, should always be used. Fishing charts adapted for fishing should be used for that purpose only and should not be used for navigation. Fishing charts concentrate on marking the nature and bottom of the sea bed and usually are of small scale and should not be relied upon for coastal navigation where detail of lights and shore marks may either be omitted or incorrect. Similarly, Admiralty small scale charts omit much detail which is provided on large scale Admiralty charts, because the cautious navigator is expected to use the large scale chart for coastal work.

The normal chart used is the Mercator chart, which shows longitudinal meridians as vertical lines running north and south and lines of latitude running at right angles to the meridians in an east and west direction. To compensate for this distortion of the earth's curvature, it will be seen that the scale of latitude on the side of a Mercator chart increases in direct proportion as the latitude increases, *ie* as the observer moves north in the northern hemisphere. Therefore when measuring long distances between two points which do not have the same latitude, the navigator must use the scale at the mean latitude of the two places. (See *Fig 96* showing Rhumb Line and Great Circle)

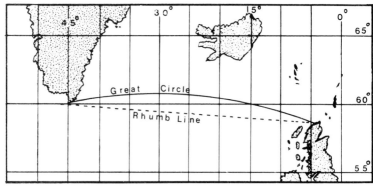

Fig 96 Mercator chart, showing rhumb line and great circle tracks

Gnomic charts are those upon which great circles appear as straight lines, *ie* all meridian lines and the equator. Consequently lines of longitude converge towards the pole. The shortest distance between two points on the surface of the earth is that followed by a great circle, and is curved. A great circle is a line circumscribing the earth, the plane of which passes through the centre of the earth. The Mercator chart (*Fig 96*) shows the rhumb line or course from Cape Wrath, Scotland to Cape Farewell, Greenland as a straight line and the shortest distance. This is in fact incorrect; *Fig 97*, the gnomic chart, shows the true distance of the rhumb line as being the longer.

Consequently, a gnomic chart should be referred to when navigating over long distances especially in high latitudes when east or west bound. A note of caution must be introduced here, however; it would be of little use saving time and fuel if bound home from Newfoundland or Greenland if the great circle track found ice on the northern arc of the circle. Far better to pass well south of the ice before making a great circle sailing.

The details shown on charts give the date of publication and large corrections, the date of which is to the right of the date of publication. Small corrections embodied in a chart, giving the year and number of the *Notice to Mariners*, appear at the bottom left of the chart near the

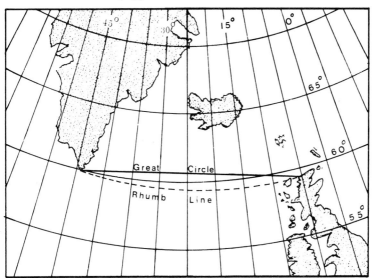

Fig 97 Gnomic chart, showing great circle and rhumb line

margin. These corrections embody in the chart either essential information for navigation by *Notices to Mariners* or information of secondary importance which shows as a bracketed correction.

Decca charts showing Decca navigator chains for coastal waters now cover many of the main trade routes of the world. They are of particular use to fishermen around the coasts of the UK, North Sea and Norwegian coasts. They are the normal Admiralty charts which have the coloured Decca lattice superimposed on them and they may be used instead of the corresponding basic navigational chart. The chart numbers for both charts are the same except that Decca chart numbers are prefixed (L(D)' followed by the chain number.

Loran charts for use in ocean navigation have Loran chains superimposed on them. The Admiralty cover the North Atlantic but the governments of Canada, Germany, and the USA also publish Loran for many areas. Loran is of particular importance to those fishing the NW Atlantic and Bear Island, Norway, and also to those out of Decca range.

Routing charts giving routing information for each month of the year include tracks, distances, meteorological and ice conditions.

The fisherman at the present time should always check that the chart he is using or going to use gives the soundings in metres or fathoms. The traditional use of fathoms and feet is being slowly discontinued and metric charts are being brought progressively into use, as are colours for the land, sand and mud, *etc*.

Large scale charts, apart from giving greater detail as previously mentioned, are usually corrected first, subsequent to a major survey of a particular coastline. This is another reason why large scale charts should always be used in preference to the small scale. In approaching the land or dangerous banks, or when taking soundings, a small error in laying down a position will show as a few metres on a small scale chart, but it may be several cables on the large scale chart.

Variation charts showing variation and its changes for the various parts of the world. Magnetic variation values shown on Admiralty charts are for the 1st July of the year mentioned, prior to 1955, and for the 1st January subsequent to 1955.

164

18   Astronomical navigation

Skippers and mates have always had a natural reluctance to study celestial navigation and have generally regarded it as being something mysterious and mathematically beyond them. Nothing could be further from the truth. By using a DR or Chosen Position and with the use of tables, the taking of an altitude of the sun will give the observer a position line. An understanding of what one is doing is necessary and it is quite simple to understand the basic principles of celestial navigation. It is also necessary to be able to use a sextant and apply the simple corrections, also found from a table, to be able to finish with a true altitude.

Because UK fishermen at present follow their occupation in the northern hemisphere, all illustrations and calculations will be in this area, and as previously mentioned in the part of this book dealing with tides, the student is asked to accept that the earth is at the centre of the universe. Surrounding the earth is the celestial sphere or concave. The earth is very small compared to the distances we are using, realtive to the sun and stars etc. In *Fig 98*, the large circle represents the celestial sphere and the small circle is the earth with C as the centre of the earth. If a vertical line is drawn from the centre of the earth through the geographical pole P and continued until it meets the celestial sphere, we have the celestial pole P¹.

If a line is drawn from C through the observer's position, it will meet the celestial sphere at the observer's zenith Z.

If a third line is drawn from C through to X which is the sun, we have a geographical position on earth G. Therefore GX is the sun's zenith line.

We now have a triangle P¹ZX, the classical navigational spherical triangle. The three sides of this triangle are arcs of great circles whose planes pass through the centre of the earth.

By using the chosen or estimated position of the observer as a basis on which to work, we can, using tables, establish the following data:

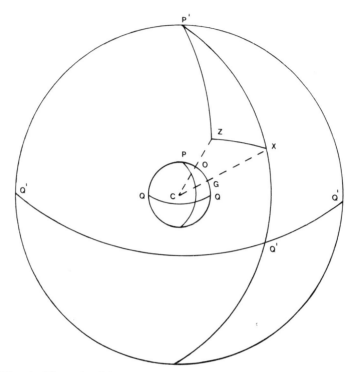

Fig 98 The celestial sphere with the earth at its centre

P¹X   = Co-declination
P¹Z   = Co-latitude from the chosen position
Angle ZP¹X = Local hour angle

An explanation on how to find this important data will follow; for the present the simple basic principles of celestial navigation are being established. Because we have two sides and an angle, it is now possible to calculate the side ZX and thereafter the calculated altitude of the sun from the DR position.

We now turn to the altitude taken by sextant and, after correction, we have a true altitude. We can, by using simple azimuth tables, find the true bearing of the sun for the time when the sight was taken.

By comparing the true altitude and the calculated altitude we will find a difference, which is the intercept away or towards the sun. In *Fig 98* if we imagine a small circle proscribed from X with its circumference running through Z, the arc of the circle at Z is the calculated position line with ZX the zenith distance as its radius. The true ZX is found by subtracting the true altitude from 90°, which will be explained later. By calculating the true bearing of the sun and laying down the bearing on the chart, we are now able to place the intercept either towards the sun or away from it and at right angles across the bearing. This is the position line on which the observer stands.

Requirements for finding and calculating a position are a sextant, a chronometer keeping GMT, a nautical almanac and nautical tables. We may now proceed with the calculation on how to find the observer's zenith distance from a dead reckoning position.

We return to the celestial triangle and first we will find side PX. From the nautical almanac, with the exact time of the day on which the observation was taken, the declination of the heavenly body can be ascertained. The declination is the distance north or south of the equator of the heavenly body, given in degrees, minutes and seconds. In this case we find the declination for the sun. Look at *Fig 98* again and we have QX. Because the sun is north of the equinoctial we can subtract the declination from 90° (PXQ) and we have solved the first side of the triangle.

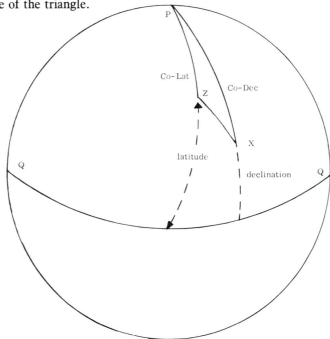

Fig 99   The PXZ celestial triangle

The observer has taken a DR position, which of course will be in terms of latitude and longitude. We can now subtract our latitude from 90°, and we will have the second side of the celestial triangle PZ. Our latitude on earth has been projected to our zenith and the measurement of latitude from the celestial equator is the same.

We must now find angle ZPX at the pole, which is the local hour angle. We have the chronometer time which is Greenwich Mean Time (GMT), and by using the nautical almanac we can take out the sun's Greenwich hour angle. This is the angle subtended at the pole between the Greenwich meridian and the sun's meridian at that particular time. The sun's Greenwich hour angle is measured 0°–360° in a westerly direction from the Greenwich meridian and is given for every two hours of time. Depending on the time of observation, accurate interpolation must be made to get this angle right. Now to find the local hour angle or ZPX. We have the DR longitude; if the longitude is east, then you must add it to the Greenwich hour angle; if the longitude is west, subtract it from the Greenwich hour angle. In triangle ZPX we now have the following data, which is all the information required to find ZX.

Local hour angle	LHA	(ZPX)
Co-latitude	PZ	Polar distance
Co-declination	PX	Sun's polar distance

The formula is:

Nat Hav ZX = (Log Hav ZX × Sine PZ × Sine PX) + Nat Hav (Lat ± Dec).

In order to save one step of work in this formula and to make it simpler for the navigator, instead of finding the observer's polar distance PZ and then finding the sine of PZ, the formula can be slightly altered to use the cosine of the latitude which is the same as the sine of the co-latitude. The same thing can be done with the declination. Let us suppose we are in latitude 60°N and have the sun with a declination of 20°N. To find the two sides PZ and PX we would subtract the 60° latitude and the declination of 20° from 90° (the distance from the equinoctial). To avoid this step, and the added chance of making a mistake, it is simpler to use the latitude directly but the formula has to be changed so that we look up the cosines of 60°N latitude and the declination of 20°N. If the reader looks up in his nautical tables the sine of 30° and the cosine of 60° he will find that

168

they are both the same figure *ie* 9.6990

The formula is therefore changed to:

Nat Haversine ZX = (Log Hav L H A × Cos Lat × Cos Dec) + Nat Hav (Lat ± Dec)

Now it can be seen that in practice all the navigator needs to know to find ZX to compare it with his sextant altitude is a DR latitude and longitude, the sun's declination and the LHA which can be found by the intelligent use of nautical tables and the correct GMT.

Let us now take a practical example and work out the calculated zenith distance of the sun and see how quickly it may be executed after a little practice.

Example (1).   An observation of the sun's lower limb gave an altitude of 36° – 20.3′, height of eye 25′, chronometer reading 9hrs 10m 30s, Sunday 23rd July 1978. The ship's DR position was 60°-10′N, 06°-30′W.

Find the intercept.

Calculation. Sunday 23.7.78

GMT 09hrs 10m 30secs.	0800 =	298°–24.0′	Even hrs below
Use nautical almanac	+ 1hr 10m =	17°–30.0′	Correction Table
to find Greenwich hour angle	30secs =	7.5′	
		‾‾‾‾‾‾‾‾‾‾	
To find local angle apply longitude		316°–01.5′	
If easterly add to GHA, westerly subtract		– 6°–30.0′W	
		‾‾‾‾‾‾‾‾‾‾	
	LHA	309°–31.5′	(1)
		‾‾‾‾‾‾‾‾‾‾	
	LAT	60°–10′N	(2) Data
		‾‾‾‾‾‾‾‾‾‾	
From nautical almanac	*DEC*	20°–07′N	(3)
find declination		‾‾‾‾‾‾‾‾‾‾	

continued on next page

Formula

Nat Versine ZX = Log Vers LHA × Cosine Lat × Cosine Dec × (Nat Hav (Lat ± Dec))

Use nautical tables

(1) Log Vers 309°–31.5'	=	9.25958
(2) Log Cos 60°–10'	=	9.69677
(3) Log Cos 20°–07'	=	9.97266

Log Versine   8.92901

Change to Nat Versine	.08491
Lat-dec 40°–03'	.11726
Nat Versine	

Lat and dec
Same name minus, opposite name add

Obs altitude	36° – 20.3'	Co-altitude ZX	= 0.20217

Total Correction +	10.2' (Ht of eye 25')	Co-altitude	= 53°–26.5'
		True altitude	= 36°–30.5'

36°–30.5'

Less than 90°	89°–57.0'
therefore away	90°–00.0'

Intercept away   3.0'

To take the observation, use the necessary shades to avoid glare, and with telescope adjusted, the index at zero, look at the sun. Make sure that you can see the sun clearly as a pale orb. Release the clamp and, with index arm steady, bring the sun down to the horizon as described in *Chapter 16*. When the sun is at or near the horizon, release the clamp with the left hand and adjust the micrometer until the lower limb is just touching the horizon. Swing the sextant gently from side to side to make sure that the sun is just touching the horizon. Adjust the micrometer as necessary and when satisfied take the time on the chronometer. It is recommended that the observer should have someone standing by the chronometer to take the time when the word time is called.

Having taken the observation, the altitude should be corrected using the sun's total correction table in the nautical almanac, with the height of eye and the observed altitude in order to take out a total correction. The total correction allows for dip, refraction, parallax and the semi diameter of the sun and is always added.

The observer has now found from the previous example that he is three miles further away from the sun than calculated from his dead reckoning position. We must now find what the true bearing of the sun was at the time the observation was made. The true bearing, or azimuth, may soon be found, we have all the information which was needed to calculate the co-altitude in the P¹ZX triangle.

By using nautical tables, ABC, go to table A with the previously found local hour angle of 309½° along the top of the table and the latitude of 60° down the side and pick out the value of A = + 1.45

By using table B in the same way, except that declination 20°N is used instead of latitude, we find by interpolation that B = -.43. Because latitude and declination are both north and the same name B value is minus. Therefore A 1.45 - B .43 = 1.02 = C.

From table C with the value 1.02 and the latitude 60°N we find that the true azimuth was S63.4°E or 116°T.

By drawing a line 116° on the chart through the DR position and measuring the intercept found, three miles away from the sun, we can now draw a position line at right angles to the bearing or azimuth and the ship is somewhere on that line.

By taking another sight later, possibly in the afternoon, the position line already found may be transferred and used as a running fix. Better by far for the navigator to observe the altitude of the sun at noon so as to get an accurate position line which will be his latitude and transfer his morning position line thereto. The finding of one's latitude by meridian altitude is a simple procedure and with a little practice is very reliable. The finding of the intercept as described appears to be lengthy and detailed but with practice and perseverance the average skipper and mate would soon become proficient.

Meridian altitude

Time, as we know it, is governed by the sun and is the interval between two events. We have what is widely known as Greenwich Mean Time, from which it is commonly thought that at noon each day the sun crosses the meridian of Greenwich. But this concept is far from true. The earth rotates on its axis once every twenty four hours but because the earth is orbiting elliptically and not on a perfect circle it will invariably pass the meridian of Greenwich several minutes before or after noon depending on the time of the year and the earth's orbital position. For the sake of good order we have universally adopted a mean time but the earth in rotation will only occasionally have the sun on the Greenwich meridian at 1200 GMT. From the nautical almanac we find that the sun can cross the Meridian of Greenwich at times which vary from 11.44 to 12.16 GMT. Therefore, for navigational purposes we have to use the Greenwich apparent time, that is the time when the sun is actually on the meridian of Greenwich.

If we look back to our celestial triangle it will be obvious that we must use the apparent time at Greenwich to find our local apparent time or local hour angle. Similarly, if we wish to find our latitude by meridian altitude, we must have some idea when the sun will cross our meridian, the noon local apparent time. If we again take 23rd July 1978 to enter the nautical almanac table which gives the equation of time, we will find that on 23rd July, the equation of time for the sun's meridianal passage at Greenwich is + 6m.24s, and the time of the transit in relation to GMT is 12.06. If the ship were on the Greenwich meridian, then we would have the sextant ready to take the altitude at about 12.06 GMT.

But let us suppose we are in a position $60°-35\frac{1}{2}'N$ $5°-54'W$ then because we are to the west of the Greenwich meridian, the sun will not cross our meridian until some time later. The amount of time we will have to wait for noon to occur will obviously depend directly on the amount of the longitude. In this case it is $5°-54'W$. Longitude in degrees and minutes can also be expressed in time, *ie* hours, minutes and seconds. The earth revolves on its axis 360° every 24 hours, that is 15° every hour, 1° every four minutes, $\frac{1}{4}°$ for one minute, *etc*. So that for the position given above $60°-35\frac{1}{2}'N$, $5°-54'W$, the longitude which is nearly 6°W can be expressed as 23m.36s, or nearly 24 minutes. Nautical tables have conversion of arc into time.

We already know that the sun's transit at the Greenwich meridian will take place at 12.06 GMT, and because we are west of Greenwich we add 24 minutes, which gives a time of 12.30 GMT for the sun's meridian passage in longitude 5°-54'.

Nautical almanac, July 23rd 1978,
Sun's transit Greenwich	12.06 GMT
Nautical tables, convert 5°-54' arc into time 23 m 26 s	+ 24
	———
Time of sun's meridian passage	12.30 GMT

If the longitude was east then noon at the local position would occur before that at Greenwich and the allowance for longitude would be subtracted. This small calculation is simple and very easily done.

172

Taking a meridian altitude of the sun

Having calculated from the DR position the time that the sun will cross the meridian, the sextant should be ready at some time before 12.30 GMT. Drop the necessary shades so that the sun appears as a clear but pale ball and bring it down so that the sun's lower limb is just touching the horizon. By watching the sun carefully it will be seen to slowly rise above the horizon until it reaches its highest point at noon local time and bears due south. Until this happens, keep bringing the sun down to the horizon. Swing the sextant to and fro in a small arc to see that the lower limb is just touching the horizon. At noon, and only for a few seconds, the sun's altitude will remain steady, the sun will remain on the horizon and will then begin to slowly fall below. When it is seen to be steady and neither rising nor falling, then is the time to read the altitude (12.30 GMT approx). When the altitude has been read, look at the sun on the horizon again to check that it is falling. We now have only a simple calculation to find the latitude.

By taking a corrected altitude when the sun is on the meridian we are working on an arc of 90° from the observer's zenith through the sun and down to the horizon. (See *Fig 100*) By subtracting the altitude from 90° we find the zenith distance which is the length of the arc from the observer's zenith to the sun.

With this information we can now move to *Fig 101*, the celestial sphere. Here the zenith distance has been illustrated to fit on to the celestial sphere in conjunction with the heavenly pole and equinoctial. By applying the declination of the sun to the zenith distance, the latitude is found.

Fig 100 Meridian altitude of the sun

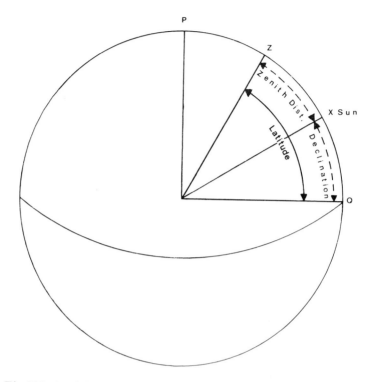

Fig 101 Applying zenith distance and declination to find latitude

Example (2).   A ship soon after 12.30 GMT latitude 60°–35.5′N
5°-54′W DR observes the sun at noon on the meridian with an altitude
of 49°-16′ on Sunday 23rd July 1978. Find the latitude.

Noon transit Greenwich	=	12.06	Sextant alt		49°–16.0′
Long. 5°–54′ + W	=	+ 24	Index error		Nil
Noon transit at ship	GMT	12.30	Obs alt		49°–16.0′
			Total corr		+ 10.3′
			True alt		49°–26.3′
					90°–00′
Same names N or S + ⌈	Zenith distance		N		40°–33.7′
Opposite names N or S − ⌊	Declination		N +		20°–05.3′
	Latitude				60°–39.0′

174

The position line found in *Example (1)*, if drawn 3′ away from the original DR position at 09.10 may now be transferred to the newly found position line of latitude after laying off the course and distance steamed. (See *Fig 102*)

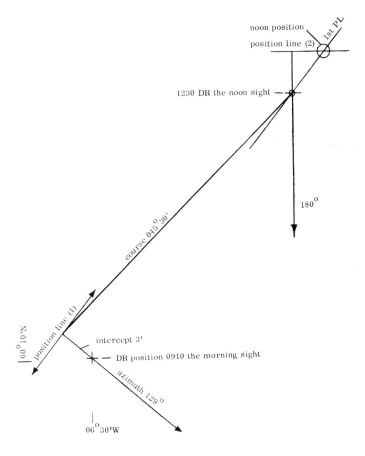

Fig 102 Transferring position line to the noon latitude

Ex-meridian by short method tables

It may be that at noon local time the sun may be obscured by cloud and that the taking of a meridian altitude is not possible. If this occurs, the skipper or mate may take a sextant angle of the sun just before or just after the sun's meridian passage. As seen before the quick method of finding the sun's meridian passage can soon be found. By using the DR position and declination as in the previous example and by taking an altitude, let us suppose exactly 20 minutes before apparent noon, we can from Table 1 of the ex-meridian tables, latitude and declination same name, take out the value contained therein (Lat 60°-34'N, Dec 20°-05'N). With this value from Table 2 with 20 minutes as the hour angle before the meridian passage take out a value in minutes and seconds, known as a reduction to apply to true altitude:–

Example 3

Table 1	Table 2		
Dec 20'N $\Big\}$ = 1·40 Lat 60½°N	Hour before 20m $\Big\}$ = 9·4 Value 1·40 reduction		

Obs alt	49°–09'
Total correction	+ 10.3
True alt	49°–19.3'
Reduction +	9.4

The latitude found here is 2.8 miles north of DR lat and in the previous example the noon latitude 20 mins later gave a position 2.5 miles north of noon DR position.

	49°–28.7'
	90°–00
Zenith distance	40°–31.3' N
Declination	20°–05 N
11.40 Local time lat	60°–36.3'

The use of the ex-meridian tables makes the procedure simple but the correct tables must be used *ie* lat and dec same names and different names. The 'reduction to the true altitude' is always added on the upper transit and subtracted on the lower transit. The cautious trawler officer in cloudy conditions simply takes from the nautical almanac the sun's transit time, *ie* in this case 12.06 GMT, and applys the longitude in time, + 24m, to get 12.30 GMT as the sun's transit time at the ship. He will then be prepared to take an ex-meridian prior to this time, for use if the sun is obscured by cloud at noon local time.

176

Finally, the method of working out the latitude at noon in a few seconds will be demonstrated. By preparing in advance, the latitude can be found almost instantaneously once the sight has been taken, by working in reverse as follows using the figures from Example 2.

Quick method		Ordinary method	
90°–00'		Obs Alt	49°–16'
–10.3	Total correction	Total correction	+ 10.3'
89°–49.7'		True altitude	49°26.3'
+ 20°–05.3'	N Declination		90°–00'
109°–55.0'	Prepared for noon	Zenith distance N	40°–33.7'
– 49°–16.0'	Obs mer alt (Write in at noon)	Declination N	+ 20°–05.3'
60°–39'N	Lat of ship	Lat of ship	60°–39.0'

The example on the left, prepared before noon, enables the navigator to observe the meridian altitude at noon, enter the sextant reading on the second line from the bottom and, by subtracting, find the latitude at once. This is common practice at sea and is very simple.

Navigation by stars and planets

It can be seen that navigation by the sun can only be carried out if the navigator has certain data, *ie* a DR latitude, declination, longitude and local hour angle. This information, by use of the PZX triangle, gives a calculated altitude. The true altitude obtained by the sextant may then be compared with the calculated altitude from the DR position and enables the navigator to lay off a position line at right angles to the azimuth towards or away from the sun. To be able to work out the calculated altitude, the haversine or versine formula is used. This formula may also be used in conjunction with the true altitude to find the true hour angle and longitude.

The same formula is used when using other celestial bodies, *ie* planets or stars. The important difference in using stars for navigational calculations is that the declination is found in a slightly different way to that of the sun and the computing of the local hour angle is quite different to the method used for that of the sun.

To find the declination of a star

To find the declination of a star is quite simple. It is found by nautical almanac, wherein the star's declination is given for the first day of each month. This declination does not alter throughout the month.

To find the declination of the moon or planet

In the case of the moon, look up the day in question where the declination will be found with the mean variation per hour. Interpolate for the appropriate time. The declination of the planets Venus, Jupiter, Mars, and Saturn is given daily, and they vary to a very small amount, which can easily be interpolated. The interpolated amount must be applied correctly by noting whether the declination is increasing or decreasing from day to day.

Measuring the local hour angle of star or planet

From the previous description on how to find the Greenwich hour angle of the sun, the reader will know that the GHA of a heavenly body is the angle subtended at the pole between the prime meridian (Greenwich) and the meridian on which the body lies. By applying the longitude of the ship to the GHA of the body we find the local hour angle, which is the angle at the pole in our PZX triangle between the ship's or observer's meridian and that of the heavenly body.

The sun revolves around its axis once every 24 hours and this rotation is perfectly regular. But, because the sun in its orbit moves elliptically and irregularly, the apparent length of a solar day varies. Because the sun governs our lives, we must use solar time organised as a mean time, GMT. When taking a celestial observation the navigator accurately takes the time to the nearest second on the chronometer which keeps GMT. Stars however have a time of their own known as sidereal time. The sidereal day is the interval measured when the earth completes one rotation between transits of the First Point of Aries. The sidereal hour angle of a star is the angle subtended at the pole measured between the meridian of Aries and the meridian of the star.

The First Point of Aries is the point on the celestial equator (equinoctial) when the centre of the sun, moving along the ecliptic, changes its declination from south to north. It is known as the vernal, or spring, equinox.

The right ascension of a star is measured from this point eastward to the meridian on which the star lies and is always expressed in time 0-24 hours.

By using the nautical almanac for a particular time (GMT) and date, the navigator will be able to find the Greenwich hour angle of Aries. By finding the sidereal hour angle of the star and applying it to the GHA of Aries, the star's GHA can be found. The application of the observer's longitude will give the LHA for use with the haversine formula.

Having explained the principle involved in computing the local hour angle from the First Point of Aries, it must now be said that some nautical almanacs have tables compiled wherein the Greenwich hour angle for any of the principal stars may be picked out. The GHA is given for a particular star for the first day of each month, and careful interpolation for the instant of time when the observation is made, (the day, hour, minute and second) will give the GHA. Apply the longitude of observer in the normal way, west minus or east plus, and the local hour angle P is solved. The nautical almanac is provided with a correction table for use in computing star's GHA.

The best time for taking observations of stars is at twilight and dawn. The duration of these times varies with the declination of the sun and the observer's latitude. Trawlermen fishing North Cape Norway know that when the sun has maximum declination in June, because of the high latitudes northern Norway may have twilight lasting for many hours. In tropical latitudes dawn and twilight are short periods and they become progressively longer as the latitude increases. At these times the observer will be able to see the star and also see the horizon clearly; conditions which allow for a reliable altitude to be taken.

We have so far dealt with the use of stars in finding a position line or longitude by chronometer and we now turn to an important aspect of star navigation — the finding of one's latitude by star sight. In the northern hemisphere there is always the pole star, which must always bear approximately north from the observer who, by having an approximate latitude, will be able to set his sextant to the required reading before taking the correct altitude.

Latitude by pole star

Trawlermen in northern waters with long periods of twilight, will find

Polaris to be of the greatest value in finding latitude quickly and accurately. Because Polaris is less than 1° from the celestial pole at any time, a small correction taken from the pole star tables and applied to altitude taken by sextant will give the latitude.

The pole star with a magnitude of 2.1 is but a moderately bright star, therefore the observer should set the DR latitude on the sextant prior to twilight or dawn. With the horizon clearly defined, face true north and sweep the horizon — the star should be clearly seen. Bring the star to the horizon and take the chronometer time; to the nearest minute will suffice. If this practice is followed the observer should have no trouble in taking the altitude. If, however, the observer waits until the pole star can be visibly identified, it will be too dark to see the horizon clearly.

Obtain the local hour angle between observer and Aries in order to take out the correction to apply to the sextant altitude from the pole star tables and the latitude will be found. If the pole star tables cannot be used because of high latitude, use ex-meridian tables.

Example. A trawler fishing at Rising Bank, Orkneys in DR position 60°-00'N 05°-30'W took an altitude by sextant of the pole star, 59°-34' at 2100 hours GMT 1st June 1978. Height of eye 25 ft. What was her latitude?

GHA Aries		Obs Alt	59°-34'
1st June 2000 hrs =	220°–01.6'	Stars tot corr −	05.3'
Corr for 1 hour =	+ 15°–2.5'		
		True alt	59°–28.7'
GHA Aries	235°–04.1'		
Long west	− 5°–30'	Pole star corr +	48.1'
LHA Aries	229°–34.1'	Latitude	60°–16.8'N

To find a true bearing of Polaris refer to the nautical almanac with LHA Aries and latitude LHA = 229°. Latitude 60° gives true bearing 000.6°.

Latitude by Polaris is really an ex-meridian calculation for which the correction may be taken directly from some nautical almanacs, *eg* Reeds, or it may be found by using any ex-meridian tables.

Similarly a latitude may be found at dawn or dusk by turning ship's mean time into GMT and finding the meridian passage of a suitable star which will be on or near the meridian at that time.

Star identity is a very important part of star navigation. The fisherman who is interested should purchase a good star identity chart. These charts show graphically how stars may be identified and after a little use and study it will be found that star identity is quite simple.

Navigation—sight reduction tables

At the present time fishermen are allowed to use the quick method tables issued by the Hydrographic Department of the Admiralty. These tables and the method used therein allow the navigator to enter the tables with three arguments so that a calculated altitude may be taken out. This calculated or computed altitude when compared with the *true* altitude will give an intercept either away or towards the heavenly body which has been observed. The tables are primarily for use with the Intercept or Marcq St Hilaire method of sight reduction. By using these tables the navigator avoids the use of the haversine formula and thereby the chance of making a mistake in the use of logarithms and calculations.

The sight reduction tables are divided into six volumes. Each volume is governed by a zone of latitude of 15°, beginning 0°-15°, 15°-30° and on to the last volume six, *ie* 75°-90°. There is an overlap of 1° in the latitude scale at both ends of any particular volume.

It has already been seen from the beginning of this chapter that, in order to calculate an altitude on the PZX triangle, certain data is necessary, *ie* the LHA, the declination of the heavenly body and the latitude. The DR position of longitude is used to find the LHA. DR latitude and declination are two sides of the celestial triangle.

Because the sight reduction tables are arranged so that each whole degree of latitude and hour angle is a fixed amount, with the true declination as the only variable for interpolation, the DR position cannot be used as a basis from which to work unless the observer happens to be in a DR position which is, let us say, 60°-00′N 6°-00′W when he takes his sight, which is highly unlikely. The observer must then choose a position where the co-ordinate of latitude and longitude are in degrees and as near to his DR position as possible. This place is known as the chosen position and is the place from which the intercept will be laid off across the azimuth.

By taking a sight as before described and noting the exact time of observation by chronometer, the observer may now proceed. By applying the total correction to the altitude observed, the true altitude should be found and written down. The corrected chronometer reading will now be used, not only to find the declination of the heavenly body but also to find the Greenwich hour angle and, thence, the local hour angle by applying the longitude of the chosen position.

The observer is now ready to refer to the sight reduction tables with the latitude of the chosen position, the hour angle of the chosen position and the declination of the heavenly body.

Use the correct volume for the latitude chosen and enter the tables according to the LHA. Use the page on the left if declination and latitude are the same name; if of different name use the right hand page. Having found the page with the LHA, pick out the column headed Lat and the horizontal line corresponding to the degree of declination. Record the tabular altitude given (HA) and the altitude difference. The azimuth angle at this stage may be noted and mental interpolation made for actual declination.

Follow the instructions given in the sight reduction tables for exact interpolation of the difference in minutes of declination and apply it to the tabular altitude (HC).

The difference between the calculated altitude and the true altitude will give the intercept which should then be set off on the chart from the chosen position.

19 Electronic navigational aids and equipment

Since its first introduction to the fishing industry, radio and electronic equipment has played an increasingly important part in the seeking, catching, and safe and economic landing of fish. The facilities this equipment offers have become an essential part of modern fishing operations and trawler officers should be fully conversant with the proper operation, use and limitations of electronic aids.

Large distant water trawlers carrying radio officers usually have high power telegraphy sets capable of transmitting and receiving on high, medium and low frequencies. These sets may also be provided with a radio-telephone capability. Such equipment may be used for communication not only with coastal stations but with long range stations, eg Portishead.

Middle and near water vessels may not carry radio officers and for this type of vessel radio-telephone equipment is provided for the skipper or mate. There is a wide range of equipment that is simple to operate and efficient.

The installations on smaller near water vessels consist of medium power radio-telephone equipment with a built-in receiver and an extension speaker to the wheelhouse so that the officer of the watch is able to listen in on the calling frequency for distress or emergency calls. The speaker in the wheelhouse is also provided on fishing vessels which carry radio officers, to be used when the radio officer is not on duty.

Radio telegraphy and radio-telephone receivers are fitted with alarm signals which activate on the transmission of either a keying or two tone signal respectively. (See *Chapter 9*). The alarm signal gives the listener some warning that a distress message will follow.

Some receivers have an additional capability in that they are fitted with sensors and can be connected to a direction finding loop aerial. All these sets may be used to receive transmissions from the BBC concerning time signals, navigational/gale warning, weather forecasts, *etc*.

VHF radio

The international maritime VHF radio-telephone service is the most rapidly expanding facility available for relatively short-range interference-free efficient coastal communications. The UK coast is being planned to have shore repeater stations distributed around the shore line on suitably elevated sites to ensure complete coverage of national waters. With port operations, pilot services, harbours, docks, tugs, HM Coastguard, RNLI, lightships, *etc* an increasing volume of traffic makes the VHF band the most versatile and widely used international service.

The silence period should be strictly observed on Channel 16, the calling safety channel. Skippers and mates should make themselves familiar with the procedure when calling coast stations by knowing the particular stations working channel in advance.

Consult Admiralty radio signals as follows:
Volume 1 – Coast radio stations, SAR procedures, medical advice by radio and AMVER.
Volume 6 – Stations working with port operations service, pilot service, and traffic surveillance

Radio direction finding

There are two ways of obtaining a RDF bearing. The more usual method is for the ship which is equipped with direction finding equipment to take a bearing of a lightship or lighthouse which transmits a distinctive and identifiable signal. The second method of obtaining a radio bearing is to request a coastal radio station to take a radio bearing of the ship (QTG).

In all cases the radio bearing will be a part of a great circle, which cannot be applied to a Mercator chart. However, the great circle bearing can soon be corrected for use on a Mercator chart. By taking the position of the shore station and the ship's DR position, the mean latitude and the difference of longitude can be found. In all good nautical almanacs and nautical tables there will be half convergency tables. From these tables ascertain the mean latitude and D longitude between station/beacon and ship, then take out the correction in degrees. Apply it to the great circle bearing so that the Mercator bearing lies on the equatorial side of the great circle bearing or when using 360° compass, as follows:

	North lat	South lat
Bearing measured eastward	Add	Subtract
Bearing measured westward	Subtract	Add

Example.   The navigator of a ship in DR position 58°-30′N 2°-30′E was given a bearing of 082°(T) from Wick W/T DF station (58°-25′N 3°-10′W). Find the true bearing to lay on the chart.

Wick radio lat	58°–25′N	Wick radio long	3°–10′W
Ship's lat	58°–30′N	Ship's long	2°–30′E
Mean lat	58°–27½N	Diff long	5°–40′

Enter Burton's Table 38 for convergency angle and with mean lat 60° in the vertical column and diff long in the horizontal column, extract the correction of 2.6°. The bearing was taken from Wick Radio 082°T correct by bringing the easterly bearing towards the equator.

$$082°T$$
$$+\quad 2.6°T$$

$$084.6T \text{ from Wick Radio}$$

This line of position may now be drawn 084.6T from Wick, and the ship is somewhere on the position line. (See *Fig 103*) If the radio bearing had been taken from the ship it would have read

$$267.2(T) \text{ westerly towards equator}$$
$$\text{Correction}\quad 2.6$$
$$264.6(T)$$

Bearings of two or three coastal stations taken simultaneously will provide a good fix. If three can be taken which give a small 'cocked hat' when laid off on the chart, a reliable position is fixed.

There is, however, no reason why a radio bearing, which is a position line, cannot be crossed with another position line. If, for example, the observer was given a bearing from Wick Radio as in the preceding example and then took an observation of the sun, then both position lines could then be laid off on the chart to give a fix.

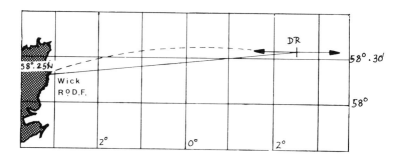

Fig 103 Position line obtained by DF bearing

Practical use of radio direction finder

There are two types of direction finding equipment, the fixed loop aerial and the rotating loop aerial. The former is the most reliable. Disconnect any other aerial circuits at their sets if the aerials are near to the loop.

Consult both chart and Admiralty list of radio signals in order to choose suitably placed stations that are within the range of reliability, *ie* 50 miles by day and 25 miles at dawn. At sunrise and sunset sky-wave errors are at their peak if the vessel is more than 25 miles from the station. If the distances are less than 25 miles reliable bearings may be taken by day or night.

Good bearings depend on the accuracy of the loop-reading, the accurate determination of the ship's heading at the time of the reading, and the range of the ship and station.

Adjust the receiver tuning for best reception on the transmitting station's frequency. Use earphones in preference to a loudspeaker. When the station's call sign has been recognised, it will usually be followed by a long dash. Swing the pointer through the long dash until the sound fades altogether and on until the sound is just heard again. This silent arc is known as the null. Repeat the swing through the null, and the mean position in the null will be the bearing.

When the precise bearing has been ascertained call out 'stop' so that the precise course on the compass is noted, because the bearing taken is relative to the ship's head. It must be stressed again that a 1° error when either taking the null bearing or noting the ship's head will result in an unacceptable error at a maximum range of say 50 miles.

Radar

Nearly all fishing vessels are now fitted with radar and in some cases the larger vessels may be provided with two sets. Radar is an invaluable aid to navigation when used properly. It must be stressed, however, that radar has its limitations and officers who ignore plotting procedures and use radar for navigation with a casual or over-confident manner, may well find themselves in a disastrous situation.

We will begin by describing in simple terms how a radio detection and range (RADAR) set works. Radio pulses are transmitted at a very rapid rate of up to 4,000 pulses per second. When these pulses strike another ship, a buoy or land, some of the pulses will be reflected back towards the transmitter, from which they were sent. The aerial from which the pulses are sent and received is known as a scanner. The radio pulses are sent out in a narrow band in one direction only, but because the scanner revolves through 360° the horizontal plane is covered on each revolution.

The pulses when returned are measured on a time scale and cathode ray tube on to which they are shown as a visible echo. This is the radar screen and because the echo or trace is illuminated on the screen with an afterglow effect, repeated on each sweep of the scanner, a continuous picture may be obtained. It is important to mention here that an echo will only be shown or indicated on the screen if pulses are returned from the target to the scanner. If pulse return is weak or non existent, it will be obvious that, in poor visibility or at night, a situation could develop which might be dangerous, particularly in coastal and landfall navigation.

The range of the radar is exactly the same as that of the human eye. The radar will not see round corners or through solids, and it has a horizon which depends on the height of the scanner. Because the radar depends on a reflected signal it will clearly indicate hills or mountains which appear above the horizon. Low lying land, beaches or shoals may only produce a weak echo, and if they lie between the ship and the high land, the imprudent navigator may mistake the contour of the high land as being the coastline.

Similarly when visibility is poor in enclosed waters such as a buoyed channel, the radar will indicate the channel buoys clearly, but if the channel is narrow and the buoys are to be passed close to, the sweep of the scanner's pulse sent out from the top of the wheelhouse will pass

187

over and above the buoy or lightship when closed. The target will not show on the screen, or it will be lost in the clutter or loom at the centre spot and a collision may occur. Most experienced seamen and pilots are aware of this situation.

A round lighthouse or a round Baltic type spar buoy designed to be conspicuously visible by eye will, because of its round shape, scatter the radar pulses and produce a very weak echo. Rain and snow clutter distort pulses and fishermen should be aware of all the limitations under the conditions as described above.

The quickly taken range and bearing of a point of land when navigating on the coast at night can be a positive danger if the observer is not absolutely sure that the point of land showing on the radar is the one required and that it is properly related to the course, distance, speed, and previous fix. Over-reliance on a radar picture and the neglect of established navigation procedures cannot be emphasised too strongly as being a dangerous practice.

A trawler bound from Hull to the south west coast of Iceland cleared the Pentland Firth and set course so that the Westman Isles were right ahead and with a distance of more than 400 miles to steam. The vessel was put on to automatic steering on the gyro-compass. The ship was fitted with a good modern radar set and it was expected that some 36 hours later the Westman Isles would be picked up. The weather was fine and clear with a fresh to strong southwesterly wind on the port side. All normal navigational procedures were then neglected. The Decca coverage from the Scottish chain, reliable for half of the run across, was not used to take an accurate fix or to determine leeway or set. The log was not set or used and the echo sounder was switched off. The sea was broken and choppy giving some degree of intermittent clutter. At about 0230 in the morning (36 hours later) a distinct echo appeared on the screen, right ahead, at a distance of 20 miles. Course was then altered to port so as to pass this target on the starboard side. It was presumed to be the Westman Isle. The trawler crossed the distinctive 100 fathom line which follows the contour line of the Icelandic coast, but the echo sounder was not in use. Soon afterwards the vessel ran aground on the low lying lava sands of Iceland and became a total loss. The echo had not been the Westman Island but a mountain peak, some eight miles inland from the coast, height 5,000 ft. The trawler had made leeway and had been set more than 25 miles to the westward on a 400 mile run. An error of $1\frac{1}{2}°$ on the gyro would have had a similar effect. Over-reliance and bad interpretation of the radar caused the loss of this ship. Fortunately no lives were lost. The reliance and confidence on this efficient radar was so great that distress signals were sent out saying that the vessel was aground on the southwest of Westman Island.

The lesson to be learnt from this incident is that constant vigilance on all navigational procedures should be the watchkeeper's and skipper's priority. They must not be neglected just because there is an efficient operational radar. The radar will only show echoes which the navigator can identify, aided by previous fixes, soundings, distance run and a knowledge of leeway, set or compass error affecting the ship.

The next most common error is the double risk an observer may make by failing to plot the movement of another vessel in fog and also to assume that the plotted target has operational radar. If for example a target is picked up ahead, then it must be plotted at regular intervals. If its bearing does not change then risk of collision exists, and a large alteration of course should be made. The large alteration will be effective on two counts. If the other vessel has radar, the large alteration of course will very soon be apparent to the observer. If the vessel seen has no working radar, then one's own vessel will move away quickly from the line of collision and the subsequent collision point, reducing the risk of collision.

Position fixing by radar

A radar position line may be obtained in one of two ways, by bearing and distance from a single point or by two or three ranges from two or three points. There is not much problem in making a fix by radar if the observer is very familiar with the local contours, *ie* the home port. Humberside mariners and fishermen have the distinctive feature of the Spurn Peninsula when approaching the Humber from seaward in fog. Fleetwood fishermen have the channel marking buoys with the point where Fleetwood lies on the bluff as well as the distinctive Wyre entrance to pick out on the radar screen. But in other places such as the Norwegian coast, with numerous rocky islets, high background mountains and inlets to fjords large and small, identity of points can be difficult. Parts of the Minch may be difficult to identify and under such circumstances with poor visibility the radar should be used to fix arcs of safe distance so as to keep off the land. Even in normal visibility, the most likely source of error will be to identify with certainty the exact position on the chart shown by the echo on the screen.

The accuracy of a radar bearing is always less than that of a visual bearing. The pulse signal transmitted by the scanner has an angular width of up to two degrees. As a result of this angle of 2°, measured at the scanner, the beam width increases in proportion to the distance off the target. Consequently a very small island or lightship, *etc* will appear as a blur on the screen. Similarly if the observer is unfortunate enough to have another target on approximately the same range and near to each other, then the echo of the one will be carried into the other. This can easily happen with a small archipelago of islands or cluster of dangerous rocks. With an unchecked range marker it is obvious that the accuracy of the radar bearing will not equal that of the visual bearing taken by gyro-repeater or standard compass.

Reflectors, racons, ramarks

It has been explained how radar pulses may reflect badly from curved lighthouses, flat low lying shores and buoys. Other targets such as wooden craft, ice, or fibre glass may reflect radar pulses badly or not at all. This can be overcome by the fitting of a radar reflector, except of course in the case of ice. Fishermen who are likely to have to fish or navigate in ice conditions are advised to read and study the *Mariners Handbook* published by the hydrographer of the Navy. In this book there is a comprehensive description of ice conditions, navigation, and shiphandling in ice, as well as detection of ice by radar.

Radar reflectors are constructed so that they may be fitted to the top of the mast or wheelhouse of a wooden boat. They may be fitted to the top of a buoy or at each end of a wooden jetty, indeed on to anything which may be thought to reflect radio pulses badly. The reflector consists of steel plates, intersecting with each other and set at different angles, so as to be able to respond readily to the radar pulse.

Ramarks

The ramark which transmits continuously from an important navigational mark, *ie* a lighthouse or lightship, will be shown on the radar picture as a continuous or dotted line. This line appears on the edge of the screen and runs towards the centre spot, and it gives the bearing but not the distance of the station transmitting the ramark signal.

Racon

The racon is a radar beacon which responds to the pulse of a radar transmission by transmitting its own pulse in a known pattern. The racon station's signal appears on the screen of the ship and the bearing is obtained. In addition to the bearing, the racon by means of its signal being of a fixed length and pattern gives the radar observer the distance off and identity of the station. The signal begins at the racon station and ends at the ship. If we take for example a lightship, fitted with racon, which emits a signal in the form of the morse letter O. Note that the morse letter from a racon invariably begins with a long dash rather than dot. The dot could be taken as being another target and not part of the code letter. By looking up the racon signal for the light vessel, it may be seen that the letter O on the screen covers a total distance of two miles with each dash .6′ and the spacing between each dash .1′ thus:

| .6 | .1 | .6 | .1 | .6 | = 2 miles |

If we know that the spacing between each letter is one mile then it will be seen that by direct read off from the screen, the distance between observer and lightship as well as the bearing will be established. Check with the range ring.

Radar types and use

There are two types of radar set and two kinds of display which may be obtained for each of the two types.

Unstabilised, ship's head up

On this display the heading marker always points to 000° on the degree scale ring surrounding the display. Bearings are always relative to the ship's head, thus two men are required to take an accurate bearing. The observer's position is always at the centre of the screen and the apparent track of another vessel will be the combined movement of the other vessel relative to one's own movement. A rapid alteration of course, *eg* swinging, will create shadow and temporary loss of definition.

Stabilised north up

By feeding the vessel's course from a gyro compass into this display unit, the ship's head marker points to the compass course in degrees on the graduated scale surrounding the screen. The picture is always shown north up, with 000° on the scale being at the top of the screen, as one would look at the true compass rose on a chart regardless of the course being steered. Bearings taken on the radar screen are relative to the north of the gyro compass and are as good as the gyro. The ease in taking bearings on this type of set is such that risk of collision with another vessel may be determined by the observer alone if he lays the bearing marker on to the target to see if there is any appreciable change.

True motion north up

The observer's position on this display does not remain at the centre of the screen but moves according to course and speed across the screen. All stationary targets, ships at anchor, buoys and shoreline are in plan view and motionless, with other vessels as well as one's own moving across the screen on their different courses. When one's own vessel nears the edge of the screen it is automatically returned to commence another traverse. If the observer is concerned as to what hazards lie ahead, his own ship's position may be returned manually to the beginning of a traverse. The advantages of this type of set are high because all movement of other craft may be seen in a true format and collision situations appreciated more readily. On the true motion display, a feathered track or afterglow indicates the course of other moving echoes.

True motion head up

A radar set fitted with stabilisation capability may be adjusted so that the ship's course is head up instead of north up. In pilotage waters there is an advantage in that other vessels ahead and astern can be seen in relation to the narrow channel and the buoyage therein.

Control settings

Whichever type of display unit is available, the user must be able to recognise loss of performance and maladjustment of the controls. The correct settings can be recognised as follows:

Brilliance. The rotating trace should be only just visible, this may require re-adjustment when changing range. The gain should be turned off when adjusting brilliance control.

Focus. The range rings should be as thin as possible.

Heading marker. This should point to 000° on the ship's head up display and to compass course on stabilised displays.

Sensitivity (gain). Correct adjustment is easily recognised on the longer ranges by the speckled background being only just visible.

Anti-clutter. Ideally this control should be set so that the sea clutter is only just visible. In practice it will probably be found that this control needs continuous adjustment so that too dark and too bright areas may be examined.

Performance monitor. The performance monitor is the only real sure means of checking that both transmitter and receiver are working properly. The watchkeeper should be familiar with the length of plume or sun effect which is displayed when the monitor is switched on.

Rain switch (differential). This control sometimes helps to pick out targets in an area of rain, but increased gain may be required when it is in use.

Use of radar

The UK Department of Trade from time to time issues '*M*' *Notices* on the use of radar. Recommendations on the use of radar agreed at the 1960 Safety of Life at Sea Conference were printed as an annexe to the 1965 *Collision Regulations*.

In the 1972 *Collision Regulations* now in force, the SOLAS recommendations have been embodied into the rules and set out within Part B, Steering and Sailing Rules, Conduct of Vessels in Any Condition of Visibility. Extracts from the current '*M*' *Notice*, Use of Radar are:

'Collisions have been caused far too frequently by failure to make proper use of radar; by altering course on insufficient information and by maintaining too high a speed particularly when a close quarters situation is developing or is likely to develop. It cannot be emphasised too strongly that navigation in restricted visibility is difficult and great care is needed even though all the information which can be obtained from radar observation is available. Where continuous radar watch-keeping and plotting cannot be maintained even greater caution must be exercised.

Clear weather practice

Whether or not radar training courses have been taken it is important that shipmasters and others using radar should gain and maintain experience in radar observation and appreciation by practice at sea in clear weather. In these conditions radar observations can be checked visually and misinterpretation of the radar display or false appreciation of the situation should not be potentially dangerous. Only by making and keeping themselves familiar with the process of systematic radar observation and with the relationship between the radar information and the actual situation, will officers be able to deal rapidly and competently with the problems which will confront them in restricted visibility.

Interpretation

(1) It is essential for the observer to be aware of the current quality of performance of the radar set (which can be most easily ascertained by a performance monitor) and to take account of the possibility that small vessels, small icebergs and similar floating objects may escape detection.

(2) Echoes may be obscured by sea or rain clutter. Adjustment of controls to suit the circumstances will help, but will not completely remove this possibility.

(3) Masts and other obstructions may cause shadow sectors on the display. *Notice No M.535* on the fitting of radar sets makes provision for the measurement and recording of such sectors.

Plotting

To estimate the degree of risk of collision with another vessel it is necessary to forecast her nearest approach distance. Choice of appropriate avoiding action is facilitated by knowledge of the other vessel's course and speed, and one of the simplest methods of estimating these factors is by plotting. This involves knowledge of one's own ship's course and the distance run during the plotting interval.

Appreciation

(*1*) A single observation of the range and bearing of an echo can give no indication of the course and speed of a vessel in relation to one's own. To estimate this a succession of observations at known time intervals must be made.

(*2*) Estimation of the other ship's course and speed is only valid up to the time of the last observation and the situation must be kept constantly under review, for the other vessel, which may or may not be on radar watch, may alter her course or speed. Such alteration in course or speed will take time to become apparent to a radar observer.

(*3*) It should not be assumed that because the relative bearing is changing there is no risk of collision. Alteration of course by one's own ship will alter the relative bearing. A changing compass bearing is more to be relied upon. However, this has to be judged in relation to range, and even with a changing compass bearing a close quarters situation with risk of collision may develop.

Operation

(*1*) If weather conditions by day or night are such that visibility may deteriorate, the radar should be running, or on 'standby'. (This latter permits operation in less than one minute, whilst it normally takes up to five minutes to operate from switching on). At night, in areas where fogbanks or small craft or unlighted obstructions such as icebergs are likely to be encountered, the radar set should be left permanently running. This is particularly important when there is any danger of occasional fogbanks, so that other vessels can be detected before entering the fogbank.

(*2*) The life of components, and hence the reliability of the radar set, will be far less affected by continuous running than by frequent switching on and off, so that in periods of uncertain visibility it is better to leave the radar either in full operation or on standby.

Radar watching

In restricted visibility it is always best to have the radar set running and the display observed, the frequency of observation depending upon the prevailing circumstances, such as the speed of one's own ship and the type of craft or other floating object likely to be encountered.

Radar training

It is essential for a radar observer to have sufficient knowledge and ability to recognise when the radar set he is using is unsatisfactory, giving poor performance or inaccurate information. This knowledge and ability can only be obtained by a full and proper training; experience alone or inadequate training can be dangerous and lead to collision or stranding through failure to detect the presence of other vessels or through misinterpretation of the radar picture.

Radar training courses have been established at a number of centres in the United Kingdom.

The Radar Observer Course is open to shipmasters, deck officers and intending deck officers of the Merchant Navy and those concerned with navigation in the Fishing Fleet. This course enables the mariner to obtain training in the operation and use of marine radar.

The Radar Simulator Course, open to shipmasters and senior deck officers, enables those officers to practise ship manoeuvring and collision avoidance on radar information. Considerable experience of realistic radar observation, interpretation and collision avoidance manoeuvres can be obtained during the five days of this course.

Information about these courses is included in *M Notices* which can be obtained, together with a list of colleges at which the courses are held, from any Mercantile Marine Office.

Radar in narrow channels and port approaches

In poor visibility, whether a pilot is carried or not, as much information on ships at anchor or moving should be obtained from the port information service. If the fairways and approaches are clear it may be considered safe to proceed, but it is not safe to leave a dock or proceed to a dock with a strong ebb or flood tide running in the same direction as the ship. It will be obvious that a vessel proceeding against the tide is under better control in poor visibility than the vessel with the tide astern, whether the channel is clear or not. To proceed up river in fog on a strong flood tide, or to sail down river from a dock on an ebb tide is to invite trouble. In an emergency, complete control of the single screw ship will be lost by going astern when running with the tide.'

Decca navigator

The Decca receiver, now widely used on nearly all ships navigating northwest Europe, has a capability of receiving radio signals from a group of stations and converting them into readings on dials. The readings, identified by colour as well as numerically, may be read off at any instant and plotted on a Decca lattice chart. The accuracies of position fixing are good and more than enough for coastal navigation.

The UK and continental coasts are covered by groups of stations for different areas known as chains. Each chain has a master and three slave stations, each Master/Slave gives a hyperbolic pattern and position line which can be referred to the chart quickly and accurately for position fixing. Lane identification is provided so that the receiver can be set up and charts are marked according to the chain for which they are latticed. The range of reliability is for about 240 nautical miles from the master station.

There is a Decca Marine Automatic Plotter which, when linked to the Decca Navigator, provides a visual record of the ship's progress on paper. This is a most useful facility when fishing on the edge of a bank and when on fish.

When navigating in poor visibility, homing along lanes towards a particular point such as a light vessel or fairway buoy can be dangerous in that other vessels may have adopted the same procedure on similar or reciprocal courses.

The echometer

Originally produced as a navigational aid by showing the depth of water beneath the vessel between the sonar transmission points and the bottom, the echometer soon proved itself capable of indicating the presence of fish. This latter facility was pursued in the design and development of later models and unfortunately the echometer is now regarded by many fishermen as being primarily an aid to fish catching and they neglect to use the machine as an aid to navigation. Most large fishing vessels are fitted with two sounders, the visual type and the recorder, which traces the depths in a pattern on a paper roll. The graph shown on the paper roll depicts the contour of the sea bed and consequently indicates wrecks or other fasteners on which fouling of gear may occur.

The echo sounder works by reason of an underwater sonic transmission emitted from the bottom of the ship, so that when reflected from the ground it is received at the bottom of the ship and the time interval is measured. The speed of sound through sea water is known for varying temperatures and salinity. Normally it is 4920 ft per second, thus the time interval is converted to distance in feet, fathoms or metres. Continuous signals are shown as continuous depths and may be displayed on a dial to be visually observed, or they may be shown on a sounding trace, to be seen as well as recorded on paper.

In shallow water with only a few feet under the bottom, an echo sounder may show greater depths than actual by reason of the signal reflecting several times between the ship's bottom before being received and transferred into a distance. For dock and harbour soundings special echometers capable of sounding to less than a foot are available but their transmission points (small craft) are placed in the fore and aft line for better pick-up and reliable depth reading. Fishermen must use the sounder cautiously when navigating in close proximity to the bottom.

A more recent development in the echo sounding equipment is that of the capability of selecting a particular band of soundings, ie 150 fathoms to 200 fathoms. This band selection is of particular use to fishermen in that the band chosen is expanded to be shown on a longer scale. Consequently more detail of the bottom can be seen and of course fish associated with bottom trawling can be more easily seen. Similarly a band can be selected when fishing in the pelagic mode, regardless of depth of bottom, so that pelagic fish shoals may be seen. It is important to remember to return the echo sounders mode of sounding to normal when fishing is completed and it is intended to begin steaming.

Loran

Long range aid to navigation systems (Loran) are now being more widely used on distant water fishing vessels. As these systems have been developed, a greater accuracy in position fixing has been achieved. Pulsed hyperbolic signals are transmitted from a master station and slave stations and they are time measured by the receiver on board a ship.

The relative time difference between the signals sent out from the Master/Slave No 1 station is represented by a hyperbola and can be put on a chart as a position line. Similarly the measured time difference between the signals sent out simultaneously from the Master/Slave No 2 station give a second position line. Where these two position lines intersect is the position of the receiver. Reference to a Loran chart which is specially marked with these hyperbolic lines of position, usually 100 microseconds apart, establishes the geographical position.

It is important that fishing vessel officers should know and understand the basic working of Loran so that a proper degree of confidence can be felt, relative to the operational circumstances.

Both systems Loran A and C utilise pulsed hyperbolic signals. Loran A stations send out a signal pulse. Each Loran C station sends out a group of eight signal pulses. This is done to improve the signal-to-noise ratio and thereby increase range and accuracy.

Loran A   stations send out a signal pulse and receivers use only the pulse envelope to measure the time difference; as a result accuracy and fine resolution inherent in the Loran C system cannot be achieved. Because Loran A chains have only one slave station the receiver must be manually tuned. Accuracy of position is from 200 — 2,000 yards, range 700 miles max.

Loran C   chains have several slave stations but the set is limited to provide a readout of two position lines so that the two that provide the best intercept are selected for display. Loran C receivers first measure the pulse envelope, this is called pulse matching, and obtain an approximate time difference reading. They then use an RF carrier to achieve fine resolution, this is called cycle matching, and in ground wave areas at a distance of at least 1,000 miles accuracy of fixes can be within 50-500 yards.

Full service Loran C sets automatically track and display two time difference readings, either simultaneously, or alternatively every few seconds. Watchkeeping fishing vessel officers, before using Loran C, should determine from the Loran C chart which chain is appropriate for their approximate position and set the pulse rate code for this chain on the chain select switches. For example, N Atlantic SL7, set SL on the basic and 7 on the specific control switch. A new numbered system for chain selection is soon to become operative. Switch on and allow ten minutes for the set to stabilise. In good ground wave cover the set should lock on to the appropriate stations.

Further adjustments for signal interference, extended range and station change can be made easily, and watchkeepers should study the operator's manual.

Skippers and mates having switched on the Loran C set in plenty of time should check the position obtained against a known position taken from Decca Navigator or shore bearing before leaving the land or passing beyond the Decca Navigator range of reliability.

They will then know that the set is synchronised and they will appreciate that it is important for fishing vessels to obtain a high degree of accuracy in position fixing, which enables them not only to fish efficiently but to keep clear of closed fishing areas enforced by the government of other nations.

Automatic plotters are available for use with Loran C receivers. If, at night or on extended range, the ground wave signals are not being received properly, the Loran C set will continue to track on sky wave and give out TD readings. Depending on the make of the set, warning lights will be shown on the display unit indicating that sky wave is in use and that positional accuracy has deteriorated.

Watchkeepers should not work to fine limits under these circumstances because positions may be inaccurate by a greater amount than expected.

Omega worldwide navigation system

Omega is a system which measures the phase difference of very low frequency radio waves. From eight appropriately sited radio stations around the world, transmissions are made which give global soverage. The stations designated from A to H can provide a ship with digital lane information for use on an Omega chart from any two stations anywhere in the world, by night and by day with an accuracy of up to two miles.

Because the signals from each station cannot be discriminated if they are transmitted simultaneously, each of the eight stations sends out the signal having the same phase but at separate times in the transmitting sequence at 10 second intervals.

Before using Omega the starting position ± 4 miles must be entered into the receiver which then tracks automatically on the appropriate predetermined stations. Some Omega receivers have a provision for a supplementary third line of position which may be used as a cross check on the accuracy of the first two lane readings.

There is an error which must be applied to Omega readings which is known as a propagational correction. This error is caused by the very low frequency reflecting layer (ionosphere) changes in height, as by day and night, so that a small difference in the readout position line and the actual position line occurs. This propagation error may be entered into the set so that a true readout of position may be obtained from the receiver and the error to apply is obtained from propagation correction tables.

The Omega receiver operation is designed to be simply and quickly mastered, even by the inexperienced, when used in conjunction with Omega charts.

Satellite navigation

In orbit around the earth are five navigational satellites. From each satellite, data is transmitted defining the orbit with accurate time markings. This information, both orbital and time, is updated by the ground stations. The ground stations track the orbiting satellites constantly and any changes in the satellite's orbital parameters are put into effect by re-transmissions from the satellite.

The satellite receiver on board ships locks on to a satellite when it appears on the horizon; accepts orbital information, time, and doppler shift; and computes this data to produce an exact position in degrees, minutes, and decimals of a minute in terms of latitude and longitude. No corrections are necessary.

Between satellite passes the computer will supply a continuous display of DR positions if course and speed are input. On the next satellite pass the set will update the DR position with a new positional fix.

Accuracy and reliability standards are very high except for small areas near the poles. Accuracy is said to be within 400 ft.

Part IV Watchkeeping, shiphandling

20 Officer of the watch

The officer of the watch is responsible for the safety of the ship and the lives of all those on board, whether the ship is under way, on passage, at anchor, or moored in a harbour with watchkeeping maintained.

Skippers of fishing vessels must understand that they are at all times responsible for the safe handling, navigation and management of the vessels put in their care by their owners, and that they may be called to account for any mismanagement or misdemeanours of themselves or crew.

Consequently it is in the skipper's own interests to give every facility to his officers to read '*M*' *Notices, Notices to Mariners* and instructions from owners which may concern them. Deck officers should always have access to charts, nautical books/documents and equipment. Skippers and their officers must be fully conversant with the IMCO booklet *Recommendation on Basic Principles and Operational Guidance Relating to Navigational Watchkeeping.*

The skipper of the fishing vessel is therefore bound to ensure that the watchkeeping arrangements are adequate for maintaining a safe navigational watch. Under the skipper's general direction, the officers of the watch are responsible for navigating the ship safely during their periods of duty when they will be particularly concerned to avoid collision and stranding.

Before taking into consideration the composition of the watch, which may vary with circumstances, it will be necessary to organise a watch system in such a manner that the efficiency of the watchkeeping members is not impaired by fatigue. Therefore, the duties should be so organised that the first and subsequent relieving watches are rested and fit prior to going on duty. It is well known that fishing vessels, because of heavy fishing, may have had an officer on deck for a long time if he was the officer responsible for the care and stowage of the fish. It would be wrong therefore for a man in these circumstances to have to take over a long spell of watchkeeping when tired, simply because it happened to be his watch. The skipper, under such circumstances, would have to make alternative arrangements. The care and attention given to the catching and stowing of the fish would count for nothing if the ship were to be put into danger by a tired watchkeeper.

When deciding the composition of the watch the following points should be taken into account:

(1) The officer of the watch should be a certificated and/or a competent person capable of complying with the *Regulations for the Prevention of Collisions at Sea*.
(2) At no time should the bridge be left unattended.
(3) Weather conditions, visibility, whether darkness or daylight, traffic congestion.
(4) The proximity of navigational hazards which may make it necessary for the officer in charge to carry out additional navigational duties.
(5) The use and operational condition of navigational equipment such as Radar, Decca, Loran, echo sounder, gyro or any other equipment likely to affect the safe navigation of the ship.
(6) Whether the ship is fitted with operational automatic steering.
(7) Any additional demands on the navigational watch which may arise from special circumstances.

Taking over the watch

The officer of the watch should not hand over the care of the ship to the relieving officer if he has reason to believe that the latter appears to be under any disability which would preclude him from carrying out his duties.

The officer taking over the watch should only do so when his vision has fully adjusted to conditions of light or darkness. Standing orders, special night orders or instructions left by the skipper in the night order book or deck log should be read and understood by the relieving officer, who should then satisfy himself on the following points:

(1) Position, course, speed and draught of the vessel. Gyro and compass errors.
(2) Direction and speed of tides, currents, weather, visibility and effect on the ship, related to (1).
(3) Landmarks and/or seamarks in sight or expected to come into sight.
(4) Vessels in sight, their movements and bearings.
(5) The lights and signals being shown.

(6) Navigational aids in use and operational.

(7) State of weather and that expected; hazards likely to be met during the watch.

(8) Charts in use and those to be used readily available.

If at the time when watches are being changed, an alteration of course or other action is being taken to avoid a hazard, then the changeover must be deferred until the manoeuvre has been completed.

Keeping the watch

The watchkeeping officer should, whenever possible, fix the ship's position at regular intervals by whatever means possible. When coasting, fixes should be taken and laid off hourly, with the fixes being made by more than one method. Log readings should be taken at the time of the fix. Any set or drift away from the course to be made good should be allowed for by adjustment of the course steered.

The compass error must be checked regularly when conditions permit and especially after a course alteration. Bearings of approaching vessels should be taken frequently in order to establish the existence of collision risk, with early and positive action taken as required by the Collision Regulations.

By regular position fixing, both by compass and/or electronic aids, with regular log readings and course adjustment, the trawler officer will conform to good navigational practice, which will enable him to pick out and positively identify landmarks/seamarks as they are approached and come into sight.

Similarly the good watchkeeping officer when on duty and expecting to sight a landmark, lightship or buoy, will inform the lookout of the characteristics and approximate bearing of the mark expected to be seen.

In clear weather, when circumstances allow, the radar should be switched on and used for practice and expertise which can be evaluated against visual fixing, bearings and collision risks.

Restricted visibility

If the officer of the watch knows that visibility is deteriorating and suspects fog conditions, it is his duty to comply with the Collision Regulations and take the following action whenever possible before the fog is encountered:

(*1*) Call the skipper

(*2*) Post look-outs and helmsman (if on automatic steering)

(*3*) Proceed at a safe speed, sound fog signals, exhibit navigation lights

(*4*) Warn the engine room, be prepared for manoeuvring, man the bridge controls if fitted

(*5*) Operate and use the radar before entering the fog, to detect other vessels which may be unsighted.

When proceeding parallel to a coast, a course should be chosen which leads the vessel away from, rather than towards, the land. Turning points at lightships or headlands should be approached with caution. Fairway buoys, port approaches and narrow navigable waters such as the Dover Straits and Pentland Firth are convergency areas with high traffic density where the utmost skill and caution must be used in poor visibility in order to avoid collision.

Lookouts

In fog or reduced visibility a second and additional lookout should be posted so that the officer of the watch may give his full attention to the navigation of the ship. The word 'lookout' is now defined in the Collision Regulations as being a term which means a lookout being kept by sight, by hearing and any other available means. The latter term can be applied to a radar lookout.

When the skipper has been called for any reason at all he may come to the bridge and assess the situation. When fully aware of the conditions, he may take over from the officer of the watch. There should never be any doubt between the officer of the watch and the skipper when such circumstances arise. When the skipper feels that he has evaluated the situation, when all data and information has been given to him and he is ready to take over then he must so inform the officer of the watch. Experience shows that accidents have taken place when the skipper came to the bridge because the officer of the watch assumed that the skipper was in charge immediately, even before he had time to become orientated with the situation and when no clear hand-over took place.

205

Calling the skipper

The officer of the watch should call the skipper immediately when the following circumstances arise:

(*1*) If visibility deteriorates or is suspected to deteriorate.

(*2*) In traffic congestion or if other vessels are causing concern.

(*3*) When there is difficulty in maintaining course.

(*4*) Failure to sight land or navigation marks as expected. An unexpected change in soundings.

(*5*) If land or navigation mark is seen unexpectedly.

(*6*) Any breakdown of engines, steering or essential navigational equipment.

(*7*) In heavy weather, where doubt exists on damage being caused by taking seas, pounding or engine racing.

(*8*) If in any situation which gives rise to any doubt whatsoever.

In consideration of the above circumstances the officer of the watch should not hesitate to take immediate action in the interests of the safety and care of the ship, *eg* if pounding heavily or if heavy seas are coming on board, the OOW should act at once. Similarly if an unexpected mark or signal is seen ahead then the safest action to take at once is to stop or reverse course immediately.

Deck log books

All fishing vessels are supplied with a deck log book in which a continuous account is kept of the ship's progress and position, by night and by day. The log covers the whole of the trip from leaving the berth to returning to berth in the home port. In addition to the navigational information entered in the log book, a record of the weather, fire and other safety drills and rounds is entered as well as any other incidents concerning crew or other vessels.

The log book is set out so that one page covers a single day. The first half of the page is used for the first half of the day up to noon with the second half of the page covering the time from noon to midnight.

The two halves of the page are lined horizontally for each hour of the day with vertical lines providing columns for time, course, compass, error, gyro, log, wind, barometer, sea state, surroundings, and in some cases a column is provided for fire and integrity rounds. There is a space provided for remarks, where one would expect to find a routine note on where a course alteration was made and there is usually a column on the extreme right of the page for the OOW to enter his initials. In the middle of the page separating the forenoon and afternoon there is space provided for the noon position to be entered along with the skipper's signature.

Deck log books must be properly written up during and at the end of each watch by the OOW. These log books are very important to owners, skippers, Department of Trade and other interested parties. When points of law occur they are likely to be called for in evidence.

All other incidents occurring during a fishing trip, including incidents on the fishing grounds, such as casualties to personnel or vessels, however slight, losses of gear, breakdowns, or damage to property must be fully written up immediately after the incident giving time, position, compass heading, engine and wheel movements and any other relevant data.

Notes on keeping the log

(1) The wind, sea and visibility columns must be filled in at the end of each watch in accordance with accepted scales. (*ie* Beaufort).

(2) In bad weather, take and enter the barometer reading hourly. Note the change. At other times enter the barometer reading at the end of each watch.

(3) Enter the course to be made good, true course steered, standard and steering compass courses with applied error of deviation/variation proving the true course.

(4) Check the patent or electric log early in the voyage against a known distance so as to obtain the error, if any. Express this error as a percentage, fast or slow. Enter the actual log reading every hour and at course alterations.

(5) The OOW must initial the log book when going off watch. By so doing this will avoid considerable mental effort later when trying to ascertain who was on duty at a particular time.

(6) As before stated the log constitutes a continuous record and must be fully kept up when on passage. When not on passage, *ie* when fishing, a continuous record of weather conditions must be entered. The 'Remarks' column should contain details of other activities such as 'fishing', 'dodging', 'alongside', 'at anchor', *etc*.

(7) Where a fire detection system is fitted, the OOW should check the annunciator panel at the same time as fire and integrity rounds are made. Enter in log book.

(8) Erasures should not be made in the log book. If it is necessary to make an alteration, rule out and initial.

(9) When going on duty, the OOW should see that the previous OOW has initialled the log book and should check to see if the skipper has written in any night orders at the foot of the page in the space provided.

The officer of the watch, when either on passage or at anchor, must always remember that the engines and the ship's whistle or siren are there for his use as well as the steering gear. In the majority of cases risk of collision and stranding may be avoided by a timely alteration of course but the OOW should not hesitate to use engines and whistle signals in case of need. He should also keep in mind the manoeuvring capabilities of his ship, *ie* turning and stopping distances.

At anchor

When a fishing vessel is at anchor it is normally considered necessary to maintain bridge and engine room watches as if the vessel were at sea. The following procedures should be observed:

(1) Determine and plot the ship's position by visual bearings and plot on the largest scale chart. When possible, note shore or navigational marks in transit, for speed and convenience of checks.

(2) Note the time of HW/LW strength and direction of flood and ebb. Note soundings on echometer.

(3) Take radar bearings and distance of prominent and identifiable shore mark when visibility is good. Note the readings as they may become useful if fog develops and the vessel remains at anchor.

(4) Maintain a proper lookout.

(5) Maintain fire and integrity rounds.

(6) Call the skipper if the vessel is thought to be dragging the anchor. Use engine and steering as necessary.

(7) Call the skipper in the event of fog developing and comply with fog signals applicable for vessels at anchor in the Collision Regulations.

(8) Exhibit appropriate lights and shapes for a vessel at anchor in the Collision Regulations.

OOW with pilot embarked

Despite the duties and obligations of a pilot to both the ship and her owners, his presence on board does not relieve or exonerate either the skipper or the OOW from his duties and obligations for the safety of the ship. They should co-operate closely with the pilot and keep an accurate check on the vessel's position and movements.

If there is any doubt as to the pilot's intentions or actions, clarification should be sought from the pilot, and if doubt still remains, the skipper should be called immediately and action taken at once as the OOW or the skipper considers necessary.

OOW and personnel

The OOW should give the members of his watch all appropriate instructions and information which will ensure the keeping of a safe watch, a proper lookout and regular fire and integrity rounds of the vessel.

When men are working either on deck or aloft, the OOW must remember that he is responsible for their safety. If weather conditions worsen so that the movement of the ship is likely to create a risk to men aloft, or if shipped water becomes a hazard to men working on deck, then the OOW should not hesitate to bring the men down from aloft or in from the open deck. Lifelines should always be rigged when considered necessary.

21　Shiphandling

Shiphandling in port and at sea

Within the meaning of the word shiphandling, there are two basic practices, *ie* handling a ship in narrow confined waters, such as a dock, tidal or non tidal river or estuary, channel, *etc* and, secondly, the handling of a ship at sea in bad weather. It is therefore proposed to divide shiphandling into two parts as described.

Shiphandling in harbour

The art and skill of shiphandling varies to a large degree on the type of vessel one is called upon to handle. Experience in shiphandling is a valuable asset, as in any skill.

There are different degrees of skill required for different ships. The twin screw vessel with a bow thrust is probably the easiest type of vessel to handle. This type of vessel is usually a passenger ferry, oil rig or perhaps a naval vessel and it will usually be a high-powered vessel. At the other end of the scale there is the large single screw vessel with a large cubic capacity and low power. When heavily laden, these vessels with a low power to weight ratio are the most difficult to handle, both at sea and, particularly, within the confines of a port. Because trawlers and other fishing vessels are nearly all single screw vessels without bow thrusts, we will describe only the handling of single screw vessels, on the assumption that if one is capable of handling a single screw ship, then the technique of handling a twin screw vessel will not give rise to any problems.

Much has been written and illustrated on shiphandling which is largely geometrical and theoretical. Let it be said that the basic principle involved in successful shiphandling is that a vessel should have as little headway as possible when swinging or on the approach run to a lock, berth or jetty. Too much headway when manoeuvring is the cause of nearly all shiphandling accidents. In most cases the skipper will realise that there is too much headway on his ship when the lock or quay is neared. By going astern in a single screw ship in order to take off the headway, all control will probably be lost; the ship may cant violently and a collision with the quay or lock will be inevitable. Judgment of a vessel's headway plays an important part in assessing movement, and only concentration and practice will improve judgment. The normal method of judging a ship's speed or headway prior to manoeuvring is to look at the shore marks abeam to see how quickly the ship is passing them. However, if the ship is several hundred feet away from the shore it would seem that the vessel is hardly moving. But if the ship is within a hundred feet of the bank or shore it will appear to be passing the marks very quickly. Judgment of a ship's speed by eye can be related to the distance of ship from shore. It is advisable, if possible, to run all the way off or go astern, before an approach run is made directly to open lock or jetty.

If we take a practicable example of this and suppose that a fishing vessel arriving at Hull at high water is to proceed head into Albert Dock. When off Alexandra and Victoria Dock, out in the middle of the river, it would appear that the ship is just moving ahead at a crawl. But as the vessel is angled in so as to pass close to Corporation Pier, the skipper may very well find that the ship is moving ahead far too quickly for entry into the lock. By going astern between Victoria Pier and Albert Dock, entrance with headway is dangerous. Far better to approach with only enough way so as to be able to steer. A similar approach is also advisable when wishing to swing off Albert Dock.

If Fleetwood is taken as a second example, here a vessel has to come from sea and enter the lockpit. The distance from the Fairway Buoy to the lock is less than three miles. It would not be wise under these circumstances to ever come up to full speed considering that a slow speed is required when passing vessels on the north end berths. Minimum headway on passing the Ro-Ro corner is necessary for a sensible approach to the lockpit. If the vessel sheers on the approach to the lock then the prudent skipper can put the engines ahead and, by use of full rudder, bring the ship under control again. Skippers may well say that from Ro-Ro corner to Slades corner, the vessel would set on to Tiger's Tail. The solution to this is:

(1) Pass as close as possible to Ro-Ro Corner (50 ft), the tide will then set towards the channel

(2) Do not come into the river too early on the flood tide.

If the reader refers to *Chapter 15* it will be seen that the tide runs strongest between three hours and two hours before high water, reducing in velocity down to zero knots at high water. It is prudent therefore to approach and manoeuvre off a tidal dock as near to high water as possible. The way cannot be taken off a ship which is proceeding up river on a strong flood tide, consequently direct entry into a lock or the swinging of a vessel under such circumstances (depending on swinging room) will be difficult.

The basic lessons to be learnt by the shiphandler are:
(1) Do not begin any manoeuvre with too much way on the ship. If in doubt stop the ship and begin from a stopped position.
(2) Avoid an approach to a dock, harbour or swinging area on a strong flood tide and where space or distance is limited.
(3) Learn and practice the judgment of speed over the ground on approach runs on slack or non tidal water. When approaching a jetty, always stem the tide so that headway may be easily adjusted.

Remember that the quickest manoeuvre is that which is carried out slowly.

Transverse thrust, single screw

In the previous description of approach to a lock, it was stated that by having too much headway on approach to a lock or jetty, making it necessary for the engines to be put astern, control of the ship might well be lost by the vessel canting to one side. This sheering effect is peculiar to single screw vessels and is known as transverse thrust. Conventionally, ships have been fitted with engines so that the shaft and propeller, when turning ahead, rotate in a clockwise direction, when looked at from astern.

If we look at a righthanded propeller from aft which is going ahead (*Fig 104a*), it will be seen that a greater pressure of water on the ship's hull is engendered by the blade in the top position and a weaker effect follows the blade at the lower position. This pressure effect on a ship's hull is created by the shape of the hull in the area of the stern. The width of the ship at the bottom of the propeller aperture is minimal, *ie* the width of the sole piece. Because of the hull shape being very fine at the bottom there is less suction behind the bottom blade. But on the top blade and above, the hull is shaping outwards vertically and horizontally, causing a greater suction effect behind the blade as it turns to the right, or to starboard when going ahead. If the right-handed propeller is moved anticlockwise into the astern position (*Fig 104b*) the opposite suction force is effected so that the stern moves bodily to port.

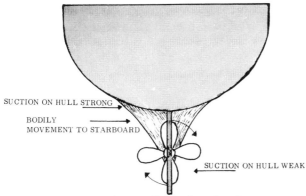

Fig 104a Right handed propellor going ahead

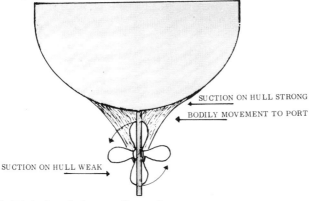

Fig 104b Right handed propellor going astern

This latter movement is the one which is important to the shiphandler. In the modern trawler the stern of the ship is full down to the water line, and below in the stern trawler. In calm conditions with still water, the engines of a righthanded ship when put astern will draw the stern to port and the head to starboard, and we have a starboard swing. When the engines are put ahead, the ship will have a tendency to swing to port. But if the shiphandler wishes to swing a righthanded ship in a limited space, then he must go ahead with full starboard rudder and then astern, which will not only maintain the swing but also the position of the vessel within the swinging area. Conversely, the lefthanded ship will swing to port when the engines are put astern. The shiphandler now has the following rule for swinging his ship and should, when possible:

213

(1) Swing the righthanded ship to starboard.

(2) Swing the lefthanded ship to port.

(3) When going alongside, port side to, make the approach run to the berth with only a little headway, and the fore and aft line of the ship finely angled towards the quay. When closing the quay, the righthanded ship will square up with the jetty when engines are put astern. If the swing to starboard is too great, then, by reason of having no way on the ship after the astern movement, a touch ahead and port helm will stop the swing and keep the vessel parallel to the quay. (See *Fig 105a*)

(4) When going alongside, port side to, in the left-handed ship, make the approach run as before in (3). On this occasion it is even more important that headway should be minimal. When sufficiently near to the berth for a line to be put ashore from forward, put the wheel hard to starboard and, with a short turn ahead on the engines, develop a starboard swing; stop the engines when the swing begins. When approximately parallel to the quay, come astern so that the ship and the starboard swing come to a simultaneous stop. (*Fig 106c*)

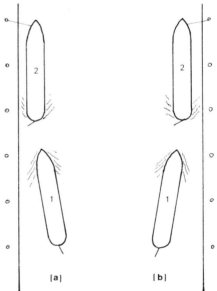

Fig 105 Going alongside, right-handed screw (a) port side to (b) starboard side to

214

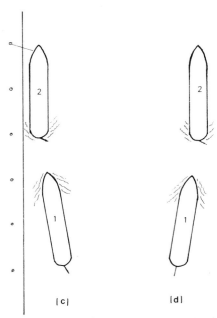

Fig 106 Going alongside, left handed screw (c) port side to (d) starboard side to

(5) When going alongside starboard side to, in the left-handed ship, make the approach run with minimal headway towards the quay. When near enough to pass a line ashore from forward put the engines astern. The ship's head will swing to port away from the quay and the stern will swing towards the quay. When approximately parallel to the quay put the wheel/rudder hard to starboard and with a short turn ahead on the engines the swing will be stopped. (See *Fig 106d*)

In all the above cases, crew should be at stations fore and aft, with heaving lines and mooring ropes ready. Breast ropes should be put out as soon as possible and the ship brought alongside easily on to fenders prior to mooring up properly shown in *Fig 107*.

Effect of wind

In windy conditions the skipper should have anchors ready when going alongside. Wind, if fresh enough, may overcome transverse

215

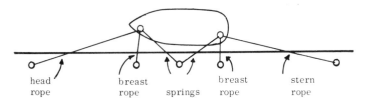

Fig 107 Correct mooring of a vessel

thrust by blowing the bow down on to a quay. If the stern sets towards a quay, the engines and helm used appropriately will keep it off. If, however, the wind blows the bow quickly down on to the quay, then only an anchor dropped on to the bottom will save the situation. If it is known prior to berthing that the wind is strong and that there is no tug to assist, then an anchor should be used to control the bow. High sided stern trawlers, are particularly vulnerable to a lot of wind.

There are two methods of using an anchor when going to a lee berth. If in dock or mooring in shallow water, then the ship may be brought abreast of the quay at a considered safe distance. By dropping the anchor on to the bottom on a short stay, the ship's head will slowly pay off to leeward controlled by the anchor dredging along the bottom. The length of cable may be judiciously increased if movement towards the quay is too great. This method may be found useful for trawlers in that they have a high raised whaleback with a much lighter forward draught than aft. The approach to the lee berth may be made at a broader angle when the anchor is used, thus keeping the stern up wind a little. If at any time too much cable is used, then the anchor may hold and bring the ship's head up into the eye of the wind. It is wise therefore to put the anchor on the bottom in good time, so that its braking effect on the ship's head can be seen and adjusted.

Anchors may be dropped and cable paid out abreast of a berth when it is known that a strong prevailing wind is likely to blow on to the quay. The anchor can then be used to heave the ship off when sailing. It is as well to know when the ship is sailing however, because an anchor laid out on the flood tide could be an embarrassment if the ship is to sail on the ebb tide.

A typical example of using an anchor to assist in dock work was the use of anchors in Albert Dock, Hull, prior to its conversion to a fish dock. The larger vessels which were unable to swing in the dock because of length were brought through the lockpit stern first, with a single tug aft on a bridle. When clear of the inner end of the lockpit, an

216

anchor was dropped on to the bottom. This anchor kept the fore end of the ship in the middle of the dock. The tug towed the vessel down the middle of the dock and towards the berth, where by use of engines, helm and tug, the vessel would be safely and properly berthed.

Use of anchor when swinging

If a vessel has to be swung with a flood tide running with the ship in a narrow channel, then an anchor should always be made ready before arriving at the place where the swing is to be made. (See *Fig 108*) Run all the way off the ship by slowing and stopping the engines well in advance. Go astern on arriving at the swinging area. If swinging to starboard, keep as close as possible to the port side of the fairway and have the starboard anchor ready. After having gone astern to reduce the effect of the flood tide, the skipper should not be surprised to see that the effect of transverse thrust is nil. This is because the flood tide

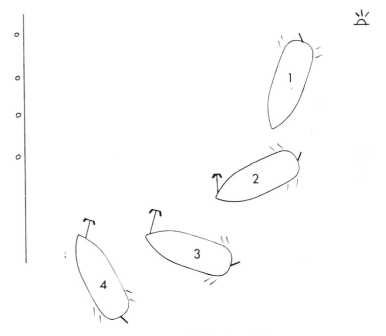

Fig 108 Use of anchor when swinging in a tideway

is strong and the fore and aft direction of flood down the ship's side is far greater than the low power of the transverse thrust. With all the way off put the helm hard over to starboard and with engines ahead bring the vessel athwart the tide. Drop the starboard anchor on to the bottom so that it just runs clear of the ship's side. Take off any surplus headway and hold on to the dredging anchor and the tide will do the rest of the work by swinging the ship on the dredged anchor, which should only be bumping and snatching at the bottom. The important part of this operation is that of letting go the correct amount of cable. The mate should let the anchor go when ordered to do so. When the anchor hits the bottom the cable will become slack and at this stage the brake should be applied. There are two reasons for applying the brake at this point. The cable is slack and the brake will take its weight easily. If a little more cable is required it can be paid out slowly by easing the brake. If, however, too much cable is run out, the anchor may hold on the bottom, the brake will be applied, and because the ship is athwart the tide, a tremendous weight will be taken by the windlass brake. If this happens, the brake may not hold; the cable will continue to run out and part at the end. The brake linings could burn out and the ship would swing violently.

Throughout this chapter it has been stressed that a shiphandler should never have too much way on the ship when manoeuvring. This is true, and it is the basis for adept and skilful ship control. The reader should not gain the impression however that whilst handling a ship, full power either ahead or astern should not be used.

There are often occasions when bold and decisive action is necessary to avoid a hazard, when a temporary burst of full ahead, with the wheel hard over will avoid a danger. For example let us suppose that a trawler is to leave a dock and pass through a 300 ft lock, with both sets of gates open and with the dock and lock lying on an east to west direction. If we also suppose that a strong to gale force wind is blowing from the north across the lock it will be clear that on a reduced speed approach towards the lock the ship will have to be steered well up into the wind to make a good fetch at the lock. The dock being wide enough allows this to be done, but if the lockpit is only 50 ft wide, then bold action will be necessary to take the ship through the lockpit unscathed. When the ship's head is about to enter the lock, full speed will have to be used to hold the ship up to wind and steer the ship through without scraping the lee side. The full speed thrust of the propeller would give responsive and accurate steering through the lock and when clear of the lockpit the vessel would still not have gathered much headway, so that speed could be reduced again. If the beam of the ship was such that the lock was not much wider than the ship's beam, then it would be unwise to try to pass through the lock without tug assistance, and with the tugs on short bridles.

By learning and studying tides, skippers and mates leaving their home port on tidal estuaries will become proficient shiphandlers and may learn the art of letting the tide assist a manoeuvre where possible. A ship is always under better control and manageable when head to tide and it is fundamental that approaches to jetties, locks, buoys, *etc* should always be made head to tide.

Stern to tide

When leaving a tidal jetty, head down river with the ebb away, there are dangers to be looked for. If there is plenty of room and water abreast of the jetty, the manoeuvre of letting everything go aft and holding on to a tightly set forward backspring will allow the ship's stern to cant off the jetty into the river. Let go of the spring when sufficiently well angled and at the same time put the engines astern. The funnel effect of the ebb running down river between the quay and the ship's bow will normally keep the stern away from the jetty. Transverse thrust would most likely have little effect. When leaving a jetty on the ebb as described, too large a swing should not be allowed to develop, so that as soon as the bow is sufficiently clear from the jetty with helm and engines ahead, the swing should be counteracted and the ship headed down river. If the ebb is strong and the stern of the ship swings quickly off into mid-channel, back off from the jetty and maintain the swing by going ahead to bring the ship head up into the ebb. If there is sufficient width, keep the vessel swinging until head down river.

If it is seen that there are ships at anchor abreast of or down river from the berth, then under no circumstances should the above manoeuvre be carried out. The best method under these circumstances would be to take a tug aft to hold the ship's stern up river until the vessel cleared the jetty. The tug could then be let go and the ship could proceed down river, once the tow rope was clear.

In the event that no tug was available and the ebb was not too strong, providing that there was sufficient room on the jetty, the ship might be swung on the quay. By putting out a suitably strong back spring from the fairleads at the bow, setting it tight and letting go all the after mooring ropes, the stern would swing right round for 180°, thence alongside again, leaving the ship head up river to the ebb. In small ships, such as trawlers might be considered to be, this manoeuvre is not difficult. The bow should be well fendered and the back spring sound. When this operation is carried out, it may appear that the stern will describe the 180° turn at an alarming speed, but as the stern closes the quay, there will be a cushion (pressure) effect between stern and quay. This effect, with the spring now a forward leading bow rope and the use of engines/helm, will prevent any impact of the stern on the quay.

Shallow water shiphandling

When a ship is taken into very shallow water with way on, the following effects will warn the shiphandler of the vessel's proximity to the ground:

(1) The bow wave and frictional wake down the side of the ship will disappear and the water will appear to be flat and calm.

(2) If the ship is by the stern on draught, on entering the shallow water the ship's head will visibly go down when looked at against the shore or horizon. The engines, wheelhouse, mast and superstructures will vibrate violently. The engine revolutions will drop. Only by reducing engine speed to dead slow will the vibration be stopped.

(3) When a vessel touches the bottom with the keel, if the bottom is of soft mud, the touch will be felt, if the bottom is hard sand, shingle, stone, *etc* it will be heard as well as felt.

It will be seen from the above that when a vessel is knowingly taken through a channel or dock approach where there is only a little more than sufficient water to float, the chance of hitting the bottom and losing control of the ship varies directly with the engine speed plus the speed of the ship through the water.

What is actually happening is that when a ship's hull is propelled forward through water, the bow action pushes water away from the bows. This displacement is followed by a trough towards the after end of the ship. At full speed, even in deep water, the after draught increases, or it is said 'the ship pulls down'. In shallow water, the trough becomes deeper, because the water displaced by the hull is not so easily replaced. There is little or no water under or around the ship in a narrow enclosed and very shallow channel, the propeller at full speed is thrusting water away from itself and the result is that the propeller and rudder are working in a partial water vacuum. This sets up vibration throughout the ship and increases draught, so that if the ship does not ground in the channel, she may well ground just out of the channel because of lack of steering control.

A typical example of this type of channel is that of the Wyre Dock Channel at Fleetwood. This channel, some 740 metres (2420 ft) in length, extends from the dock gates in the form of a dog's leg, to the main channel where the water deepens. The Dock Channel has mud banks on each side which dry out at low water as does the channel which is also very narrow.

At high water neap tides there is only sufficient water to float a trawler, drawing 16 to 18 ft if the vessel is accurately kept within the narrow channel. Yet experienced skippers who have grounded their ships in or near the channel have later said that on leaving the lock, full speed was rung on in an attempt to force the vessel over the muddy bottom. The proper and more seamanlike procedure is to leave the lock at dead slow speed so that displacement of water effect is minimal. If and when the ship appears not to be steering either straight in the channel or at the turn of the dog leg (Slades Corner), then a short, sharp burst of speed and thrust on the rudder by the screw should bring the ship under steering control again. Speed should again be reduced immediately. By proceeding slowly, the water displacement is slowed right down and the flow return to the after end is assisted. If the vessel were to ground in the channel at dead slow then there would not have been sufficient water to sail in the first instance and the vessel should not have left.

Variable pitch propellers

The forces of a propeller when turned in water are two-fold. By far the largest component is that force which drives the ship either ahead or astern. There is a minimum component which has already been described, ie transverse thrust. The effect of the transverse thrust component has been explained for the traditional engine/power transmission to the propeller, where there is an engine which can be reversed in order to go astern.

During the last decade a new form of transmission known as the variable pitch (VP) propeller has increased in use. The ship's engine is

221

so arranged that it runs in one direction only. The engine revolutions may be controlled from an appropriate minimum speed to the maximum full speed. The engine is geared to the propeller shaft in such a manner that at slow speed, by means of a gear change, the direction of the shaft will be reversed (similar to the reverse gear of a car). The effect of transverse thrust at this stage is the same as that of the traditional vessel except for the fact that to the geared shaft there is a propeller fitted which has a variable pitch facility.

The VP propeller fitted on a geared shaft can be moved in one direction only, that is from a full pitch down to a zero pitch, or vice versa. Because the direction of the drive shaft can be reversed, a reverse pitch is unnecessary. Consequently a vessel wishing to go full speed will have maximum pitch on the propeller blades and maximum revolutions on the engine.

But at slow speed, not only is the engine slowed down to its minimum, the pitch may also be reduced by degrees until zero pitch is attained, when the propeller is turning as a wheel in the water, with no bias on the blades. This then is the stopped position even though the engine, shaft and propeller are turning at slow speed. The propeller is said to be feathering when turning on zero pitch.

Referring back to *Figs 104a* and *b* we will see that with the VP propeller it may still be considered as righthanded or lefthanded as is the conventional propeller, depending on whether the drive shaft turns clockwise (RH) or anti-clockwise (LH) when going ahead. The suction still presses on the hull shape and follows the blade direction. But the suction diminishes as the pitch of the propeller is reduced, because the angle of the blade as a thwartship component is less, the suction behind the blade is less. When on zero pitch, however, there is still a little bias which may be described as wheeling effect. So now it can be seen that transverse thrust on a VP propeller is not quite so effective, once the shiphandler begins to reduce pitch from full. Transverse thrust either ahead or astern is effected by

(*1*) Reduction of engine speed

(2) Reduction of pitch.

VP propellers, reversible

There is at the present time in wide use within the fishing fleet the fully controllable pitch propeller which is reversible. In this type of vessel both the engine and propeller shaft are uni-directional, *ie* they

222

run continuously in one direction. The continuously running engine and shaft have speed control between slow and full speed, *ie* say 200 revs up to 600 revs.

The directional thrust of the propeller, ahead or astern, is altered by means of a reversible pitch propeller. In short, the propeller and blades always turn in the same direction, but the pitch or angle of the blade in the vertical plane is altered so that the thrust effect in the water surrounding the propeller gives ahead propulsion or astern propulsion.

If, for example, we take a variable pitch propeller in a ship which a skipper is to join for the first time. The skipper, before handling the ship, must find out in which direction the engine (shaft) turns. Let us suppose it is clockwise. Then because the propulsion is unidirectional, the ship will have a tendency to go to port when put ahead and astern because the transverse thrust is uni-directional, *ie* the screw always turns to the right, only the blade bias changes.

In conclusion we have in the case of fully reversible pitch propellers on a uni-directional shaft and engine giving the following effects for shiphandlers:

(*1*) Vessel with clockwise propulsion, transverse thrust of stern to the right on ahead and astern manoeuvre, port swing.

(*2*) Vessel with anti-clockwise propulsion, transverse thrust of stern to the left on ahead and astern manoeuvre, starboard swing.

Pitch

The pitch of the screw is the distance it would move the ship ahead in one revolution, supposing that the propeller is turned in a solid and not in water. If one imagines an ordinary wood screw being turned by a screwdriver into wood, then the depth gained by one round turn is comparable to the pitch of a propeller. The greater the angle of the blades, the greater the pitch.

Slip

Slip is the difference between the actual distance covered by the ship and the pitch of the propeller/engine revs. It is mainly due to the fact that unlike a solid, water yields to the pressure exerted on it by the screw as it thrusts the ship ahead. This is important in shiphandling. If we suppose that a ship is proceeding down river on a strong ebb of five knots, then we have a situation where the water is carrying the ship at five knots regardless of engines. But because the water is moving downstream and against the after part of the propeller blades the slip will be negative or nearly so as the propeller turns against it. But what happens when, in the case of an emergency, the engines are put astern? The ebb tide continues to run past the propeller and the stern movement of the screw is in water which is passing the blades because of its own velocity. The percentage of slip becomes very high and the engines must be kept running astern for some considerable time before headway is lost.

Engine speed

Engine speed is the rate at which the propeller would drive a ship if there were to be no slip. Speed = pitch × rpm × 60m ÷ ft in a nautical mile.

Rudder

The rudder in trawlers is usually placed behind the propeller so that the water thrust astern by the propeller may steer the ship. In contrast to the propeller, the greater the slip, the greater the efficiency of the rudder. To illustrate this we may look at a vessel with engines stopped and at anchor. With a strong tide running the vessel can be steered. With a strong following tide and a ship proceeding at slow speed, the rudder is less effective, there is less slip, and less water running past the rudder.

Shiphandlers should also bear in mind that in a sudden emergency, whereby engines are put astern in order to get the way off, putting the wheel hard over helps the ship to pull up. The flat surface of a rudder on maximum angle being dragged astern causes some loss of headway.

Pivoting point

The average vessel will pivot approximately one third of the length of the ship measured from the bow. This is useful to know when going alongside or when swinging a single screw vessel.

Turning circle

When the helm on a vessel is put hard over she will turn on a circular path through 360°. If at sea and steaming at full speed the turning circle will be greater than that made under other circumstances, of particular interest to the shiphandler. At sea and under full speed there is a greater side slip away from the centre of the turning circle. When shiphandling, the skipper will normally be interested only in half of the turning circle, *eg* when swinging. Suppose a vessel has just picked up her anchor, is head to tide and has to turn round to proceed up or down river. The ship will have no headway so by putting the wheel hard over, engines to full ahead, the smallest turning circle will be achieved. Because the ship begins the turn with no headway, there is no side slip or moment of centrifugal force and the ship's speed over the ground will never reach maximum by the time she has swung 180°. Once again when proceeding with the tide even with engines stopped prior to swinging, because the trawler is being carried ahead the centre of gravity of the vessel will create the centrifugal force or side slip when the turn begins. As previously suggested, have the anchor ready when turning with the tide in confined waters.

When opportunity allows, a skipper should, when at sea and on full speed make a turning circle so as to be able to judge the performance of his vessel. In fine weather and with time to spare before catching the tide, a quiet area at sea with no traffic would be a suitable time to assess the swinging of a vessel when on full speed and also from a standing start.

Use of rudder when going astern

When a vessel has gathered sternway on swinging and the swing is to continue, experience shows that by stopping the engines and by putting the helm no more than halfway over in the direction of swing the vessel will be more likely to follow the rudder than if it were put hard over.

Going alongside a vessel at anchor

By looking back to *Fig 75* on page 103 it will be seen that a vessel at anchor will pivot around her stem to a degree depending on wind, tide and swell. A vessel in an anchorage which is not sheltered from wind and/or swell, or one in open waters, will certainly be moving in a figure of eight motion either large or small.

Fishing vessels which are called upon to go alongside a vessel at anchor should exercise the utmost degree of caution and skill before doing so. The first task before going alongside of the anchored vessel, after having decided that it is safe to do so, is to establish communication by VHF and maintain it throughout the operation.

The approach run to the anchored vessel should not be made at a fine angle from the stern, nor should it be made with very much headway. As the bow of the approaching vessel nears the stern of the anchored vessel, even in a calm, interaction between the ships will be set up, depending on the way of the approaching vessel. The displacement effect at the bow will put pressure on the stern of the anchored vessel and push it away. The ship at anchor will pivot at an angle across the approaching vessel's bows and a collision will probably occur. If contact is made at the forepart of the anchored ship, both vessels will sheer away forward and a second contact will take place between the quarters.

It is far better to approach an anchored vessel on her beam at a suitable distance and pass breast ropes across. By doing so the ships may be brought together under the control of the breast ropes and by winch. If the anchored vessel takes a sheer when the two ships are abeam, it can be corrected by the use of helm and engines. The vessel about to moor must also take action to avoid impact and if necessary steam away altogether.

Once having moored alongside an anchored vessel it is of primary importance to be sure that the vessels are well fendered. It will also be seen that any two vessels are unlikely to have the same characteristics insofar as draught, length, beam and stability conditions. Consequently, in any sea, swell, or wind, the ships will have different roll and pitch periods, and they will range differently. In moderate to good conditions, good fendering may be adequate to prevent damage, but the prudent skipper will have the ship ready at all times so that he is ready to cast off in the event of worsening wind, sea, or swell and so avoid damage to his ship.

The pressure effects of water around a ship when steaming in a river, canal or channel, can be appreciated and will be clearly seen by watching the shore. Suppose that there is a tide gauge on the river bank, jetty or dolphin and the reading is taken well before the ship comes up to it. (This is the proper time to read a tide gauge). Further suppose that a depth of 20′ is showing on the gauge as the ship approaches, and before the bow is abeam of the gauge there is a surge of water which may well rise to about 23 ft. or 24 ft. As the bow passes the gauge the water level will drop quickly to about 17 ft (the trough) and then rise once more (the stern wave) before settling down at 20 ft.

When passing a jetty at which a ship is moored, these pressures or water surge may damage the vessel or her moorings and that is why it is necessary for vessels to slow down before and until a jetty is passed.

When a ship passes close to a bank and at full speed, this movement of water is restricted by the proximity of the bank and the trough becomes deeper towards the bank. Because the water on the bank side is in the form of a narrow band deepening to a trough its velocity is increased and the bow is pushed or cushioned away from the shore. The stern will be sucked towards the bank by reason of the deep trough, and the whole effect is known as interaction, canal effect.

Interaction between two ships will take place more readily when one vessel overtakes another in a fairway or channel when too close together. The overtaking ship may suck the other into her side when abeam and experience shows that a vessel on full speed passing another on slow speed will draw the overtaken vessel along for a great distance, if the channel is narrow and/or shallow.

Shiphandling at sea

In good weather at sea shiphandling is mainly knowing how quickly the ship will react when turning, steering and stopping during an emergency.

Shiphandling at sea is primarily concerned with the safety of lives on board and the safety of the vessel in bad weather. The largest British fishing vessel is about 260 ft in length; most vessels are trawlers of some 200 ft in length or less. So when considering bad weather, length of sea, and swell, the trawler may be thought to be a small ship relative to the prevailing weather conditions. Large vessels in a short sea behave well and are more comfortable than small vessels.

Primarily, the capacity of a trawler to ride in heavy weather in a reasonable manner without risk of damage depends on the course and speed. Secondary considerations affecting good sea behaviour in heavy weather are stability range, weight distribution, and wave period. Though secondary, these conditions are very important.

Roll and pitch

There is probably little the trawlerman can do immediately insofar as

227

altering either stability or weight distribution when heavy weather is encountered and risk of damage and seaworthiness becomes apparent. But by altering course and/or speed, the roll and pitch period will be altered. By reducing speed or altering course, the pitch and roll period will change the ship's position and direction relative to the waves.

At the present time there are many stern trawlers of varying size which are so constructed that their engine rooms are well forward, probably only one third of the ship's length from the bow. When steaming into heavy weather these ships are particularly susceptible to pounding or slamming damage. There have been numerous cases when vessels have pushed on at full speed into a head sea when pounding occurred, and severe damage has been caused to bottom plating, twisted frames and damaged holding-down bolts on the engine. Skippers are aware that when steaming against high winds and heavy seas, water will be taken over forward causing damage on deck which will be seen. Portholes, bridge windows, bent ladders, indents to deckhouse plating are some of the deck damage which has been suffered by trawlers before the ship was eased down. The vessel should always be eased down as soon as water is being taken on board in appreciable quantities. When pounding and slamming takes place, steps should be taken at once to reduce speed. This cannot be stressed too strongly; unseen and unknown damage may be done to bottom plates and frames, especially in stern trawlers with engine rooms well forward. A stern trawler steamed north through the Minch, where she had been sheltering from bad weather from the west. When rounding the Butt of Lewis, heavy seas from the west were encountered and the vessel pounded heavily before being eased down. This modern vessel on return to port had all bottom plates under the engine room set up between frames, several frames were distorted along the bottom and up the ship's sides, three deck supporting pillars were buckled in the engine room and the engine and shaft were put out of alignment. All this damage was caused in a very short length of time when the vessel left sheltered water and turned into head seas at full speed. In case the reader should gain the impression that being head to sea is a hazardous position in bad weather, let it be said that this is not so. By design, shape, construction and stiffening, a trawler put head to sea at the right speed is likely to be much safer, less vulnerable and better to handle, than with the sea astern or on the beam. If the weather is bad enough, the trawler will be less vulnerable even if speed is reduced

228

until only steerage way is maintained and the vessel is hove-to or is dodging. By reducing speed in heavy weather from ahead, not only does the prudent seaman avoid the risk of damage being caused forward, but also the damage which may be done to engine, gearbox and shaft which can be caused by the propeller racing, ie the propeller wholly or partly emerging from the sea loses the normal frictional resistance present when turning in water. As a result, propeller, shaft and engine will race at excessively high speeds.

The degree to which a vessel will roll on any given wave period, when such waves are abeam, will depend upon the ship's stability. If the centre of gravity is low in the vessel there will be a large metacentric height. If the centre of gravity is high in the vessel there will be a small metacentric height. In the first case, the low centre of gravity will make the ship stiff and resistant to the waves. The roll period will be short and quick and waves will break over the ship causing damage. The quick roll will be uncomfortable, with a greater strain on lashings, stays, clips and other holding down gear due to the quick thwartship direction change.

The counterpart to the stiff ship is the ship with the high centre of gravity, which vessel is described as tender. The roll of the tender ship will be longer and slower than that of the stiff ship. If water is taken on board a tender ship, with high bulwarks and jammed freeing ports, the weight of water winged out to the sides on a long, large angled roll will dangerously reduce stability. Both extremes of condition, stiff and tender, are undesirable. Skippers should therefore always study the stability plans on board in order to understand the ship's condition with regard to behaviour in bad weather.

Pooping and quartering seas

When a ship is steaming and the sea is on the bow, she will roll and pitch simultaneously. The vessel will encounter the waves by putting the bow or shoulder into the wave and the resistance offered reduces the angle of roll. When running with the sea on the quarter the opposite effect takes place, the roll increases because there is less resistance forward and the wave runs past the ship more slowly because ship and wave run in nearly the same direction. This combination produces a pronounced roll and pitch effect which results in heavy seas being taken on board from aft. Because the seas are moving from aft and traversing the ship, the rudder is less effective and the ship may be slewed across the wave direction and broach-to. The added weight of water taken on deck when pooped and broached-to on a large angle of heel could result in a loss of positive stability and capsizing.

This situation will have arisen because of the pronounced heeling effect of the sea on the quarter; the large amount of water allowed to come on board because the ship remains under the crest of the breaking wave for a long period; or poor steering qualities.

In circumstances such as these the skipper must take immediate action by varying both the course and the speed to avoid synchronisation of ship/wave speed and direction. It may be decided to turn head to sea.

Turning a trawler, heavy weather

The decision to turn a trawler in heavy weather should not be left until it is too late, *ie* when a lee shore enforces the decision. Turning from a following sea until it is ahead requires skill and judgment. It should be done on a chosen time, the manoeuvre being started as soon as the last wave crest has passed the vessel. The engine speed should be reduced to a minimum, this will allow the last sea to pass quickly. With everything on deck and below secure, the wheel should be put hard over and the ship turned in the trough between wave crests. The trawler should be turned as quickly as possible in the trough so that she is head on or nearly head on to the next wave in the cycle. This will only be done in the lull immediately following one wave and the next. By use of full rudder the turn will be started, full speed may be used to turn short round, so long as too much headway is not gathered, before meeting the next sea. By studying the cycle of wave crests, the opportune time to turn may be chosen. Oil spread from aft prior to turning will assist greatly. Do not commit the ship to turning when water has been taken on deck. Try to turn when the wave crest has just passed and only a comparatively small amount of water has been taken. By starting the turn at this stage on easy engine revolutions, the ship may, when athwart, be pushed round into wind and sea on full revolutions when in the trough. As soon as the trawler is nearly head up to wind and sea, engine speed should be reduced and the vessel steadied to meet the next sea. The prudent skipper will always turn head to sea before being forced to do so by reason of extensive damage, loss of stability due to heavy shipping of seas, or proximity of a lee shore.

230

A stern trawler may find that it is necessary to turn, when running before heavy seas, much earlier than the conventional side trawler, by reason of her ramp. At slow speed with a following or quartering sea, a wave will readily run up a ramp and break on to the after deck. On a heavy heel and pitch motion the water on the after deck would effect a loss of stability on the downward roll. The high bulwarks which run from right aft to the midship accommodation block on the stern trawler provide a comfortable working space in normal conditions, but in a following sea, a natural water trap exists. Freeing ports must be kept clear and in working order and pooping avoided at all times.

22   Basic elements of stability

From the previous chapter on ship handling at sea, it will have been noted that heavy weights of water taken on deck would endanger the safety of the vessel by adversely affecting and reducing stability. Heavy icing on deck and superstructure will also have the same effect.

Transverse stability

Dynamic stability is the moment of force which will return a ship to its normal equilibrium when it is moved by an outside force such as wind or wave motion. When a vessel is placed in water it will displace a volume of water equal to that of its own weight. If the weight of the vessel and its contents exceeds the weight of the volume of water displaced, it will sink.

The buoyant volume of a ship is that part of the vessel which is enclosed and is watertight. This is the total buoyancy force, and that part which is normally above the water plane is known as the reserve buoyancy.

To be able to understand stability, the fisherman must understand the meaning of the following terms as they are related to a ship: the centre of gravity, the centre of buoyancy and the metacentric height. When a ship is built, the designer, because he knows the hull form or shape of the vessel, is able to calculate the position of the centre of buoyancy B. Because he is able to calculate the displacement of the newly built ship, which gives him the weight, and he is aware of weight distribution, the designer will be able to calculate the centre of gravity of the ship G. From this data he will now be able to find M, the metacentric height. If we look at *Fig 109(a)* which illustrates a ship in an upright position of equilibrium, we will see that B the centre of buoyancy has its force directed initially upwards through the centre line of the ship. G, the centre of gravity will be seen to be above B, with its gravity exerted downwards; both forces being placed from the keel. *Fig 109(b)* shows the righting moment and directional force

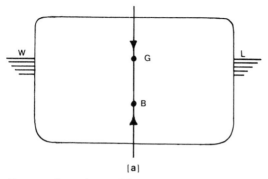

Fig 109a Centre of gravity and buoyancy

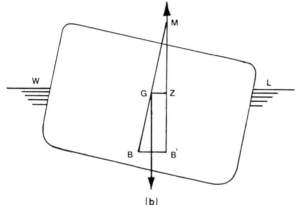

Fig 109b Righting lever GZ when heeled by an outside force

when the vessel has been heeled by an outside force such as wind or wave.

B. The position of B is the centre of gravity of the underwater volume of the ship and it is the point through which the forces of buoyancy act vertically upwards. The force of buoyancy is equal to the amount of water displaced.

G. The centre of gravity is a point within a body where the force of gravity is said to act vertically downwards. The force is equal to the weight of the body.

M. If we now suppose that the vessel is heeled to an angle of 10°, it will be seen on *Fig 109b* that the shape of the hull below the waterline has now altered. There is more of the hull on the right of the centre line below the waterline than that on the left and B must change its

233

position to B^1. If we now draw a vertical line through B^1, it will be seen that it intersects the original buoyancy line at M, and we have a triangle GMZ.

(1) The distance GM is a measure of the initial stability of the ship at small angles of heel.

(2) GZ is the righting lever which is the force required to bring the ship back to an even keel when heeled by an outside force. *Fig 109b* illustrates the righting moment where GZ is the lever.

(3) GMZ equals the angle of heel.

Because we know the length of GM and θ the angle of heel, it is now possible to calculate GZ ($GZ = GM \sin \theta$). If GZ is multiplied by the displacement we then have the moment of force in foot tons which will bring the ship back to the upright when she has been heeled by an outside force.

The designer of the vessel can calculate the position of B, G and M because he knows exactly the underwater form or shape of the vessel at a fixed draught. He may confirm his calculations by means of a heeling test when the ship is launched.

The metacentre M may be regarded as a fixed point but only at small angles of heel, and for a particular draught. At large angles of heel the draught and underwater shape change quickly and other more complicated calculations have to be made. If the designer arranges the hull dimensions so that at small angles of heel there is a good safe margin of stability and there is a reasonable stability factor for different but normal loading conditions, then it may be assumed that the conventional form of vessel will have sufficient transverse stability to correct heel when rolling in heavy weather.

If a vessel has a large transverse metacentric height (GM), she will develop a short but rapid roll and in very bad weather it may be described as violent. Such a ship is said to be stiff and because of the rapid roll may damage herself by shifting cargo, machinery, *etc*.

A vessel with a small GM will develop a long slow transverse motion and is said to be tender. The ideal condition is somewhere in between with a reasonable stability factor that would make the ship neither stiff nor tender.

The fisherman must have a basic understanding of the fundamental concepts of stability as described before we look at stability and how it can be affected adversely. When a vessel sails and she is fully bunkered and stored, the position of M the metacentric, which has been determined by the designer for that draught, is fixed. It is fixed for various draughts and M will be tabulated and often shown as a diagram which will show BM, *ie* the distance of the transverse metacentre M from B the centre of buoyancy. Its height will also be shown as a distance from the keel.

G, the centre of gravity, can, however, be altered by moving stores, fuel or ballast. Traditionally, trawlermen would sail from their home port bound for distant waters and they would be at sea for some 20 days. A large sized distant water vessel would carry some 180 tons of fuel, several tons of fresh water and stores. During the three week period of fishing an average daily fuel consumption might be six tons. The water and stores would also be slowly used up and the vessel would return with about 50 tons of fuel on board.

But during this period the trawler would be progressively catching fish, which would be carefully stowed in shelves and packed in the fishroom. It would be carefully packed, boarded off in a loading process which began at the bottom of the fishroom working upwards. The progressive fish catching balances out the consumption of fuel, *etc*. A catch of 2,000 – 2,500 kits of fish would equal 125-155 tons in weight. This would approximate with the stores and fuel used.

Traditionally, stability has not posed many problems for either trawlermen or trawler managers except in exceptional circumstances, as follows:

(*1*) Heavy icing on deck and superstructure, when G would be raised until there was little or no righting moment and positive stability. Draught will increase and freeboard will reduce.

(*2*) The shipping of heavy and successive seas in abnormally bad weather. If the heavy volume of water on deck is not free to spill quickly from a well deck, it will have the effect of raising the vessel's G, increase the draught, and reduce the freeboard, the centre of gravity of the sea water will move from side to side if the vessel is rolling. Partially filled tanks (slack tanks) will have a similar effect as that of water on deck.

Except for these circumstances it will be seen that under normal conditions with a ship sailing full of bunkers, stores, ice, *etc*, there is nothing that the fishermen can do which is likely to affect B or M. He may alter the position of G by transferring or using fuel but this change is only small and in any case is allowed for in designs.

With the advent of the pelagic mode of fishing, circumstances concerning the stability factor have been changed considerably and pelagic fishing must now be carefully considered in relation to stability. The basic reasons for these changes are that pelagic fishing allows for a large weight of catch to be brought on board in a very short time. In the traditional demersal fishing it might take eleven days of continuous fishing to produce 130 tons of fish, which would be systematically and carefully stowed. This weight of fish may now be caught pelagically in two or three hauls and in a matter of hours. The factors adversely affecting stability are as follows:

(1) The extra weight of equipment, net drum and gear may add 10-20 tons of top weight to a vessel, depending on size of ship. This will raise G.

(2) As much as 30-40 tons of fish may be brought on deck in one haul in a stern trawler, depending on the size of ship. This will raise G.

(3) The stowage of the fish should be such that it is contained within compartments around the centre line and towards the bottom of the fishroom. If the fish is bulk stowed and not divided properly it will move if the ship heels or rolls so that G will move proportionally.

(4) By reason of only having to be at sea for a very short time the vessel may only be lightly stored and bunkered. The double bottom tanks may be slack because of the minimum fuel on board. Some tanks may be empty. This will raise G.

(5) The cubic capacity required to stow one ton of demersal fish such as cod and haddock, iced and shelved is high. The cubic capacity to stow one ton of pelagic fish in bulk with the water element is low. By filling the fishroom and taking fish on deck, the vessel could be overloaded, with a consequent increase in draught and decrease of stability and freeboards.

(6) The side trawler which has been converted to fish pelagically will not, of course, be able to drag a heavy bag of fish on board as does the stern trawler.

If a side trawler lifts large weights of fish by derrick or gilson wire, then she will reduce her stability considerably. The G of the bag of fish is exerted downwards from the derrick head. Because of its height and horizontal distance from the centre line, the centre of gravity of the ship moves proportionally towards the derrick head and a small trawler picking up a large net of fish will list heavily when the weight comes on the derrick head.

Providing that the skipper has an understanding of stability and the danger factors there is no reason why trawlers should not be able to catch and stow large weights of fish. It is only prudent, however, to have new stability data drawn up by the shipbuilder or other authority showing GM for the new conditions. Various recommendations may be made for different ships, *ie* a ship may have to have permanent ballast in order to increase her GM when in light condition in order to offset a large weight of fish on deck. The prudent skipper will study the stability plans, curves and information, and will not overload his vessel.

Stability information, which includes typical conditions of loading, is provided for use by the skipper on board. This will allow him to acquire a general understanding as to how the stability of his vessel will fluctuate during a typical voyage and will also provide the basis for any adjustment he may wish to make for a special or particular condition of loading. An 'icing-up' weight will usually be given for distant water trawlers.

Before looking at plans or conditions of loading, the fisherman should understand that at this stage we have been looking at the transverse stability of a ship. Transverse stability is related directly to the vertical height of the centre of gravity measured from the keel. In ships' plans or tables it will be shown as VCG. Its height influences the speed and degree to which a ship will roll or heel. VCG will move up or down towards a weight taken on board, depending where the weight is placed. It will move when a weight is taken out of a ship, away from the position of the weight. It will move sideways towards a weight if the weight is loaded off centre. *Fig 110* shows the effect of picking up a bag of fish from over the side by derrick or gilson. It demonstrates that the centre of gravity moves not only vertically but horizontally

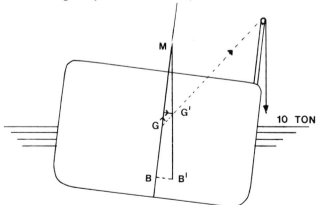

Fig 110 Suspended weight loss of GM

towards the derrick head. If we suppose M to be fixed it will be seen that the value of GM and the righting lever has been considerably reduced. If the above effect as described is combined with an increased movement of G when the ship is listed owing to a slack tank as shown in *Fig 113* an aggravated situation will arise.

The centre of gravity is also measured longitudinally between the forward perpendicular, from the centre of flotation (CF). CF or tipping centre is the geometrical centre of the water plane about which the vessel will trim. It is important to the fisherman to know that the longitudinal centre of gravity will affect trim. When a heavy bag of fish is hauled on to the ramp of a stern freezer, the vessel will increase the mean draught because of the extra weight being taken on board. But because the weight is taken on to the ramp at the extreme distance from the CF then a considerable change in trim will take place. The ship's draught will increase aft and decrease forward. In the ship's plans the longitudinal centre of gravity will be seen as LCG with the vertical centre of gravity as VCG.

From the first part of this chapter on stability it will be seen that the dangers facing the fisherman may be a complete loss of GM and /or GZ, the righting lever. The causes may now be separated into different categories for description, action and correction, *ie* list, loll, free surface, suspended weights.

List

List is caused by off centre loading. The ship's centre of gravity will move towards the weight in a ratio dependent upon the weight loaded or moved, its distance from the centre line, and the vessel's displacement. The list may be corrected by adjustment and movement of the weight or other weights about the centre line so that the vessel will return to an upright position. (See *Fig 111*)

If a list is not corrected, however, the listed position becomes the initial condition of stable equilibrium and the vessel will roll about this position. If we suppose that a trawler has an uncorrected list of 10° to starboard, then in the event of rolling due to bad weather, the vessel would roll symmetrically about the inclination of 10° to starboard. Let us suppose that the vessel began to roll to an angle of 10°, then when rolling to port she would reach the vertical and when rolling to starboard she would be heeled 20° from the vertical. This would not be desirable and the list should be corrected by adjusting weights around the centre line of the ship.

238

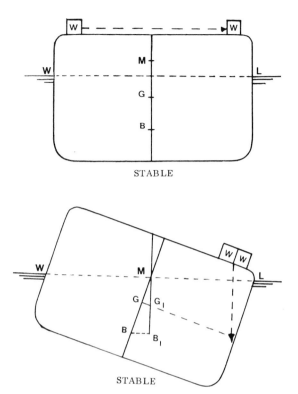

Fig 111 Effect of a moved weight creating a list

In conclusion, it must be understood that a list is the angle to which a vessel heels because of off-centre weights and when the vessel initially had positive stability when upright. It is quite different to loll which is caused by being unstable when upright.

Loll

A vessel which is unstable in the upright position may have little or no positive stability. She may even have negative stability with G above the metacentre. It might well be thought that the vessel would capsize. This would happen if large weights were added very quickly and very high up in the ship and heavy beam seas were encountered. Fortunately, there is a counter action for the vessel which has unstable equilibrium which takes place when a vessel with a small or negative GM heels.

239

The condition of loll is of course unsatisfactory and is caused by either too much top weight, too little bottom weight or by free surface liquid anywhere in the ship. By reducing the top weight and reducing free surface, G may be lowered. It is important that counter weights which would correct a list should not be used. In using counter measures such as filling a side tank on the high side or removing weight from the low side, it must be remembered that because of the low stability factor or wind/wave action, the vessel could easily roll to the other side and the momentum gained in the roll may take her past the angle of loll and she may not recover. G can be lowered by:

(1) Filling a small divided double tank on the *low* side. If it is already slack, well and good. If empty, G will rise at first but as the tank becomes full G will fall. The angle of heel may now be a list which can be eliminated by filling the opposite tank on the high side.

(2) Jettison weights from the *high* side. If the loll has been caused by icing up on the trawler's masts, stays, *etc*, remove the ice beginning on the centre line, masts, *etc*, then on the high side, before starting on the low side.

In both cases as set out above, G is lowered and the angle of heel may at first increase. Remember that the waterplane area increases from the ship's vertical position as she heels and reaches its maximum at approximately 45° to 50° in the average ship.

At the beginning of this chapter, set out numerically, were certain factors concerning the pelagic mode of fishing. These factors included heavy weights taken on deck with empty and/or slack bottom tanks. Any combination of these factors might lead to a loll condition. Beam seas would further aggravate the situation.

To be able to understand why a vessel with a small or negative GM does not immediately capsize, the formula $BM = \dfrac{I}{V}$ must be analysed.

BM = The distance between the centre of buoyancy and metacentre.

I = The transverse moment of inertia of the water-plane $(L \times B^3)$

V = The volume of the ship's displacement.

If we ignore the factor of co-efficient fineness (CF) of the vessel, we have BM $= \dfrac{I}{V} = \dfrac{L \times B^3}{L \times B \times D} = \dfrac{B^2}{D}$ where L, B and D = length, breadth and draught.

We are now left with BM $= \dfrac{B^2}{D}$. By looking at *Fig 112* it can be seen that as the vessel heels to the position of loll the waterplane area increases by reason of the increased breadth. The above formula BM $= \dfrac{B^2}{D}$ shows that BM increases in a ratio directly as the square of the breadth and inversely as the draught. When the ship heels, the draught increases slightly on the low side but decreases on the high side; the mean draught will therefore remain constant. But the beam of the ship measured across the waterplane has increased and B² at the angle of loll will raise the position of M until it is above G. This is the angle of loll about which the vessel will move. (See *Fig 112a* and *b*)

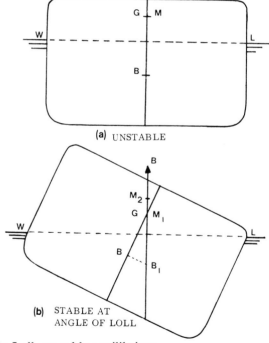

(a) UNSTABLE

(b) STABLE AT ANGLE OF LOLL

Fig 112a Loll, unstable equilibrium
Fig 112b Stable at angle of loll, owing to increased waterplane area

241

Free surface effect

Provided that a tank is at least 98% full of liquid, no movement of the liquid is possible, and the tank may be regarded as being filled with a solid material. When a quantity of liquid is drawn off, however, the stability of the ship is adversely affected by what is known as 'free surface effects'. Regardless of where the tank is situated within the ship, either high or low, there is a rise of G and a loss of GM depending on the length and breadth of the tank and the relative density of the liquid.

The liquid in an undivided tank running across the breadth of the ship and partially filled with liquid must be regarded as a weight which is free to move from side to side as the ship heels when steaming at sea. The G of the liquid moves from side to side and the G of the vessel consequently moves proportionally from side to side of the centre line. If we examine *Fig 113a* it will be seen how a slack tank reduces GM.

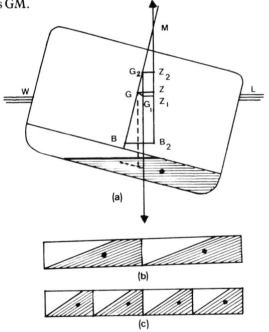

Fig 113(a) Loss of stability due to slack tanks

(*b*) & (*c*) show reduction in stability loss with the greater number of tanks

The formula for finding loss of GM is $\dfrac{i}{V}$. However, the slack tank may contain either fresh water, salt water or fuel oil and i would need to have the relative density applied before calculation. For the purposes of illustration let us assume that the vessel floats in salt water and the tank partially filled with salt water.

Double bottom tanks, loss of GM $= \dfrac{i}{V}$ $\qquad (i = \dfrac{L \times B^3}{12})$

∴ when $\quad$ L = length of tank
$\qquad\qquad$ B = breadth of tank
$\qquad\qquad$ V = displacement of the ship
$\qquad\qquad$ N = number of divided tanks

∴ Loss of GM in an undivided tank $= \dfrac{L \times B^3}{12 \times V}$

∴ Loss of GM in divided tanks $= \dfrac{L \times B^3}{12 \times V \times N^2}$

If, however, the tank is divided at the centre line and we have two separate tanks, the loss of GM is reduced to 1/4 of that of the undivided tank, *ie* the square of the number of tanks. If the tank was divided longitudinally into four tanks the loss of GM would be reduced to $^1/_{16}$th of the undivided tank. (See *Fig 113b* and *c*)

Suspended weights

The principle of suspended weights is that when a weight is picked up by a derrick, the centre of gravity G of the weight moves immediately to the derrick head and this happens regardless of the position of the weight, *ie* whether it is just clear of the water or right up at the derrick head. Therefore, we have two stability factors to consider. (See *Fig 110* on page 237)

The weight of a bag of fish taken from the water will be imposed at the derrick head which is a considerable distance vertically from G the ship's centre of gravity. The ship's G will be raised by the weight of the bag in a vertical direction.

The second stability factor will be that the ship's G will move sideways towards the weight and because the derrick head is outboard, the distance from the centre line will be considerable. Depending on the weight of the fish in the cod-end a list will develop. Once again we must compare traditional fishing methods with the pelagic mode at present being used. If a side trawler fishing demersally picked up a cod-end containing 100 baskets of fish equally about $1\frac{1}{4}$ tons in weight, then picking this up from over the side by gilson or derrick would have little effect on stability.

But a large pelagic net with 15-20 tons of fish would very much affect the stability of a trawler in the 500 ton displacement range. Far better to pump the fish on board hydraulically from the net from its buoyant position alongside. It may be brought on board by scoop or basket as in seine net fishing but this would be a long and tedious operation.

Hints on practical stability for trawlermen

A fairly safe estimate for GM which might be found useful is that the GM of any fishing vessel might be considered to be reasonable if it lies somewhere about 4% of the ship's breadth. If a table of a small, medium and large stern trawler is made up it will be seen that 3%-4% gives a reasonable margin of stability in a properly loaded vessel. It is a rule of thumb method only.

Trawler	Beam	%	GM
Small 'Providence'	6.01m or 20 ft	4%	.24m or 0.8ft
Medium 'Navena'	8.5m or 27.89ft	4%	.34m or 1.12ft
Large 'Junella'	12.2m or 40ft	4%	.49m or 1.6ft

System Internationale units of measurement

The standard system of measurement which has been in existence for some years now is the System Internationale (SI) unit. All ships' plans and documents are written up in SI units. Set out below is the data for the new system. Specific gravity is now known as relative density, fresh water $= 1.000$.

Multiply by	To convert from	To obtain	—
0.03937	Millimetres	Inches	25.400
0.03937	Centimetres	Inches	2.5400
3.2808	Metres	Feet	0.3048
2.2046	Kilogrammes	Pounds	0.4536
0.0009842	Kilogrammes	Tons (2240 lbs)	1016.047
0.9842	Metric tons (*ie* Tonnes of 1000 kg)	Tons (2240 lbs)	1.016
2.4998	Metric tons per centimetre immersion	Tons per inch immersion	0.4000
8.2014	Moment to change trim one centimetre	Moment to change trim one inch	0.122
187.9769	Metre radians	Feet degrees	0.0053
—	To obtain	To convert from	Multiply by above

All ships' plans and calculations now use the SI units of measurement. For examinations, the SI unit is used. For those familiar with the metric system of weight and measurement the System Internationale will be simple to follow. For those who are used to the traditional system of weights, measures and distances, *ie* lbs, gallons, yards and feet, the new system should be learnt and understood. A table setting out the conversion of units to and from SI is shown above, but it is far better to become familiar with the new system which is established so that length, mass, weights and density are co-related to a standard unit of one and down to three places of decimal, *ie*:

Length

1 metre (m)	= 10 decm. (dm)	=	1m	By writing down a
1 decm.	= 10 cent. (cm)	=	.1m	length of say
1 centi.	= 10 milli. (mm)	=	.01m	22.345m, a distance
1 milli		=	.001m	has been accurately set out in metres, *etc*.

Weight

1,000 grammes (g)	= 1 kilogramme (kg)	By writing down a
1,000 kilogrammes	= 1 metric ton or	weight of say 22.345,
	1 tonne.	we have an accurate
		weight in tonnes and
		kilogrammes.

Relative density

In the past relative density (RD) was referred to as specific gravity. It is the comparative ratio of the weight of a substance shown against the weight of fresh water when both weights occupy similar volumes. As an example, one tonne of fresh water has a measured volume of one cubic metre. Therefore we have

1 tonne fresh water = 1 cubic metre or $1T/m^3$ = RD fresh water

∴ the RD fresh water = 1,000

Salt water occupying one cubic metre of space has a weight of 1025 kg or 1.025 tonnes so that its relative density may be expressed RD = 1.025. It can be seen that any weight of substance measured in tonnes per cubic metre will give a density relative to that of fresh water.

$$\therefore RD = \frac{\text{Density of substance}}{\text{Density of fresh water}}$$

It is important to understand this formula. Let us suppose we have a DB tank, 10m × 10m × 1 m. How much bunker oil, RD 0.9 or salt water, RD 1.025, would it contain?

Volume of tank L × B × D. 10 × 10 × 1 = 100m³

$$100 \times \frac{0.900\,(\text{oil})}{1.000\,(\text{FW})} = 90 \text{ tonnes oil}$$

$$100 \times \frac{1.025\,(\text{SW})}{1.000\,(\text{FW})} = 102.5 \text{ tonnes salt water}$$

From the above it will be seen that the metre, the tonne and the relative density have an accurate, simple and convenient method of relation, one to the other.

Moments

Moment is the product of force and distance. In simple terms 'force' is the attraction of a body and its acceleration, because of gravity, towards the centre of the earth. So that we have 1 metric ton force = 1 tonne or i metric ton in weight.

Therefore by multiplying larger weights involved in ship stability by the distance they are moved, moments may easily be expressed as tonnes/metres. If for example a 40 tonne bag of fish is taken on to the trawl deck, which is 10 metres from the keel (K), then we have a vertical moment of 400 (tonnes/metres). By using either the ship's stability tables or a simple formula, the rise of G may soon be found with the loss of GM.

Useful stability formulae

GG_1 (loading a wt) $\quad \dfrac{w \times d}{W + w} \quad$ when w = weight loaded

$\qquad\qquad\qquad\qquad\qquad\qquad$ d = distance from G

GG_1 (discharging a wt.) $\quad \dfrac{w \times d}{W - w} \qquad$ W = displacement

$\qquad\qquad\qquad\qquad\qquad\qquad\qquad$ volume (tonnes)

GG_1 (shifting a wt) $\quad \dfrac{w \times d}{W}$

$$GZ_1 \times GM \times \sin \theta = \text{angle of heel}$$

$$\text{New KG} = \frac{\text{Sum of moments above the keel}}{\text{Sum of the weights}}$$

(The moments may be applied to the ship's tabular plan for a condition of loading.)

$$\text{Change of Trim} = \frac{\text{Moments about CF}}{\text{MCT. 1CM}}$$

CF = Centre of flotation

MCT = moment to change trim: $\text{MCT.1CM} = \dfrac{W \times GML}{100L}$

GML = longitudinal metacentric height

L = length of Vessel

$$BM = \frac{I}{V}$$

Loss of GM due to free surface in a rectangular tank = $\dfrac{L \times B^3}{V} \times \dfrac{1}{n^2} \times \dfrac{RD}{RD^1}$

when:–

L and B = length and breadth of tank
V   = displacement tonnes
n   = number of compartments if the tank is divided
RD   = contents of tank density
RD_1 = density of water in which vessel floats

23 Meteorology

Surrounding the earth and revolving with it through space we have an atmosphere which lies in the form of an envelope through which we can see other heavenly bodies. The layer of atmosphere nearest to the earth is known as the troposphere and has an average depth of from 5 to 10 miles.

Within the troposphere there are air pressure and temperature variations. There is heat radiation from the sun as well as heat diffused by the earth itself. The earth revolves on its axis and we have large areas of ocean with irregularly shaped land masses. These factors all contribute to meteorological conditions and approximate behaviour patterns of weather systems. At this stage it must be said that this chapter cannot contain a full explanation of all the variables which affect weather systems. In order to understand meteorology fully it is recommended that a more detailed study be made of text books dealing solely with meteorology. The *Mariner's Handbook* is a book from which the student and the practising seaman might well read to advantage.

The barometric pressure, the temperature, and weather forecasts which are broadcast regularly are the aids by which the fisherman may preserve the safety of his ship and crew. The distribution of air pressure over the globe when laid off in isobaric form reveals that the atmospheric pressure around the earth's surface is roughly divided into about five main sea areas. Over ocean tropical areas we have moderately low pressure areas to the north and south of the equator. To the north and south of the equatorial zones in latitudes 20°-40° we have high pressure areas, *ie* in the Pacific, Atlantic and Indian Ocean. Because our interest is mainly focused on the north Atlantic it will now be seen that the north Atlantic high pressure area (Azores) extends from approximately the latitude of the Straits of Gibraltar down to the beginning of the tropical zone, 22°N with the centre lying towards the eastern half of the ocean. The winds of the system, because of the earth revolving from east to west, revolve around the high in a clockwise direction. In the south Atlantic winds will revolve in an anti-clockwise direction. The first rule of meteorology may now be set out as:

North hemisphere	Anticyclone (high). Wind revolves clockwise.
	Cyclone (low). Winds revolve anti-clockwise.
South hemisphere	Anticyclone (high). Wind revolves anti-clockwise.
	Cyclone (low). Winds revolve clockwise.

Referring once again to the anticyclone areas in the north Atlantic, it will be seen that the prevailing winds around this centre are the northeast trade winds blowing towards the tropics on the east of the system, Easterly winds on the south of the system, southerly winds on the USA side of the system, and finally southwest to westerly winds to the north of the system blowing towards Europe. These are the prevailing winds.

The influence of the sun

The influence of the sun is such that the centre of the anticyclone varies with its declination. The calm belt of the tropical zone is the developing ground for tropical revolving storms which form as the result of interaction between relatively cool dense air on the one hand and warm light air on the other. The boundary between two such air streams is known as a polar front because the cold air has a tendency to push its way forward in the form of a wedge under the warm air so that a bulge developes. A depression is formed with a frontal system which is preceded by a warm front closely followed by the cold front with the tip of the front being at the centre of the low. The path of the tropical revolving storm follows the line of least resistance by moving in a westerly direction below the north Atlantic high, curves on the approach to the American land mass towards the north and then moves in a west to northwest direction towards Europe. A depression forming in the tropical zone will at first intensify and move at varying speeds, the average speed near to the West Indies being about 300 miles per day. On their approach to, or when crossing, land they tend to fill and dissipate because the supply of warm moist air necessary to their existence is no longer present.

The fishermen of the UK who fish mainly in the northwest Atlantic zone will already know that depressions or lows in the majority of cases move in a west to east direction across the north Atlantic towards northwest Europe. A diagramatic explanation of general weather patterns with approximate depression movement is shown in *Fig 114*.

Depressions or lows

The wind around a low in the northern hemisphere circulates in an anti-clockwise direction. In the southern hemisphere the reverse applies. By joining up lines of equal barometric pressure, an isobaric line is formed which is known as an isobar. The direction ahead of a depression is the path with the track coming behind. At right angles to this line running through the centre of the depression we have a

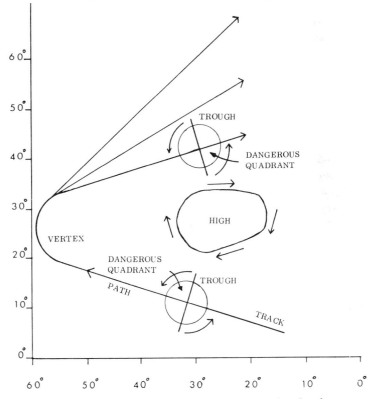

Fig 114 Path of low pressure systems in the north atlantic

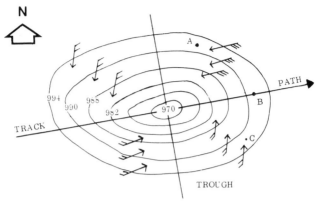

Fig 115   Storm centre, giving 3 ship positions relative to the centre

trough. From *Figs 115* and *116* it will be seen that the winds circulating around a depression blow slightly inwards towards the centre at an angle which is known as the angle of indraught. It will also be seen why in an intense depression it is hazardous to be caught in the dangerous quadrant. The following meteorological terms are set out below in order that the figures and explanation may be fully understood.

Isobar. A line joining places of equal barometric pressure.

Pressure gradient. The difference in pressure in unit distance measured at right angles to the isobars.

Path. The expected course or direction which the storm might take.

Track. The course over which the storm centre has already passed.

Vertex. The furthest point in the west which the storm reached before turning.

Indraught. The angle between the isobars and wind direction, always towards the eye.

Eye. The storm centre, usually an area of temporary calm.

Dangerous semi-circle. The half of the storm which lies to the right of the path in the northern hemisphere. (To the left in the southern hemisphere).

Dangerous quadrant. The leading quadrant of the dangerous semi-circle wherein the wind blows towards the path.

Navigable semi-circle. The half of the storm field which lies to the left of the path in the northern hemisphere.

Trough line. The line drawn through the eye of the storm at right angles to the path.

252

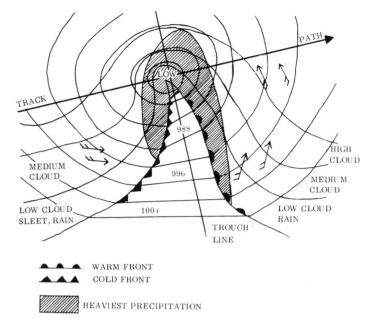

WARM FRONT
COLD FRONT
HEAVIEST PRECIPITATION

Fig 116 Typical frontal system of a storm

Veer. A wind is said to veer when it changes direction in a clockwise movement from whence it blows, *ie* from south to west.

Back. A wind is said to back when it blows from a point and changes direction in an anti-clockwise movement, *ie* from south to east.
It should be emphasised that all storm centres which approach northwest Europe do not necessarily come from the southwest-west. A number of tropical storm centres follow a path leading towards Iceland/Greenland area. When this occurs the storm centre may take the line of least resistance by either recurving so as to pass south of Iceland or pass through the Denmark Straits and then recurve. These depressions may well intensify by reason of the lee given by the Greenland mountains and/or vertical instability resulting in a deep depression approaching northwest. Europe or the Norwegian Sea. Distant water fishermen will have experienced these storms.

All depressions are not necessarily of tropical origin and may be of non-frontal origin, being formed by a large amount of surface heating, in the lee of very high land and/or when there is atmospheric vertical instability. This will be explained later.

253

Action — storm centre

Fishermen having made themselves familiar with the circulation of winds around a storm centre must also be able to recognise a frontal system and the approach of a frontal system. The obvious and easiest way in which to learn of the existence, position and path of a depression relative to one's own position is by listening carefully to the weather forecast and synopsis broadcast by the BBC on domestic channels and by listening to European coastal stations which broadcast weather reports in plain language (UK, Norway, Holland, Germany, Iceland, Canada, *etc*).

If, however, the fisherman has to determine whether a depression is approaching, then the barometer and thermometer are his best aids when used together. Even if it is known that a low is approaching, one can never be sure of its path.

If we look at *Fig 116* and suppose that the fishing vessel is in the dangerous quadrant of a storm moving from west to east, the pressure will fall slowly as the temperature rises, the wind will veer from south to southwest, the sky will become overcast with drizzle and a swell will become noticeable. The clouds will be high and possibly broken. The wind will continue to veer, the pressure will fall steadily, and there will be a continuing rise in temperature and heavier rain. Medium to low cloud and strong winds from the west will indicate the approach of the warm front. The time taken for these changes depends on the pressure gradient and distance away from the vortex.

In the warm sector between the warm and cold fronts, the barometer will remain steady as will the thermometer. The wind will be steady with poor visibility in drizzle or light rain.

On the cold front the first indications will be a sudden drop in temperature with a rising barometer, a sudden veer of the wind towards the northwest in squalls, and heavy rain or sleet with an improvement in the visibility as the rain turns to showers when the front has passed. Thereafter the weather will improve with the barometer and thermometer steadying, but with the sea and swell remaining.

The dangerous quadrant has been described above and it is so called because the wind direction will tend to keep the vessel within the storm area regardless of her course (if she is able to maintain course). If hove-to, the winds will carry the vessel towards the path and subsequently towards the storm centre.

The position of the storm centre relative to the ship's position must be established when a gale is believed to be approaching. In order to take a bearing of the storm centre, we have to use Buys Ballot's Law which says that if an observer faces the true wind, then he will have the eye of the storm centre approximately 10 points to the right in the Northern hemisphere. (To the left in the Southern hemisphere). This is one of the most reliable rules in meteorology. To obtain this bearing, the vessel should be stopped in order to obtain the direction of the true wind. If and when the wind changes and a second bearing were to be taken, whilst the distance away from the centre would not be known, an indication of its approximate path would be obtained.

If we look at *Fig 115* we will see the letters A, B, C shown as observers on the leading edge of a storm field:

(A)   By facing the easterly wind the observer would know that the storm centre lies to his right. If the wind backs to the left, the observer would know that he was in the left hand or navigable semi-circle. The action to take in this case would be to run with the wind on the starboard quarter until the barometer began to rise and it was confidently felt that the storm centre had passed.

(B)   If the wind at position B remained constant by direction, but increased steadily in force, observer B would know that he would be on the path of the storm centre. If the vessel remains here she will be overtaken by the storm centre and her experience can be imagined if the reader traces back the path of progression.
        The action to take is similar to that taken by A: run to the north with the wind on the starboard quarter until the barometer begins to rise and until confident that the vortex is past and clear.

(C)   Being in the dangerous quadrant, the observer should steam his vessel away from the path in a southerly direction as soon as he is aware of his position relative to the storm centre. If left until too late, high seas and swell may force the ship to heave to and fall back towards the passing storm centre. A falling barometer, rising temperature and backing wind will show that C is in the dangerous quadrant.

Southern hemisphere, tropical storms.

In the northern hemisphere the winds revolve around the centre of a tropical storm or low pressure area in an anti-clockwise direction. In the southern hemisphere however, the winds revolve around the storm centre in a clockwise direction. As previously stated the breeding ground for tropical storms is in an area which is but a few degrees north or south of the equator, usually where there is a large expanse of ocean.

The track followed by tropical storms in both hemispheres is towards the west and away from the equator until a latitude of 20° to 30° north or south is reached when they recurve towards the east, and polewards. In the South Pacific the cyclone will usually generate to the North East of the Fiji Islands, then follow a WSW path until latitude 20°S is reached before recurving to follow a South East path.

Because of the clockwise wind circulation the dangerous semi-circle of the cyclone in the southern hemisphere is the left hand quadrant. The vortex of the storm may be estimated by facing the wind and measuring approximately 8 to 10 points to the *left*. This will indicate the direction of the storm centre. See *Fig 117* which shows the path of

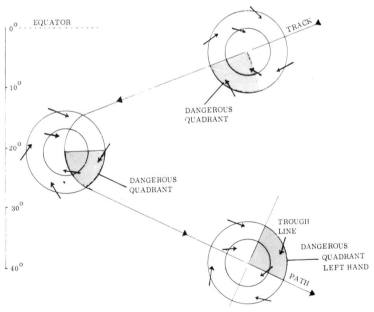

Fig 117   Path of a typical storm in the southern hemisphere

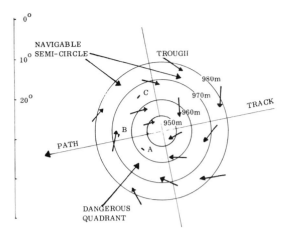

Fig 118 Locating ships position relative to storm centre in the southern hemisphere.

a tropical storm in the southern hemisphere and application of Buys Ballot Law for the southern hemisphere.

By looking at *Fig 118* and supposing that three ships are at positions A, B & C it will be seen that they will find their positions relative to the storm centre by firstly noting a rapidly falling barometer, increased seas and stronger winds.

(A)   By facing the wind when hove-to ship A will note that the storm centre is approximately 90° — 110° to the left, because the wind is blowing from the East. If the wind backs with a continuing fall in pressure then A must assume that she is in the dangerous quadrant and steam to the southward with the wind on the port quarter.

(B)   Ship B hove-to and facing the wind will find the barometer falling very rapidly and if the wind remains constant in direction from the south but increasing in force then the storm centre in relation to the rule must remain constant relative to the ship's position. B must assume that she is near to or on the path of the storm and should steam in a northerly direction into the navigable semi circle, keeping the wind on the port quarter so as not to be drawn by the angle of indraft towards the vortex.

(C)   Ship C will find the barometer falling quickly with increased wind speed from a SSW direction changing to SW and will know by using Buys Ballot Law that the storm centre will pass south of her position. She may run with the wind on the port quarter away from the storm centre or if circumstances allow heave to until the trough line passes and the barometer begins to rise again. The wind will veer through West and thence North.

From all that has been written so far, the student might think that all depressions are likely to be dangerous. This is not so; depressions or lows are a common occurrence in and around the British Isles and in many cases the centre of a depression may have a barometric pressure of 1004 or 1008 in a large field, with the isobars well spread (low gradient). At the centre, winds will probably be less than 30 knots, force 6 possibly force 7. Experienced fishermen will be aware of this type of depression. These depressions should be carefully watched in case they deepen. They are known as shallow depressions.

It is the gale warning for gale force, storm and hurricane strength winds against which precautions should be taken. Fishing vessels should not be caught in the dangerous quadrant. In high latitudes in winter the passing of a frontal system in a storm becomes dangerous for two reasons. Firstly because it is a storm or intense depression the isobars will be close and there will be high winds and rough seas. The vessel will possibly ship water and a lot of spray. Secondly, when the cold front passes the ship's position, there is a sudden and appreciable drop in air temperature. If the air temperature drops to -2° Centigrade ($28\frac{1}{2}$°F), salt water when airborne will freeze. Consequently masts, derricks, stays, deckhouses and winches will become covered with ice. Conditions in the storm will be such that it will not be possible for men to go out on deck in order to remove the ice. The ship will become overloaded with the top weight of ice and may capsize.

The prudent fisherman will listen carefully to radio gale warnings and in the event of a storm warning, especially in high latitudes in winter, will watch the barometer, thermometer and the wind to avoid being caught in the dangerous quadrant and associated frontal system, which will give rise to freezing spray, rain and sleet.

Prevailing winds

Because the majority of low pressure systems pass to the north of the

British Isles, we are subjected to a fair amount of southwest to westerly winds. The associated fronts of the low pressure system passing to the north from west to east are a predominant feature of British coastal weather. Fishermen who have experience of fishing in the western approaches to the English Channel will know that southerly winds freshening, with an accompanying swell, indicate the approach of bad weather with the wind backing to the southwest to west and then northwest when the low has passed, thence moderating and leaving the swell.

Anticyclones

Anticyclones or high pressure areas are mainly considered to be good weather systems. The air around the centre circulates in a clockwise direction in the northern hemisphere (the reverse applies in the southern hemisphere).

Anticyclones are associated with small pressure gradients and light winds. They may be formed by either cold or warm air gathering over a sea or land mass. The warm anticyclone forms when the air in the troposphere is warmer than the surrounding air, the pressure being caused by the great vertical height of the warm air. An example of these types are the high pressure areas, previously mentioned, in the north Atlantic (*Fig 114*) with their source near to the Azores. This is known as a maritime tropical anticyclone. In the same latitude there is the continental tropical anticyclone with its source in the Sahara. Towards the pole we have cold anticyclones which form because high pressure is created when the air is colder in one particular area compared to the cold surrounding air. Typical example of these cold anticyclone systems is the maritime polar of Greenland and the Arctic. The continental polar is the well known high in Siberia. Because the air in permanent areas of high pressure, *eg* Greenland and the Arctic. is unstable, depressions may form, as mentioned earlier in this chapter. The very cold air at the centre of the high will diverge at the base by pushing out into the relatively warmer air surrounding the high, and a depression will form. Experienced fishermen will be aware of depressions moving away from Greenland and across Iceland.

Anticyclones are good weather systems, with good visibility and very light winds. However, they have one drawback — fog. Fog may form when warm air from a warm high system passes over the sea which has a lower temperature, conduction takes place and fog forms.

With a very cold anticyclone the cold air meeting the relatively warmer Arctic water will create fog or Arctic smoke. This occurs in places other than the arctic and can actually be seen to happen in rivers and estuaries in the UK. There is insufficient wind to disperse fog in anticyclonic conditions, but the sun may absorb the fog by its heat. In winter, however, there is usually little heat from the sun and the fog may well persist for long periods.

During summer in high pressure systems when there is little or no cloud cover, the land which has been heated during the day by the sun will radiate this heat at night when the air has cooled, and fog will form during the night. Sea fog will develop in summer where warm tropical maritime air crosses cold sea surfaces; the air is cooled below its dew point and fog forms.

Record of weather conditions

It is imperative to keep a continuous record of weather conditions in the bridge log book. Wind direction, force, barometer readings and temperature should be recorded accurately and regularly so that they can be referred to and used at any time when a storm is expected.

Tables of weather conditions follow:

Beaufort force	Description of wind	Wind speed (knots)	Appearance of sea
0	Calm	Less than 1	Sea like a mirror.
1	Light air	1–3	Ripples with the appearance of scales are formed but without foam crests.
2	Light breeze	4–6	Small wavelets, still short but more pronounced. Crests have a glassy appearance and do not break.
3	Gentle breeze	7–10	Large wavelets. Crests begin to break. Foam of glassy appearance. Perhaps scattered white horses.

4	Moderate breeze	10–16	Small waves, becoming longer. Fairly frequent white horses.
5	Fresh breeze	17–21	Moderate waves, taking a more pronounced long form. Many white horses are formed. Chance of some spray.
6	Strong breeze	22–27	Large waves begin to form. White foam crests are more extensive everywhere. Probably some spray.
7	Near gale		Sea heaps up and white foam from breaking waves begins to be blown in streaks along the direction of the wind.
8	Gale	34–40	Moderately high waves of greater length. Edges of crests begin to break into spindrift. Foam is blown in well marked streaks along the direction of the wind.
9	Strong gale	41–47	High waves. Dense streaks of foam along the direction of the wind. Crests of waves begin to topple, tumble and roll over. Spray may affect visibility.

10	Storm	48–55	Very high waves with long overhanging crests. The resulting foam, in great patches, is blown in dense white streaks along the direction of the wind. On the whole, the surface of the sea takes a white appearance. The tumbling of the sea becomes heavy and shock-like. Visibility affected.
11	Violent storm	56–63	Exceptionally high waves. (Small and medium sized ships might be for a time lost to view behind the waves.) The sea is completely covered with long white patches of foam lying along the direction of the wind. Everywhere the edges of the wave crests are blown into froth. Visibility affected.
12	Hurricane	64–71	The air is filled with foam and spray. Sea completely white with driving spray. Visibility very seriously affected.

State of sea

Appearance	Height (approx)
Calm (glassy)	0
Calm (ripples)	0 – 1 ft (0–0.3 m)
Smooth (wavelets)	1 – 2 ft (0.3–0.6 m)
Slight	2 – 4 ft (0.6–1.2 m)
Moderate	4 – 8 ft (1.2–2.5 m)
Rough	8 – 13 ft (2.5–4 m)
Very rough	13 – 20 ft (4.0–6.0 m)
High	20 – 30 ft (6.0–9.0 m)
Very high	30 – 45 ft (9.0–14.0 m)
Phenomenal	Over 45 ft (Over 14.0 m)

State of swell

Length	Height	
–	None	Low
0–300 ft (0–90 m)	Short	7 ft approx
Over 600 ft (over 183 m)	Long	(about 2 m)
0–300 ft (0–90 m)	Short	Moderate height
300-600 ft (90–183 m)	Average	7–13 ft approx
Over 600 ft (over 183 m)	Long	(2 – 4 m)
0–300 ft (0–90 m)	Short	Heavy
300–600 ft (90–183 m)	Average	Over 13 ft approx
Over 600 ft (over 183 m)	Long	(over 4 m)
–	Confused	

Visibility Scale

Dense fog ⎤	Less than 55 yd (about 50 m)
Thick fog ⎟ *	Approx 55–220 yd (50–200 m)
Fog ⎟	″ 220–550 yd (200–590 m)
Moderate fog ⎦	″ 550 yd – ⁵/₈ nautical mile
	(590 m – 1.2 km)
Mist or haze	″ ⁵/₈–1 nautical mile (1.2–1.8 km)
Poor visibility	1–2 nautical miles (1.8–3.6 km)
Moderate visibility	2–6 nautical miles (3.6–10.8 km)
Good visibility ⎤	6–12 nautical miles (10.8–21.6 km)
Very good visibility ⎟	† 12–30 nautical miles (21.6–55.0 km)
Excellent visibility ⎦	30 nautical miles or more
	(55.0 km or more)

* Grouped together as 'fog'
† Grouped together as 'good visibility'

Sky and Weather Notation

b	Blue sky (up to one-quarter covered)	o	Overcast (completely covered)
bc	Partly clouded (quarter to three-quarters covered)	p	Passing showers
		q	Squalls
c	Mainly cloudy (not less than three-quarters covered)	Q	Heavy squalls
		r	Rain
		rs	Sleet
d	Drizzle	s	Snow
e	Wet air without rain	t	Thunder
f	Fog	tl	Thunderstorm
g	Gale, force 8 or 9 maintained for not less than 10 minutes.	u	Ugly sky
		v	Abnormal visibility: objects at a distance unusually clearly seen
h	Hail		
l	Lightning	z	Haze
m	Mist		

BBC weather forecasts

The BBC broadcast weather forecasts on Radio 4 200 kHz at 0015,

0625, 1355 and 1750 hrs GMT. Forecasts for the areas shown on the map below are usually given in the order: Viking, Forties, Cromarty, Forth, Tyne, Dogger, Fisher, German Bight, Humber, Thames, Dover, Wight, Portland, Plymouth, Biscay, Finisterre, Sole, Lundy, Fastnet, Irish Sea, Shannon, Rockall, Malin, Hebrides, Bailey, Fair Isle, Faroes, South East Iceland.

A forecast for 'Trafalgar' (southern Spain, not shown on map) is given at 0015 hrs only.

Broadcasts follow the order:
    (1) Gale warnings in force
    (2) General weather synopsis and expected changes
    (3) 24 hour weather forecast for home waters.

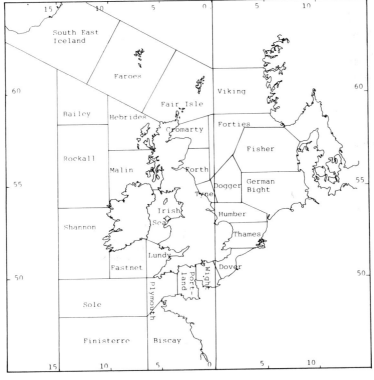

Fig 119 Coastal weather forecast areas

265

24 Collision avoidance regulations

Taken from Command Paper 5471.

International Regulations for Preventing Collisions at Sea, 1972

PART A. General
Rule I
Application

(*a*)   These Rules shall apply to all vessels upon the high seas and in all water connected therewith navigable by seagoing vessels.

(*b*)   Nothing in these Rules shall interfere with the operation of special rules made by an appropriate authority for roadsteads, harbours, rivers, lakes or inland waterways connected with the high seas and navigable by seagoing vessels. Such special rules shall conform as closely as possible to these Rules.

(*c*)   Nothing in these Rules shall interfere with the operation of any special rules made by the Government of any State with respect to additional station or signal lights or whistle signals for ships of war and vessels proceeding under convoy, or with respect to additional station or signal lights for fishing vessels engaged in fishing as a fleet. These additional station or signal lights or whistle signals shall, so far as possible, be such that they cannot be mistaken for any light or signal authorised elsewhere under these Rules.

(*d*)   Traffic separation schemes may be adopted by the Organisation for the purpose of these Rules.

(*e*)   Whenever the Government concerned shall have determined that a vessel of special construction or purpose cannot comply fully with the provisions of any of these Rules with respect to the number, position, range or arc of visibility of lights or shapes, as well as to the disposition and characteristics of sound-signalling appliances, without interfering with the special function of the vessel, such vessel shall comply with such other provisions in regard to the number, position, range or arc of visibility of lights or shapes, as well as to the disposition and characteristics of sound-signalling appliances, as her Government shall have determined to be the closest possible compliance with these Rules in respect to that vessel.

Rule 2

Responsibility

(*a*) Nothing in these Rules shall exonerate any vessel, or the owner, master or crew thereof, from the consequences of any neglect to comply with these Rules or of the neglect of any precaution which may be required by the ordinary practice of seamen, or by the special circumstances of the case.

(*b*) In construing and complying with these Rules due regard shall be had to all dangers of navigation and collision and to any special circumstances, including the limitations of the vessels involved, which may make a departure from these Rules necessary to avoid immediate danger.

Rule 3

General definitions

For the purpose of these Rules, except where the context otherwise requires:

(*a*) The word "vessel" includes every description of water craft, including non-displacement craft and seaplanes, used or capable of being used as a means of transportation on water.

(*b*) The term "power-driven vessel" means any vessel propelled by machinery.

(*c*) The term "sailing vessel" means any vessel under sail provided that propelling machinery, if fitted, is not being used.

(*d*) The term "vessel engaged in fishing" means any vessel fishing with nets, lines, trawls or other fishing apparatus which restrict manoeuvrability, but does not include a vessel fishing with trolling lines or other fishing apparatus which do not restrict manoeuvrability.

(*e*) The word "seaplane" includes any aircraft designed to manoeuvre on the water.

(*f*) The term "vessel not under command" means a vessel which through some exceptional circumstance is unable to manoeurvre as required by these Rules and is therefore unable to keep out of the way of another vessel.

(*g*) The term "vessel restricted in her ability to manoeuvre" means a vessel which from the nature of her work is restricted in her ability to manoeuvre as required by these Rules and is therefore unable to keep out of the way of another vessel.

The following vessels shall be regarded as vessels restricted in their ability to manœuvre:

(i) a vessel engaged in laying, servicing or picking up a navigation mark, submarine cable or pipeline;

(ii) a vessel engaged in dredging, surveying or underwater operations;

(iii) a vessel engaged in replenishment or transferring persons, provisions or cargo while underway;

(iv) a vessel engaged in the launching or recovery of aircraft;

(v) a vessel engaged in minesweeping operations;

(vi) a vessel engaged in a towing operation such as severely restricts the towing vessel and her tow in their ability to deviate from their course.

(*h*) The term "vessel constrained by her draught" means a power-driven vessel which because of her draught in relation to the available depth of water is severely restricted in her ability to deviate from the course she is following.

(*i*) The word "underway" means that a vessel is not at anchor, or made fast to the shore, or aground.

(*j*) The words "length" and "breadth" of a vessel mean her length overall and greatest breadth.

(*k*) Vessels shall be deemed to be in sight of one another only when one can be observed visually from the other.

(*l*) The term "restricted visibility" means any condition in which visibility is restricted by fog, mist, falling snow, heavy rainstorms, sandstorms or any other similar causes.

PART B. Steering and Sailing
Rules
Section I. Conduct of vessels in any condition of visibility

Rule 4
Application

Rules in this Section apply in any condition of visibility.

Rule 5
Look-out

Every vessel shall at all times maintain a proper look-out by sight and hearing as well as by all available means appropriate in the prevailing circumstances and conditions so as to make a full appraisal of the situation and of the risk of collision.

Rule 6

Safe speed

Every vessel shall at all times proceed at a safe speed so that she can take proper and effective action to avoid collision and be stopped within a distance appropriate to the prevailing circumstances and conditions.

In determining a safe speed the following factors shall be among those taken into account:

(*a*) By all vessels:
  (i) the state of visibility;
  (ii) the traffic density including concentrations of fishing vessels or any other vessels;
  (iii) the manœuvrability of the vessel with special reference to stopping distance and turning ability in the prevailing conditions;
  (iv) at night the presence of background light such as from shore lights or from back scatter of her own lights;
  (v) the state of wind, sea and current, and the proximity of navigational hazards;
  (vi) the draught in relation to the available depth of water.

(*b*) Additionally, by vessels with operational radar:
  (i) the characteristics, efficiency and limitations of the radar equipment;
  (ii) any constraints imposed by the radar range scale in use;
  (iii) the effect on radar detection of the sea state, weather and other sources of interference;
  (iv) the possibility that small vessels, ice and other floating objects may not be detected by radar at an adequate range;
  (v) the number, location and movement of vessels detected by radar;
  (vi) the more exact assessment of the visibility that may be possible when radar is used to determine the range of vessels or other objects in the vicinity.

Rule 7

Risk of collision

(*a*) Every vessel shall use all available means appropriate to the prevailing circumstances and conditions to determine if risk of collision exists. If there is any doubt such risk shall be deemed to exist.

(*b*) Proper use shall be made of radar equipment if fitted and operational, including long-range scanning to obtain early warning of risk of collision and radar plotting or equivalent systematic observation of detected objects.

(*c*) Assumptions shall not be made on the basis of scanty information, especially scanty radar information.

(*d*) In determining if risk of collision exists the following considerations shall be among those taken into account:

    (i) such risk shall be deemed to exist if the compass bearing of an approaching vessel does not appreciably change;

    (ii) such risk may sometimes exist even when an appreciable bearing change is evident, particularly when approaching a very large vessel or a tow or when approaching a vessel at close range.

Rule 8

Action to avoid collision

(*a*) Any action taken to avoid collision shall, if the circumstances of the case admit, be positive, made in ample time and with due regard to the observance of good seamanship.

(*b*) Any alteration of course and/or speed to avoid collision shall, if the circumstances of the case admit, be large enough to be readily apparent to another vessel observing visually or by radar; a succession of small alterations of course and/or speed should be avoided.

(*c*) If there is sufficient sea room, alteration of course alone may be the most effective action to avoid a close-quarters situation provided that it is made in good time, is substantial and does not result in another close-quarters situation.

(*d*) Action taken to avoid collision with another vessel shall be such as to result in passing at a safe distance. The effectiveness of the action shall be carefully checked until the other vessel is finally past and clear.

(*e*) If necessary to avoid collision or allow more time to assess the situation, a vessel shall slacken her speed or take all way off by stopping or reversing her means of propulsion.

Rule 9

Narrow channels

(a) A vessel proceeding along the course of a narrow channel or fairway shall keep as near to the outer limit of the channel or fairway which lies on her starboard side as is safe and practicable.

(b) A vessel of less than 20 metres in length or a sailing vessel shall not impede the passage of a vessel which can safely navigate only within a narrow channel or fairway.

(d) A vessel shall not cross a narrow channel or fairway if such crossing impedes the passage of a vessel which can safely navigate only within such channel or fairway. The latter vessel may use the sound signal prescribed in Rule 34 (d) if in doubt as to the intention of the crossing vessel.

(e) (i) In a narrow channel or fairway when overtaking can take place only if the vessel to be overtaken has to take action to permit safe passing, the vessel intending to overtake shall indicate her intention by sounding the appropriate signal prescribed in Rule 34 (c) (i). The vessel to be overtaken shall, if in agreement, sound the appropriate signal prescribed in Rule 34 (c) (ii) and take steps to permit safe passing. If in doubt she may sound the signals prescribed in Rule 34 (d).

(ii) This Rule does not relieve the overtaking vessel of her obligation under Rule 24.

(f) A vessel nearing a bend or an area of a narrow channel or fairway where other vessels may be obscured by an intervening obstruction shall navigate with particular alertness and caution and shall sound the appropriate signal prescribed in Rule 34 (e).

(g) Any vessel shall, if the circumstances of the case admit, avoid anchoring in a narrow channel.

Rule 10

Traffic separation schemes

(a) This Rule applies to traffic separation schemes adopted by the Organisation:

(b) A vessel using a traffic separation scheme shall:

(i) proceed in the appropriate traffic lane in the general direction of traffic flow for that lane;

(ii) so far as practicable keep clear of a traffic separation line or separation zone;

(iii) normally join or leave a traffic lane at the termination of the lane, but when joining or leaving from the side shall do so at as small an angle to the general direction of traffic flow as practicable.

(*c*) A vessel shall so far as practicable avoid crossing traffic lanes, but if obliged to do so shall cross as nearly as practicable at right angles to the general direction of traffic flow.

(*d*) Inshore traffic zones shall not normally be used by through traffic which can safely use the appropriate traffic lane within the adjacent traffic separation scheme.

(*e*) A vessel, other than a crossing vessel, shall not normally enter a separation zone or cross a separation line except:

(i) in cases of emergency to avoid immediate danger;

(ii) to engage in fishing within a separation zone.

(*f*) A vessel navigating in areas near the terminations of traffic separation schemes shall do so with particular caution.

(*g*) A vessel shall so far as practicable avoid anchoring in a traffic separation scheme or in areas near its terminations.

(*h*) A vessel not using a traffic separation scheme shall avoid it by as wide a margin as is practicable.

(*i*) A vessel engaged in fishing shall not impede the passage of any vessel following a traffic lane.

(*j*) A vessel of less than 20 metres in length or a sailing vessel shall not impede the safe passage of a power-driven vessel following a traffic lane.

Section II. Conduct of vessels in sight of one another

Rule 11

Application

Rules in this Section apply to vessels in sight of one another.

Rule 12

Sailing vessels

(*a*) When two sailing vessels are approaching one another, so as to involve risk of collision, one of them shall keep out of the way of the other as follows:

    (i) when each has the wind on a different side, the vessel which has the wind on the port side shall keep out of the way of the other;

    (ii) when both have the wind on the same side, the vessel which is to windward shall keep out of the way of the vessel which is to leeward;

    (iii) if a vessel with the wind on the port side sees a vessel to windward and cannot determine with certainty whether the other vessel has the wind on the port or on the starboard side, she shall keep out of the way of the other.

(b) For the purposes of this Rule the windward side shall be deemed to be the side opposite to that on which the mainsail is carried or, in the case of a square-rigged vessel, the side opposite to that on which the largest fore-and-aft sail is carried.

Rule 13

Overtaking

(a) Notwithstanding anything contained in the Rules of this Section any vessel overtaking any other shall keep out of the way of the vessel being overtaken.

(b) A vessel shall be deemed to be overtaking when coming up with another vessel from a direction more than 22.5 degrees abaft her beam, that is, in such a position with reference to the vessel she is overtaking, that at night she would be able to see only the sternlight of that vessel but neither of her sidelights.

(c) When a vessel is in any doubt as to whether she is overtaking another, she shall assume that this is the case and act accordingly.

(d) Any subsequent alteration of the bearing between the two vessels shall not make the overtaking vessel a crossing vessel within the meaning of these Rules or relieve her of the duty of keeping clear of the overtaken vessel until she is finally past and clear.

Rule 14

Head-on situation

(a) When two power-driven vessels are meeting on reciprocal or nearly reciprocal courses so as to involve risk of collision each shall alter her course to starboard so that each shall pass on the port side of the other.

(*b*) Such a situation shall be deemed to exist when a vessel sees the other ahead or nearly ahead and by night she could see the masthead lights of the other in a line or nearly in a line and/or both sidelights and by day she observes the corresponding aspect of the other vessel.

(*c*) When a vessel is in any doubt as to whether such a situation exists she shall assume that it does exist and act accordingly.

Rule 15

Crossing situation

When two power-driven vessels are crossing so as to involve risk of collision, the vessel which has the other on her own starboard side shall keep out of the way and shall, if the circumstances of the case admit, avoid crossing ahead of the other vessel.

Rule 16

Action by give-way vessel

Every vessel which is directed to keep out of the way of another vessel shall, so far as possible, take early and substantial action to keep well clear.

Rule 17

Action by stand-on vessel

(*a*) (i) Where one of two vessels is to keep out of the way the other shall keep her course and speed.

(ii)The latter vessel may however take action to avoid collision by her manœuvre alone, as soon as it becomes apparent to her that the vessel required to keep out of the way is not taking appropriate action in compliance with these Rules.

(*b*) When, from any cause, the vessel required to keep her course and speed finds herself so close that collision cannot be avoided by the action of the give-way vessel alone, she shall take such action as will best aid to avoid collision.

(*c*) A power-driven vessel which takes action in a crossing situation in accordance with sub-paragraph (*a*) (ii) of this Rule to avoid collision with another power-driven vessel shall, if the circumstances of the case admit, not alter course to port for a vessel on her own port side.

(*d*) This Rule does not relieve the give-way vessel of her obligation to keep out of the way.

Rule 18

Responsibilities between vessels

Except where Rules 9, 10 and 13 otherwise require:

(*a*) A power-driven vessel underway shall keep out of the way of:

    (i) a vessel not under command;

    (ii) a vessel restricted in her ability to manœuvre;

    (iii) a vessel engaged in fishing;

    (iv) a sailing vessel.

(*b*) A sailing vessel underway shall keep out of the way of:

    (i) a vessel not under command;

    (ii) a vessel restricted in her ability to manœuvre;

    (iii) a vessel engaged in fishing.

(*c*) A vessel engaged in fishing when underway shall, so far as possible, keep out of the way of:

    (i) a vessel not under command;

    (ii) a vessel restricted in her ability to manœuvre.

(*d*) (i) Any vessel other than a vessel not under command or a vessel restricted in her ability to manœuvre shall, if the circumstances of the case admit, avoid impeding the safe passage of a vessel constrained by her draught, exhibiting the signals in Rule 28.

    (ii) A vessel constrained by her draught shall navigate with particular caution having full regard to her special condition.

(*e*) A seaplane on the water shall, in general, keep well clear of all vessels and avoid impeding their navigation. In circumstances, however, where risk of collision exists, she shall comply with the Rules of this Part.

Section III. Conduct of vessels in restricted visibility

Rule 19

Conduct of vessels in restricted visibility

(*a*) This Rule applies to vessels not in sight of one another when navigation in or near an area of restricted visibility.

(*b*) Every vessel shall proceed at a safe speed adapted to the prevailing circumstances and conditions of restricted visibility. A power-driven vessel shall have her engines ready for immediate manœuvre.

(*c*) Every vessel shall have due regard to the prevailing circumstances and conditions of restricted visibility when complying with the Rules of Section I of this Part.

(*d*) A vessel which detects by radar alone the presence of another vessel shall determine if a close-quarters situation is developing and/or risk of collision exists. If so, she shall take avoiding action in ample time, provided that when such action consists of an alteration of course, so far as possible the following shall be avoided:

 (i) an alteration of course to port for a vessel forward of the beam, other than for a vessel being overtaken;

 (ii) an alteration of course towards a vessel abeam or abaft the beam.

(*e*) Except where it has been determined that a risk of collision does not exist, every vessel which hears apparently forward of her beam the fog signal of another vessel, or which cannot avoid a close-quarters situation with another vessel forward of her beam, shall reduce her speed to the minimum at which she can be kept on her course. She shall if necessary take all her way off and in any event navigate with extreme caution until danger of collision is over.

PART C. Lights and Shapes

Rule 20

Application

(*a*) Rules in this Part shall be complied with in all weather.

(*b*) The Rules concerning lights shall be complied with from sunset to sunrise, and during such times no other lights shall be exhibited, except such lights as cannot be mistaken for the lights specified in these Rules or do not impair their visibility or distinctive character, or interfere with the keeping of a proper look-out.

(*c*) The lights prescribed by these Rules shall, if carried, also be exhibited from sunrise to sunset in restricted visibility and may be exhibited in all other circumstances when it is deemed necessary.

(*d*) The Rules concerning shapes shall be complied with by day.

(*e*) The lights and shapes specified in these Rules shall comply with the provisions of Annex I to these Regulations.

Rule 21

Definitions

(*a*) "Masthead light" means a white light placed over the fore and aft centreline of the vessel showing an unbroken light over an arc of the horizon of 225 degrees and so fixed as to show the light from right ahead to 22.5 degrees abaft the beam on either side of the vessel.

(*b*) "Sidelights" means a green light on the starboard side and a red light on the port side each showing an unbroken light over an arc of the horizon of 112.5 degrees and so fixed as to show the light from right ahead to 22.5 degrees abaft the beam on its respective side. In a vessel of less than 20 metres in length the sidelights may be combined in one lantern carried on the fore and aft centreline of the vessel.

(*c*) "Sternlight" means a white light placed as nearly as practicable at the stern showing an unbroken light over an arc of the horizon of 135 degrees and so fixed as to show light 67.5 degrees from right aft on each side of the vessel.

(*d*) "Towing light" means a yellow light having the same characteristics as the "sternlight" defined in paragraph (*c*) of this Rule.

(*e*) "All round light" means a light showing an unbroken light over an arc of the horizon of 360 degrees.

(*f*) "Flashing light" means a light flashing at regular intervals at a frequency of 120 flashes or more per minute.

Rule 22

Visibility of lights

The lights prescribed in these Rules shall have an intensity as specified in Section 8 of Annex I to these Regulations so as to be visible at the following minimum ranges:

(*a*) In vessels of 50 metres or more in length:
–a masthead light, 6 miles;
–a sidelight, 3 miles;
–a sternlight, 3 miles;
–a towing light, 3 miles;
–a white, red, green or yellow all-round light, 3 miles.

(*b*) In vessels of 12 metres or more in length but less than 50 metres in length:

–a masthead light, 5 miles; except that where the length of the vessel is less than 20 metres, 3 miles;
  –a sidelight, 2 miles;
  –a sternlight, 2 miles;
  –a towing light, 2 miles;
  –a white, red, green or yellow all-round light, 2 miles.
(c) In vessels of less than 12 metres in length:
  –a masthead light, 2 miles;
  –a sidelight, 1 mile;
  –a sternlight, 2 miles;
  –a towing light, 2 miles;
  –a white, red, green or yellow all-round light, 2 miles.

Rule 23

Power-driven vessels underway

(a) A power-driven vessel underway shall exhibit:
  (i) a masthead light forward;
  (ii) a second masthead light abaft of and higher than the forward one; except that a vessel of less than 50 metres in length shall not be obliged to exhibit such light but may do so;
  (iii) sidelights;
  (iv) a sternlight.

(b) An air-cushion vessel when operating in the non-displacement mode shall, in addition to the lights prescribed in paragraph (a) of this Rule, exhibit an all-round flashing yellow light.

(c) A power-driven vessel of less than 7 metres in length and whose maximum speed does not exceed 7 knots may, in lieu of the lights prescribed in paragraph (a) of this Rule, exhibit an all-round white light. Such vessel shall, if practicable, also exhibit sidelights.

Rule 24

Towing and pushing

(a) A power-driven vessel when towing shall exhibit:
  (i) instead of the light prescribed in Rule 23 (a) (i), two masthead lights forward in a vertical line. When the length of the tow, measuring from the stern of the towing vessel to the

after end of the tow exceeds 200 metres, three such lights in a vertical line;

  (ii) sidelights;

 (iii) a sternlight;

 (iv) a towing light in a vertical line above the sternlight;

  (v) when the length of the tow exceeds 200 metres, a diamond shape where it can best be seen.

(b) When a pushing vessel and a vessel being pushed ahead are rigidly connected in a composite unit they shall be regarded as a power-driven vessel and exhibit the lights prescribed in Rule 23.

(c) A power-driven vessel when pushing ahead or towing alongside, except in the case of a composite unit, shall exhibit:

  (i) instead of the light prescribed in Rule 23 (a) (i), two masthead lights forward in a vertical line;

 (ii) sidelights;

 (ii) a sternlight.

(d) A power-driven vessel to which paragraphs (a) and (c) of this Rule apply shall also comply with Rule 23 (a) (ii).

(e) A vessel or object being towed shall exhibit:

  (i) sidelights;

 (ii) a sternlight;

 (ii) when the length of the tow exceeds 200 metres, a diamond shape where it can best be seen.

(f) Provided that any number of vessels being towed alongside or pushed in a group shall be lighted as one vessel;

  (i) a vessel being pushed ahead, not being part of a composite unit, shall exhibit at the forward end, sidelights;

 (ii) a vessel being towed alongside shall exhibit a sternlight and at the forward end, sidelights.

(g) Where from any sufficient cause it is impracticable for a vessel or object being towed to exhibit the lights prescribed in paragraph (e) of this Rule, all possible measures shall be taken to light the vessel or object towed or at least to indicate the presence of the unlighted vessel or object.

Rule 25

Sailing vessels underway and vessels under oars

(a) A sailing vessel underway shall exhibit:

  (i) sidelights;

(ii) a sternlight.

(*b*) In a sailing vessel of less than 12 metres in length the lights prescribed in paragraph (*a*) of this Rule may be combined in one lantern carried at or near the top of the mast where it can best be seen.

(*c*) A sailing vessel underway may, in addition to the lights prescribed in paragraph (*a*) of this Rule, exhibit at or near the top of the mast, where they can best be seen, two all-round lights in a vertical line, the upper being red and the lower green, but these lights shall not be exhibited in conjunction with the combined lantern permitted by paragraph (*b*) of this Rule.

(*d*) (i) A sailing vessel of less than 7 metres in length shall, if practicable, exhibit the lights prescribed in paragraph (*a*) or (*b*) of this Rule, but if she does not, she shall have ready at hand an electric torch or lighted lantern showing a white light which shall be exhibited in sufficient time to prevent collision.

(ii) A vessel under oars may exhibit the lights prescribed in this Rule for sailing vessels, but if she does not, she shall have ready at hand an electric torch or lighted lantern showing a white light which shall be exhibited in sufficient time to prevent collision.

(*e*) A vessel proceeding under sail when also being propelled by machinery shall exhibit forward where it can best be seen a conical shape, apex downwards.

Rule 26

Fishing vessels

(*a*) A vessel engaged in fishing, whether underway or at anchor, shall exhibit only the lights and shapes prescribed in this Rule.

(*b*) A vessel when engaged in trawling, by which is meant the dragging through the water of a dredge net or other apparatus used as a fishing appliance, shall exhibit:

(i) two all-round lights in a vertical line, the upper being green and the lower white, or a shape consisting of two cones with their apexes together in a vertical line one above the other; a vessel of less than 20 metres in length may instead of this shape exhibit a basket;

(ii) a masthead light abaft of and higher than the all-round green light; a vessel of less than 50 metres in length shall not be

obliged to exhibit such a light but may do so;
- (iii) when making way through the water, in addition to the lights prescribed in this paragrph, sidelights and a sternlight.
- (c) A vessel engaged in fishing, other than trawling, shall exhibit:
  - (i) two all-round lights in a vertical line, the upper being red and the lower white, or a shape consisting of two cones with apexes together in a vertical line one above the other; a vessel of less than 20 metres in length may instead of this shape exhibit a basket;
  - (ii) when there is outlying gear extended more than 150 metres horizontally from the vessel, an all-round white light or a cone apex upwards in the direction of the gear;
  - (iii) when making way through the water, in addition to the lights prescribed in this paragraph, sidelights and a sternlight.

(d) A vessel engaged in fishing in close proximity to other vessels engaged in fishing may exhibit the additional signals described in Annex II to these Regulations.

(e) A vessel when not engaged in fishing shall not exhibit the lights or shapes prescribed in this Rule, but only those prescribed for a vessel of her length.

Rule 27

Vessels not under command or restricted in their ability to manoeuvre

(a) A vessel not under command shall exhibit:
- (i) two all-round red lights in a vertical line where they can best be seen;
- (ii) two balls or similar shapes in a vertical line where they can best be seen;
- (iii) when making way through the water, in addition to the lights prescribed in this paragraph, sidelights and a sternlight.

(b) A vessel restricted in her ability to manœuvre, except a vessel engaged in minesweeping operations, shall exhibit:
- (i) three all-round lights in a vertical line where they can best be seen. The highest and lowest of these lights shall be red and the middle light shall be white;
- (ii) three shapes in a vertical line where they can best be seen. The highest and lowest of these shapes shall be balls and the

middle one a diamond.

    (ii) when making way through the water, masthead lights, sidelights and a sternlight, in addition to the lights prescribed in sub-paragraph (i);

    (iv) when at anchor, in addition to the lights or shapes prescribed in sub-paragraphs (i) and (ii), the light, lights or shape prescribed in Rule 30.

(c) A vessel engaged in a towing operation such as renders her unable to deviate from her course shall, in addition to the lights or shapes prescribed in sub-paragraph (b) (i) and (ii) of this Rule, exhibit the lights or shape prescribed in Rule 24 (a).

(d) A vessel engaged in dredging or underwater operations, when restricted in her ability to manœuvre, shall exhibit the lights and shapes prescribed in paragraph (b) of this Rule and shall in addition, when an obstruction exists, exhibit:

    (i) two all-round red lights or two balls in a vertical line to indicate the side on which the obstruction exists;

    (ii) two all-round green lights or two diamonds in a vertical line to indicate the side on which another vessel may pass;

    (iii) when making way through the water, in addition to the lights prescribed in this paragraph, masthead lights, sidelights and a sternlight;

    (iv) a vessel to which this paragraph applies when at anchor shall exhibit the lights or shapes prescribed in sub-paragraphs (i) and (ii) instead of the lights or shape prescribed in Rule 30.

(e) Whenever the size of a vessel engaged in diving operations makes it impracticable to exhibit the shapes prescribed in paragraph (d) of this Rule, a rigid replica of the International Code flag "A" not less than 1 metre in height shall be exhibited. Measures shall be taken to ensure all-round visibility.

(f) A vessel engaged in minesweeping operations shall, in addition to the lights prescribed for a power-driven vessel in Rule 23, exhibit three all-round green lights or three balls. One of these lights or shapes shall be exhibited at or near the foremast head and one at each end of the fore yard. These lights or shapes indicate that it is dangerous for another vessel to approach closer than 1,000 metres astern or 500 metres on either side of the minesweeper.

(g) Vessels of less than 7 metres in length shall not be required to exhibit the lights prescribed in this Rule.

(h) The signals prescribed in this Rule are not signals of vessels in distress and requiring assistance. Such signals are contained in Annex IV to these Regulations.

Rule 28

Vessels constrained by their draught

A vessel constrained by her draught may, in addition to the lights prescribed for power-driven vessels in Rule 23, exhibit where they can best be seen three all-round red lights in a vertical line, or a cylinder.

Rule 29

Pilot vessels

(a) A vessel engaged on pilotage duty shall exhibit:
  (i) at or near the masthead, two all-round lights in a vertical line, the upper being white and the lower red;
  (ii) when underway, in addition, sidelights and a sternlight;
  (iii) when at anchor, in addition to the lights prescribed in sub-paragraph (i), the anchor light, lights or shape.

(b) A pilot vessel when not engaged on pilotage duty shall exhibit the lights or shapes prescribed for a similar vessel of her length.

Rule 30

Anchored vessels and vessels aground

(a) A vessel at anchor shall exhibit where it can best be seen:
  (i) in the fore part, an all-round white light or one ball;
  (ii) at or near the stern and at a lower level than the light prescribed in sub-paragraph (i), an all-round white light.

(b) A vessel of less than 50 metres in length may exhibit an all-round white light where it can best be seen instead of the lights prescribed in paragraph (a) of this Rule.

(c) A vessel at anchor may, and a vessel of 100 metres and more in length shall, also use the available working or equivalent lights to illuminate her decks.

(d) A vessel aground shall exhibit the lights prescribed in paragraph (a) or (b) of this Rule and in addition, where they can best be seen:
  (i) two all-round red lights in a vertical line;
  (ii) three balls in a vertical line.

(*e*) A vessel of less than 7 metres in length, when at anchor or aground, not in or near a narrow channel, fairway or anchorage, or where other vessels normally navigate, shall not be required to exhibit the lights or shapes prescribed in paragraphs (*a*), (*b*), or (*d*) of this Rule.

Rule 31

Seaplanes

Where it is impracticable for a seaplane to exhibit lights and shapes of the characteristics or in the positions prescribed in the Rules of this Part she shall exhibit lights and shapes as closely similar in characteristics and position as is possible.

PART D. Sound and Light Signals

Rule 32

Definitions

(*a*) The word "whistle" means any sound signalling appliance capable of producing the prescribed blasts and which complies with the specifications in Annex III to these Regulations.

(*b*) The term "short blast" means a blast of about one second's duration.

(*c*) The term "prolonged blast" means a blast of from four to six seconds' duration.

Rule 33

Equipment for sound signals

(*a*) A vessel of 12 metres or more in length shall be provided with a whistle and a bell and a vessel of 100 metres or more in length shall, in addition, be provided with a gong, the tone and sound of which cannot be confused with that of the bell. The whistle, bell and gong shall comply with the specifications in Annex III of these Regulations. The bell or gong or both may be replaced by other equipment having the same respective sound characteristics, provided that manual sounding of the required signals shall always be possible.

(*b*) A vessel of less than 12 metres in length shall not be obliged to carry the sound signalling appliances prescribed in paragraph (*a*) of this Rule but if she does not, she shall be provided with some other means of making an efficient sound signal.

Rule 34

Manoeuvring and warning signals

(*a*) When vessels are in sight of one another, a power-driven vessel underway, when manœuvring as authorized or required by these Rules, shall indicate that manœuvre by the following signals on her whistle:

–one short blast to mean "I am altering my course to starboard";

–two short blasts to mean "I am altering my course to port";
–three short blasts to mean "I am operating astern propulsion".

(*b*) Any vessel may supplement the whistle signals prescribed in paragraph (*a*) of this Rule by light signals, repeated as appropriate, whilst the manœuvre is being carried out:

  (i) these light signals shall have the following signifance:
      –one flash to mean "I am altering my course to starboard";
      –two flashes to mean "I am altering my course to port";
      –three flashes to mean "I am operating astern propulsion";

  (ii) the duration of each flash shall be about one second, the interval between flashes shall be about one second, and the interval between successive signals shall be not less than ten seconds;

  (iii) the light used for this signal shall, if fitted, be an all-round white light visible at a minimum range of 5 miles, and shall comply with the provisions of Annex I.

(*c*) When in sight of one another in a narrow channel or fairway:

  (i) a vessel intending to overtake another shall in compliance with Rule 9 (*e*) (i) indicate her intention by the following signals on her whistle:
      –two prolonged blasts followed by one short blast to mean "I intend to overtake you on your starboard side".
      –two prolonged blasts followed by two short blasts to mean "I intend to overtake you on your port side".

  (ii) the vessel about to be overtaken when acting in accordance with Rule 9 (*e*) (i) shall indicate her agreement by the following signal on her whistle:

—one prolonged, one short, one prolonged and one short blast, in that order.

(*d*) When vessels in sight of one another are approaching each other and from any cause either vessel fails to understand the intentions or actions of the other, or is in doubt whether sufficient action is being taken by the other to avoid collision, the vessel in doubt shall immediately indicate such doubt by giving at least five short and rapid blasts on the whistle. Such signal may be supplemented by a light signal of at least five short and rapid flahses.

(*e*) A vessel nearing a bend or an area of a channel or fairway where other vessels may be obscured by an intervening obstruction shall sound one prolonged blast. Such signal shall be answered with a prolonged blast by any approaching vessel that may be within hearing around the bend or behind the intervening obstruction.

(*f*) If whistles are fitted on a vessel at a distance apart of more than 100 metres, one whistle only shall be used for giving manœuvring and warning signals.

Rule 35

Sound signals in restricted visibility

In or near an area of restricted visibility, whether by day or night, the signals prescribed in this Rule shall be used as follows:

(*a*) A power-driven vessel making way through the water shall sound at intervals of not more than 2 minutes one prolonged blast.

(*b*) A power-driven vessel underway but stopped and making no way through the water shall sound at intervals of not more than 2 minutes two prolonged blasts in succession with an interval of about 2 seconds between them.

(*c*) A vessel not under command, a vessel restricted in her ability to manœuvre, a vessel constrained by her draught, a sailing vessel, a vessel engaged in fishing and a vessel engaged in towing or pushing another vessel shall, instead of the signals prescribed in paragraphs (*a*) or (*b*) of this Rule, sound at intervals of not more than 2 minutes three blasts in succession, namely one prolonged followed by two short blasts.

(*d*) A vessel towed or if more than one vessel is towed the last vessel of the tow, if manned, shall at intervals of not more than 2 minutes sound four blasts in succession, namely one prolonged followed by three short blasts. When practicable, this signal shall be made immediately after the signal made by the towing vessel.

(*e*) When a pushing vessel and a vessel being pushed ahead are rigidly connected in a composite unit they shall be regarded as a power-driven vessel and shall give the signals prescribed in paragraphs (*a*) or (*b*) of this Rule.

(*f*) A vessel at anchor shall at intervals of not more than one minute ring the bell rapidly for about 5 seconds. In a vessel of 100 metres or more in length the bell shall be sounded in the forepart of the vessel and immediately after the ringing of the bell the gong shall be sounded rapidly for about 5 seconds in the after part of the vessel. The vessel at anchor may in addition sound three blasts in succession, namely one short, one prolonged and one short blast, to give warning of her position and of the possibility of collision to an approaching vessel.

(*g*) A vessel aground shall give the bell signal and if required the gong signal prescribed in paragraph (*f*) of this Rule and shall, in addition, give three separate and distinct strokes on the bell immediately before and after the rapid ringing of the bell. A vessel aground may in addition sound an appropriate whistle signal.

(*h*) A vessel of less than 12 metres in length shall not be obliged to give the above-mentioned signals but, if she does not, shall make some other efficient sound signal at intervals of not more than 2 minutes.

(*i*) A pilot vessel when engaged on pilotage duty may in addition to the signals prescribed in paragraphs (*a*), (*b*) or (*f*) of this Rule sound an identity signal consisting of four short blasts.

Rule 36

Signals to attract attention

If necessary to attract the attention of another vessel any vessel may make light or sound signals that cannot be mistaken for any signal authorized elsewhere in these Rules, or may direct the beam of her searchlight in the direction of the danger, in such a way as not to embarrass any vessel.

Rule 37

Distress signals

When a vessel is in distress and requires assistance she shall use or exhibit the signals prescribed in Annex IV of these Regulations.

PART E. Exemptions

Rule 38

Exemptions

Any vessel (or class of vessels) provided that she complies with the requirements of the International Regulations for Preventing Collisions at Sea, 1960, the keel of which is laid or which is at a corresponding stage of construction before the entry into force of these Regulations may be exempted from compliance therewith as follows:

(*a*) The installation of lights with ranges prescribed in Rule 22, until four years after the date of entry into force of these Regulations.

(*b*) The installation of lights with colour specifications as prescribed in Section 7 of Annex I to these Regulations, until four years after the date of entry into force of these Regulations.

(*c*) The repositioning of lights as a result of conversion from Imperial to metric units and rounding off measurement figures, permanent exemption.

(*d*) (i) The repositioning of masthead lights on vessels of less than 150 metres in length, resulting from the prescriptions of Section 3(*a*) of Annex I, permanent exemption.

(ii) The repositioning of masthead lights on vessels of 150 metres or more in length, resulting from the prescriptions of Section 3(*a*) of Annex I to these Regulations, until nine years after the date of entry into force of these Regulations.

(*e*) The repositioning of masthead lights resulting from the prescriptions of Section 2 (*b*) of Annex I, until nine years after the date of entry into force of these Regulations.

(*f*) The repositioning of sidelights resulting from the prescriptions of Section 2 (*g*) and 3 (*b*) of Annex I, until nine years after the date of entry into force of these Regulations.

(*g*) The requirements for sound signal appliances prescribed in Annex III, until nine years after the date of entry into force of these Regulations.

ANNEX I

Positioning and technical details of lights and shapes

6. *Shapes*

(*a*) Shapes shall be black (the paragraph goes on to detail the sizes of the various authorised shapes).

ANNEX II

Additional signals for fishing vessels fishing in close proximity

1. *General*

The lights mentioned herein shall, if exhibited in pursuance of Rule 26 (*d*), be placed where they can best be seen. They shall be at least 0.9 metre apart but at a lower level than lights prescribed in Rule 26 (*b*) (i) and (*c*) (i). The lights shall be visible all round the horizon at a distance of at least 1 mile but at a lesser distance than the lights prescribed by these Rules for fishing vessels.

2. *Signals for trawlers*

(*a*) Vessels when engaged in trawling, whether using demersal or pelagic gear, may exhibit:
  (i) when shooting their nets:
       two white lights in a vertical line;
  (ii) when hauling their nets:
       one white light over one red light in a vertical line;
  (iii) when the net has come fast upon an obstruction:
       two red lights in a vertical line.

(*b*) Each vessel engaged in pair trawling may exhibit:
  (i) by night, a searchlight directed forward and in the direction of the other vessel of the pair;
  (ii) when shooting or hauling their nets or when their nets have come fast upon an obstruction, the lights prescribed in 2(*a*) above.

3. *Signals for purse seiners*

Vessels engaged in fishing with purse seine gear may exhibit two yellow lights in a vertical line. These lights shall flash alternately every second and with equal light and occultation duration. These lights may be exhibited only when the vessel is hampered by its fishing gear.

ANNEX IV

Distress signals

1. The following signals, used or exhibited either together or separately, indicate distress and need of assistance

(*a*)   a gun or other explosive signal fired at intervals of about a minute;

(*b*)   a continuous sounding with any fog-signalling apparatus;

(*c*)   rockets or shells, throwing red stars fired one at a time at short intervals;

(*d*)   a signal made by radiotelegraphy or by any other signalling method consisting of the group . . . – – – . . . (SOS) in the Morse Code;

(*e*)   a signal sent by radiotelephony consisting of the spoken word "Mayday";

(*f*)   the International Code Signal of distress indicated by N.C.;

(*g*)   a signal consisting of a square flag having above or below it a ball or anything resembling a ball;

(*h*)   flames on the vessel (as from a burning tar barrel, oil barrel, *etc*);

(*i*)   a rocket parachute flare or a hand flare showing a red light;

(*j*)   a smoke signal giving off orange-coloured smoke;

(*k*)   slowly and repeatedly raising and lowering arms outstretched to each side;

(*l*)   the radiotelegraph alarm signal;

(*m*)   the radiotelephone alarm signal;

(*n*)   signals transmitted by emergency position-indicating radio beacons.

2. The use or exhibition of any of the foregoing signals except for the purpose of indicating distress and need of assistance and the use of other signals which may be confused with any of the above signals is prohibited.

3. Attention is drawn to the relevant sections of the International Code of Signals, the Merchant Ship Search and Rescue Manual and the following signals:

(*a*)   a piece of orange-coloured canvas with either a black square and circle or other appropriate symbol (for identification from the air);

(*b*)   a dye marker.

Points of interest to fishing vessel officers

The 1972 Regulations which came into force on 15th July 1977 are generally compatible with the previous Regulations (1960). There are certain significant changes, however, and the attention of all fishing vessel officers is drawn to the changes and additions made in the new regulations.

The rules are divided into different sections as follows:

Part A.	General
Part B.	Steering and sailing rules
Part C.	Lights and shapes
Part D.	Sound and light signals
Part E.	Exemptions
Annex 1.	Positioning and technical details of lights and shapes
Annex 2.	Additional signals for fishing vessels fishing in close proximity
Annex 3.	Technical details of sound signal appliances
Annex 4.	Distress signals

Part A. Application and definition

Gives the circumstances under which these rules apply and the definition of different types of vessels which, because of the nature of their work, are restricted in their ability to manoeuvre.

In this section, under Rule 1 (d), it will be seen that traffic separation schemes which are or may be adopted by IMCO (Intergovernmental Maritime Consultative Organization) will become part of the rules. (See Rule 10). This is a new provision and Rule 10 particularly concerns fishing vessels and how they are affected by separation schemes.

Part B. Steering and sailing rules

The more significant changes within this section, which is concerned with the practical application of the rules, are the new or newly worded rules, *ie*:

Rule 5	—	Lookout
Rule 6	—	Safe speed
Rule 7	—	Risk of collision
Rule 8	—	Action to avoid collision
Rule 10	—	Traffic separation scheme
Rule 17	—	Action by stand on vessel
Rule 18	—	Responsibilities between vessels
Rule 21, 24	—	Towing

291

For the fishing vessel officer who has been in charge of a watch using the old rules, the new rules must be read and understood.

Rule 5. Lookout

A new rule in which there is special emphasis on the mandatory requirement to keep a proper lookout *at all times*.

The words 'by sight and by hearing' define the duties of a lookout. The lookout must use his ears as well as his eyes, he should report objects which are seen and sound signals, *etc* which are audible.

The words 'by all available means appropriate in the prevailing circumstances' is to some extent ambiguous and *must* be taken to mean a lookout where other vessels are or can be seen on the ship's radar display. This will also include information and advice passed to vessels from radar surveillance centres, and port and harbour control authorities who broadcast information and advice on ships positions, anchorage, course, speed and direction. All this information in poor visibility assists the mariner to make a full appraisal of the situation. All these factors in the broadest sense fall within the meaning of the word lookout or knowledge of the approach of or to another vessel or hazard.

Rule 6. Safe speed

This is a new term. The old expression moderate speed was an arguable and ambiguous definition of a ship's speed. Rule 6 now defines safe speed and lists the factors which will make a safe speed to be a reduction from full speed, even in clear visibility, to a slower speed which is suitable for the prevailing circumstances.

Rule 7. Risk of collision

This rule now gives instructions on how best to ascertain whether or not a collision risk exists. Emphasis is made on two methods, *ie* use of the compass bearing and radar plotting, with a warning on action taken based on scanty information. The emphasis is on correct plotting procedure.

Rule 8. Action to avoid collision

In the 1960 Steering and Sailing Rules Preliminary (i) Action to avoid collision, it was written that action *should* be positive, *etc*. It is now written that action *shall* be positive, *etc*. Stronger emphasis is made here and additionally the positive action taken shall be taken in any condition of visibility. In the old rules, the action had to be taken when vessels were in sight of one another. The use of radar is now taken into account within the new rules, so that a positive and large enough alteration of course and speed will be apparent to an observer on another ship either visually or on the radar display. This rule also states that action to avoid collision should be such that vessels will pass well clear of each other and if necessary a vessel should be stopped in order to give time to assess the situation.

Before moving on to other changes in the rules it is worth noting that the use of radar is now included in the present *International Regulations for Preventing Collisions at Sea*.

In the 1960 Regulations, the use of radar was included only as a short Annexe to the rules. The use of radar in fog is now acknowledged. Nevertheless, positive rules and instructions on its use and reliability have been made. *M Notices* give further advice and instruction on radar reliance, and the prudent fishing vessel skipper should read and assimilate both rules and *M Notices*.

Rule 10. Traffic separation schemes

These schemes which have been adopted by IMCO (Intergovernmental Maritime Consultation Organisation) are of particular interest to fishermen. Traffic separation schemes are usually laid down in high density traffic areas and are clearly shown on charts.

This is a new rule which should be read and understood. It is important to those engaged in fishing in an area where there is a traffic separation scheme and also to fishing vessels which may have to use a separation scheme when steaming.

A traffic separation scheme consists of two lanes in which traffic proceeds in opposite directions within separate lanes so as to avoid end-on situations. The two lanes will be divided centrally by a line or an area which is known as a *separation zone line*. Similarly the traffic lanes will have a *separation zone line* on the outer limits.

Vessels engaged in fishing or on passage in a separation scheme are considered to be using the scheme and must conform to the essential principles of Rule 10 b & c, *ie* proceed in the appropriate lane in the general direction of the traffic flow for that lane; so far as practicable keep clear of a separation zone or line; normally join or leave a traffic lane at the termination of the lane, but when joining or leaving at the side, vessels should do so at as small an angle to the general direction of the traffic flow as possible.

Fishing vessels may *engage in fishing within a separation zone* and they may follow any course *within the zone*.

Fishing vessels *fishing within a lane* should not impede through traffic. This means that they should not operate in such a manner that they or their gear seriously restrict the sea room available to other vessels within the lane. They should make every endeavour whilst fishing to avoid interfering with traffic; but nonetheless, if risk of collision with another ship develops, then the normal steering and sailing rules apply.

Skippers should avoid crossing lanes if possible but if obliged to do so they should cross as near as practicable at right angles to the general direction of traffic flow. Under no circumstances should a fishing vessel, whether fishing or not, proceed against the traffic flow in the wrong lane. *This is a punishable offence.*

Rule 17. Action by stand on vessel

Sub paragraph 17(a)(ii) and (c) of this rule are new. This rule covers the situation wherein two vessels are in a crossing situation and the stand on vessel is in doubt that the giving way vessel is apparently not taking any or sufficient action to avoid a collision and whereby a dangerous situation seems likely to arise.

The stand on vessel under 17(a)(ii) is now allowed, by her action alone, to take avoiding action, subject to paragraph 17(c).

This rule covers a situation whereby a vessel sees another on her port bow, the bearing of which is not changing appreciably and risk of collision is deemed to exist. If the stand on vessel fails to attract the attention of the give way vessel on her port bow and it appears that a dangerous situation may arise and the giving way vessel does not appear to be alert to the developing danger, then rule 17(a)(ii) allows the stand on vessel to take avoiding action. But such action shall not normally include altering course to port. The reasons for not altering course to port are self evident. Going astern on the engines or going hard over and around to starboard is preferable to altering course to port.

Rule 18. Responsibilities between vessels

This rule gives a comprehensive description of responsibilities on giving way between different types of vessels hampered to various degrees.

There is little change in substance to a number of rules set out separately in the old Regulations except for the addition of the new 'hampered vessel' which is constrained by her draught. Such a vessel will be identified by night by exhibiting three (3) all round red lights and by day by a cylindrical shape — Rule 28.

Rule 21d and 24 (a)(g) Towing

In addition to the extra masthead light or lights required by a vessel which is *towing another vessel*, it is now necessary to carry a yellow towing light above the white stern light. Apart from colour, this light must have the same characteristics as the white stern light and it must be vertically placed above the stern light. Towing means towing another vessel and *not* towing fishing gear.

The vessel being towed should, as in the old rules, exhibit side and stern lights but paragraph 24(g), a new rule, states: that where from any sufficient cause it is impracticable for a vessel or object to exhibit the lights prescribed for a vessel under tow, all possible measures shall be taken to light the towed vessel or at least to indicate the presence of the lighted vessel.

The Annexe to the rules is mainly concerned with technical details such as the power and positioning of lights, the size and description of shapes to be shown by day, *etc*, audibility of sound signals, distress signals.

Annexe 2, however, is new and concerns signals for use by fishing vessels when fishing in close proximity to one another. They are added as a codicil to rule 26(d) and *may* be used. They are not signals to show that the vessel is a fishing vessel. They are signals which *may* be shown so that other fishing vessels in close proximity will know that the vessel exhibiting such signals is committed to shooting, hauling, or is fast on an obstruction. There is also a signal for purse seine vessels for use when pursing the net.

Experience has shown over many years that numerous mishaps and incidents concerning the loss of lives and vessels have been caused or contributed to by bad lookout, negligent navigation and poor bridge discipline. All fishermen should make every effort to avoid dangerous situations by adhering to the Collision Regulations and by keeping good lookouts, by navigating properly and by maintaining good bridge disciplines.

25 International code of signals

Single letter signals by flag *(See front endpaper)*

A.   I have a diver down. Keep well clear at slow speed.
*B.   I am taking in, or discharging, or carrying explosives.
C.   Yes,'affirmative', or the 'significance of the previous group should be read in the affirmative'.
*D.   Keep clear of me. I am manoeuvring with difficulty.
*E.   I am altering my course to starboard.
F.   I am disabled. Communicate with me.
G.   I require a pilot.
*H.   I have a pilot on board.
*I.   I am altering my course to port.
J.   I am on fire and have dangerous cargo on board.
K.   I wish to communicate with you.
L.   You should stop your vessel instantly.
M.   My vessel is stopped and making no way through the water.
N.   No, negative or 'the significance of the previous group should be read in the negative'.
O.   Man overboard.
P.   In harbour, hoisted at the foremast. All persons should report on board 'I am about to sail'.
Q.   My vessel is healthy and I require pratique.
R.   Not allocated.
*S.   My engines are going astern.
*T.   Keep clear of me, I am engaged in pair trawling.
U.   You are running into danger.
V.   I require assistance.
W.   I require medical assistance.
X.   Stop carrying out your intentions and watch for my signals.
Y.   I am dragging my anchor.
Z.   I require a tug. (When made by fishing vessels operating in close proximity, it means 'I am shooting my nets'.)

These signals may be made by any method of signalling. Those marked by an asterisk may only be made in compliance with the *International Regulations for Preventing Collisions at Sea*.

At the time of publication the 1972 Collision Regulations introduced two new sound signals, letters (G and Z) which conflict in meaning with the International Code of Signals above when made by sound.

ie Rule 34(c) G = I intend to overtake you on your starboard side
                 Z = I intend to overtake you on your port side.

Morse Code

Alphabet				Numerals	
A	· –	N	– ·	1	· – – – –
B	– · · ·	O	– – –	2	· · – – –
C	– · – ·	P	· – – ·	3	· · · – –
D	– · ·	Q	– – · –	4	· · · · –
E	·	R	· – ·	5	· · · · ·
F	· · – ·	S	· · ·	6	– · · · ·
G	– – ·	T	–	7	– – · · ·
H	· · · ·	U	· · –	8	– – – · ·
I	· ·	V	· · · –	9	– – – – ·
J	· – – –	W	· – –	0	– – – – –
K	– · –	X	– · · –		
L	· – · ·	Y	– · – –		
M	– –	Z	– – · ·		

The 1972 *International Regulations for Preventing Collisions at Sea* provide for the following signals to be made by sound only. Those signals with an asterisk may be supplemented by a light signal as prescribed by Rule 34 and 35.

Rule 34

*E ·		One short blast, I am altering my course to starboard.
*I · ·		Two short blasts, I am altering my course to port.
*S · · ·		Three short blasts, I am operating astern propulsion.

G – – ·	I intend to overtake you on your starboard side (In a channel or fairway)
Z – – · ·	I intend to overtake you on your port side (In a channel or fairway)
C – · – ·	Indicates agreement to be overtaken and in reply to G or Z (In a channel or fairway)
*5 · · · · ·	To be sounded when vessels are approaching one another, under circumstances whereby doubt exists or there is failure to understand the intentions or actions of the other and risk of collision develops.
T –	One prolonged blast may be sounded by a vessel about to round a bend in a fairway or channel which is obscured by the intervening land. A vessel approaching the bend from the opposite direction, on hearing the prolonged blast may answer with the same signal.

Rule 35. Restricted visibility

T –	Prolonged blast, sounded at intervals of not more than two minutes by a power driven vessel making way.
M – –	Two prolonged blasts sounded at intervals of not more than two minutes by a power driven vessel under way, but stopped and not making way through the water.
D – · ·	Sounded by a vessel not under command, a vessel restricted in her ability to manoeuvre, a vessel constrained by her draught, a sailing vessel, a vessel engaged in fishing, a vessel engaged in towing or pushing.
B – · · ·	A vessel towed, or if more than one vessel is towed, the last vessel towed shall sound this signal. This signal should be sounded immediately after the signal made by the towing vessel.
R · – ·	This signal may be made by a vessel at anchor, in addition to the ringing of the bell, but only on the approach of another vessel in order to warn her of the anchored vessel's position and the risk of collision.

H · · · ·   A pilot vessel engaged on pilotage duty, whether under way or at anchor, may in poor visibility sound this signal in addition to the normal fog signals.

Rule 35 requires that a vessel aground shall give the normal rapid ringing of the bell for about five seconds at intervals of not more than one minute, and then give three separate and distinct strokes on the bell. It then says that the grounded vessel may in addition sound an appropriate whistle signal.

The advice on sounding an appropriate whistle signal might appear to be ambiguous. If the vessel is aground in fog, there is no appropriate whistle signal, so that Rule 36 must be considered. The warning signal of five short blasts may be given, Rule 34(d), but the vessels would not be in sight of one another as required by the rule.

In most ports there are local bye-laws in which there is given a whistle signal to be sounded by a vessel aground, on the approach of another vessel in poor visibility. If in doubt an appropriate signal to sound might well be the letter U, which is the single letter flag signal, meaning 'You are running into danger'. This signal has been used by light and sound for many years especially when a vessel has been seen to be running into danger.

26 Submarine telegraph cables

Running between the coastlines of the UK and the countries of Europe and America there are many telephone and telegraph cables which lie on the seabed. These submarine cables are subject to damage by ships' anchors, but bottom trawls are mainly responsible for a considerable amount of damage to these cables and the cost of repairs is very high.

There are three important reasons why trawlers should keep clear of cable areas when towing gear:

(1) Damage to modern telephone cables can cause serious disruption to world communications affecting safety of life at sea, in the air, trade, international business and affairs. Each cable is capable of carrying thousands of telephone and other messages at the same time.

(2) Most modern submarine cables carry high voltages which can prove lethal if attempts are made to cut or chop them.

(3) Loss of gear, time and in some cases a valuable catch may result if a trawler fouls a submarine cable.

Law of the sea relating to submarine cables

The International Convention for the Protection of Submarine Cables 1884, as extended by the Convention on the High Seas 1958, and agreed by member nations, stipulates that:

(a) Vessels shall not remain or close within one mile of vessels engaged in laying or repairing submarine cables or pipelines and vessels engaged in such work shall exhibit the signals laid down in the *International Regulations for Preventing Collisions at Sea 1972*. (Rule 27).

Fishing gear and nets shall also be removed to or kept at a distance of one mile from vessels showing these signals, but fishing vessels shall be allowed 24 hours after the first signal is visible to them to get clear.

Fig 120 Approximate position of submarine cables normally shown as magenta coloured wavy lines on admiralty charts

(b)   Buoys marking cables and pipelines shall not be approached within 1/4 mile and fishing gear and nets shall be kept at the same distance from them.

(c)   It is an offence for any person to deliberately, or through culpable negligence, damage or break a submarine cable and such a person is liable to a penalty of imprisonment or a fine or both. It is also obligatory that anyone who fouls a cable must sacrifice his gear rather than cut the cable.

(d)   Owners and skippers of fishing vessels who can prove that they have sacrificed an anchor or fishing gear, in order to avoid damaging a submarine cable or pipeline, shall receive compensation. A claim for such compensation should be made within 24 hours of arrival in port to the appropriate authority on Department of Trade form FSG10 giving full particulars. It is also advisable to report the incident by radio. Give the following information

(1)   The date and time of incident.
(2)   The exact position, shore bearings or readings by electronic navigation system.
(3)   Depth of water and description of cable if sighted.

The appropriate authorities are the DOT, Customs and Excise, Coastguard, and Fishery Officer. An entry made in the deck log and a statement supported by evidence of the crew should be drawn up immediately after the occurrence so as to support the claim.

Charts and position of cables

On the Admiralty navigation charts used by British fishing vessels the international symbol indicating a submarine cable is shown as a corrugated or wavy line coloured magenta. On other charts the cable may be shown as a corrugated black line. Particular importance is attached to showing cables on fishing charts obtained from other sources. (For approximate positions, see *Fig 120*)

In coastal areas normally fished by trawlers charting accuracy at about 100 miles offshore is usually better than $2\frac{1}{2}$ cables, improving to about one cable close inshore. Cables laid in mid-ocean prior to 1970 with the use of satellite navigation may be as much as two miles from their charted position, but present day mid-ocean accuracy is usually better than $\frac{1}{2}$ mile.

On very old charts which are still in existence, cables may not be shown. It has already been pointed out elsewhere in this book that skippers and mates should always use the most up to date and largest scale chart for navigation. We now have another reason, the submarine cable, which will be more clearly and accurately defined on the large scale coastal chart, than on the small.

If in any doubt as to the location of cables in a particular fishing area, application may be made to the undermentioned address for cable warning charts covering the area of interest.

> Telecommunications HQ
> Marine Division,
> Central Marine Depot,
> Berth 203, Western Docks,
> Southampton SO1 0HH.

Prevention of damage to submarine cables

Practically all cable breaks resulting from fishing are caused by otter boards or beam trawls. In most cases the cable is broken under tension without being brought to the surface. In some cases the cable armouring wires become severed and rucked up as the door or beam trawl is towed across and the broken wires then become entangled with the net. In a few cases the cable is broken but one end remains foul of the gear and is brought on board. With the more powerful trawler the cable may be brought on board and cases are known where the cable has been chopped or burnt through in order to clear.

The most obvious method by which to avoid cable fouling is to not knowingly fish over a submarine cable.

However if the trawl door is well maintained and constructed and providing that the cable conforms closely to the contours of the seabed, fouling will not normally occur. But any of the following circumstances or a combination of these, may result in fouling.

(1) Poorly maintained trawl doors and fittings
(2) Cable suspended over bottom depressions
(3) Cable turns or bight standing proud of the bottom due to excessive slack resulting from repairs in the vicinity.
(4) Door lying flat on the bottom when the trawler has turned too quickly
(5) Trawl net snagging on broken cable armour wires, as a result of trawl doors fouling the cable.

Trawl doors used in demersal fishing are designed with a rounded leading edge so that a submarine cable which lies on the sea bed will, in general, allow the door to pass over it without fastening. However, when a cable is not resting on the bottom at all points, the probability of fouling with a door may be considerable.

Skippers and mates will appreciate that a trawl door is designed to maintain the spread at the mouth of the trawl. The brackets are so constructed that a sheering angle of about 30° outwards from the ship's course is maintained. There is of course a second component of force and that is the vertical moment which positions the door above the sea bed. The position of the net and door is determined by the speed at which the ship tows and the length of warp paid out, ie the distance between the ship's towing block and the cod end. The length of warp paid out and the speed of the ship when demersal fishing is usually adjusted so that the trawl doors are either on the bottom or very close to the bottom. The vertical angle of the board relative to the sea bed depends on the position of the towing bracket. Usually the bracket is midway between the top and bottom of the door and the door is towed parallel to or along the bottom depending on the speed or catenary of the warp.

It will be seen from this data that the leading edge of a trawl door will very likely catch on a cable if the cable is in suspension over a depression and the tow is being made at approximately right angles to the line of the cable. The door will be forced over on to its side by reason of the pull on the towing bracket and the submarine cable will very likely jam between door and warp at the towing bracket.

In the event that the door passes over the cable, it is nearly certain that the bridles, footropes and ground weights or steel bobbins will foul or strike the cable causing damage to the fishing gear and the cable.

The beam trawl, by its construction and mode of operation, will almost be certain to foul a cable which is in suspension. The head of the beam trawl, with its various attachments, being dragged along the sea bed will always be a danger to cables which are proud of the bottom.

The following advice on avoidance of cable damage should be followed:
(1) Do not knowingly trawl in the vicinity of cables
(2) Do not alter course too quickly when trawling so that the trawl door on the inside leg turns over and results in it being dragged

slowly along the sea bed

(3) See that all bolt heads on the inner side of the door are round and smooth

(4) Nuts, if used, should be on the outer side of the board and project as little as possible, also have their corners rounded off

(5) The bottom of the board should not be straight throughout its length but should be well curved towards the fore end

(6) The shoe should be smooth and the bolts which secure it to the board should be counter-sunk

(7) The fore end of the shoe should be carried well up the leading edge of the board, should fit closely to the iron plates running up the front edge, and should terminate without either projection or indentation.

(8) Generally, all attachments should be as simple and smooth as possible and on every part of the door the aim should be to afford no resting place for a cable if it should be accidently picked up.

(9) The attention of skippers and mates is drawn to the importance of placing all trawl gear shackles so that the bow of the shackle faces the direction of travel.

Action to be taken if a cable is fouled

When a cable is fouled, great care must be taken in attempting to free the trawl gear. Comparatively little pressure is required to force the armouring wires through the insulation on to the copper conductor. As soon as this happens water will reach the centre conductor and the cable will be rendered unusable even though it may not be actually broken.

If the gear cannot be freed without risk of damage to the cable, then it should be abandoned and the loss claimed for as previously described.

In the event that a submarine cable is brought up either on the gear or on the flukes of an anchor and it is possible to slip the cable, then a slip rope should be passed under the cable and brought back on board. A wire should not be used for this purpose. If the anchor can be lowered clear of the cable and if the gear can be either lowered clear or brought on board, then the cable should be slipped.

The ship should be handled so that the cable does not slide along the flukes of the anchor or if caught on the gear, so that sliding or chafing does not take place. Try to avoid damage to the cable armouring and insulation.

Under no circumstances should the cable be chopped or burnt off. High voltages are fed into certain submarine cables other than power transmission cables. Serious risk of life exists due to electric shock or severe injury due to burns if any attempt to cut the cable is made. No claims in respect of injury, loss or damage suffered through interference with the cable will be accepted.

List of useful publications

Merchant Shipping Notices ('M' Notices) – issued by Department of Trade from M M Offices

Nautical College Courses (as set out in 'M' Notices)

Notices to Mariners – Admiralty

Admiralty List of Lights

IMCO Basic Principles and Operational Guidance Relating to Navigational Watch Keeping – Intergovernmental Maritime Consultative Organisation

The Fishing Vessels (safety provisions) Rules – Department of Trade

International Regulations for Preventing Collisions at Sea 1972 – HMSO

Burton's Tables

Norie's Tables

Reed's Nautical Almanac

Fires in Ships – Inst. Marine Engineers

See also the list of Fishing News Books publications at end of book.

Index

Aircraft, use of in assisting ships, 63
    dropping of equipment, 63
    droppable survival equipment, use of,
        63
    search procedure, 64
    flares, use of, 64
Anchor, bower, 34–36
Anchor, kedge, 34–36
Anchoring procedure, 29, 39
    at anchor, 30, 31
    laying out anchor, 34–39
    loss of anchor, 32
    sea anchor, 34
    weighing anchor, 31
Anchor watch, 208
Anchors and cables, 28–39
Anchor work, terminology, 28, 29
Aneroid barometer, 139
Anticyclones, 259, 260
Astronomical navigation, 165
Automatic fire detection, 94
Automatic pilot, 148, 149

Back strops, of trawl, 40
Baitings, of trawl, 40
Bang-up trawl gear, 44, 48
Barograph, 141
Beacons, radar, 190, 191
Beacons, radio, 184

Bellies, of trawl, 40
Bends and hitches, 1
Beaufort Scale, 260–262
Bobbins, trawl, 40
Bosom, of trawl, 40
Brailing, purse seine, 52
Breeches buoy, procedure and signals,
    77–79
Bulkheads, shoring of, 110
Buoyage systems, 112–120
    combined Cardinal and Lateral sys-
        tem (red to port), system 'A', 113
    International Uniform System, 112
    lateral marks, 113
    cardinal marks, 115
    chart abbreviations, 119
    light characteristics, 119, 120
Buys Ballot's Law, 255, 277

Cales, anchors and, 28–39
Cables, submarine telegraph, 301–307
    chart, marking and accuracy, 303
    compensation, lost gear, 303
    damage to cables, prevention of, 304,
        306
    fouling a cable, action taken, 306, 307
    Law of the Sea, 301
Care of the fish, 53

311

Cement boxes, to apply over leak, 108, 109
Charts, 161–164
  Decca and Loran charts, 164
  fishing charts, 162
  Gnomic charts, 163
  great circles, 163
  large scale charts, 164
  magnetic variation on charts, 164
  Mercator charts, 162
  rhumb line, 163
  routing charts, 164
Charts, buoyage abbreviations, 119
CO_2 fire smothering systems, 91
Cod end, of trawl, 40
Cod end, tying, 10
Collision avoidance, rules and regulations for, 266–296
  additional signals for fishing vessels, 289
  collision, to avoid, 270
  crossing, 274
  general definitions, 267
  head-on situation, 273
  lights, signals, 276–283
  narrow channels, 271
  overtaking, 273
  responsibility, 267
  responsibility between vessels, 275
  restricted visibility, 275, 276
  sailing vessels, 272, 273
  safe speed, 269
  sound and light signals, 284–288
  traffic separation, 271, 272
Collision damage, 110
Collisions, prevention of, International Regulations, 56
Combined Cardinal and Lateral buoyage systems, 113
Compass, magnetic, 134–136
  compass card, marks, 136
  course and bearing correction, 135
  deviation, 135
  deviation card, 135
  true and magnetic North, 135
  variation, 135
Compass, gyro, 137–139
  compass card, marks, 136, 137

  deflection, 138
  gyro error, 139
  position and operation, 137, 138
  principles, 137
Conversion tables, 245

Decca Navigator, 197
Demersal trawl, 41
Deviation, of compass, 135
Direction finding and homing, distress signals, radio, 61
Declination, 174
Disabled vessel, towage, 102, 103
  passing a line, 102, 103
  preventer, 105, 106
  towing procedure, 106–108
  towing stern first, 108
  use of anchor cable, 104, 105
Distance measuring, 133, 153, 154, 158
Distress and rescue procedures, 56
Distress signals, 56, 289
Distress procedures, 58
  aircraft, use of, 63
  auto alarms, 59
  coastal stations, 58
  direction finding, 61
  distress or urgency signals, 59
  electronic beacon, (EPIRB), 62
  helicopters, use of, 64–66
  liferaft radio, 62
  radio equipment, statutory requirement, 58
  radio frequencies, 58
  Radio Rules, Fishing Vessels, 58
  radio watch, 58
  RNLI, 63
  rocket line-throwers, danger to tankers, 72
  signals, shore stations, 74–79
  silence periods, 61
  urgency signals, 60
Duties, Officer of the Watch, 202, 203

Echometer, 197, 198
Electrical fires, 93
Electromagnetic log, 133
Emergency Station card, 80
Emergencies at sea, 96

312

Emergency Position Indication Radio
    Beacon (EPIRB), 72
Ex-meridian tables, 176
Explosives, dealing with, 96, 97
Extinguishers, fire, 89

Fire fighting and prevention, 86
    accommodation, 86
    breathing apparatus, 92
    CO_2 and steam smothering systems,
        91
    combustible liquids, 91
    dry fires, 90
    electrical fires, 93
    engine room, 87
    extinguishers, CO_2, 92
    extinguishers, dry powder, 92
    extinguishers, foam, 92
    fire drill, 87
    fire equipment, checking of, 87
    fire extinguishers, identification, 89
    fire fighting, 89
    fire pumps, 87
    muster points, 88, 89
    sprinkler systems, 94
    stability, excess water, 95
    wind direction, 95
    working spaces, 87
Fish, care of, 53
    fishroom, cleaning, 54
    freezer trawlers, 55
    gutting, 53
    icing, 54
    pound boards, 53
    stowing, 54
    washing, 53
Fishing gear, 40–52
Fix, by station pointer, 154
Fix, running, 156
Floats, of trawl, 40
Fog, 204, 205

'G' link, 42
Gear, trawl, working, 40–52
Great Circle navigation, 163
Greenwich Mean Time, 171
Greenwich meridian, 171
Ground rope, of trawl, 40

Gyro compass, 137

Hand leadline, 131, 132
Handling ship, 210–231
Hauling trawl gear, 43–44
Headline, of trawl, 40
Heaving line, knot and bend, 11
Heel, list and trim, 238
Helicopter, use of in assisting ships,
    64–67
    evacuation of sick and injured, 66, 67
    precautions by vessels, 65
    procedure, vessels, 65
    radio communication, 67
    rescue, 66
Hides, of trawl, 40
Hitches and bends, 1
H M Coastguard, 63
Horizontal angle, sextant and station
    pointer, 153–156
Hull damage, 108–110
    cement boxes, 108, 109
    collision damage, 110
    extensive damage, 110
    shoring bulkheads, 110
    stopping leaks, 108, 109

Icelandic National Life Saving
    Association, 69
IMCO (Int. Marine Consultative
    Committee), 57
Impeller log, 133
Independent piece (pennant) of trawl,
    42
Inflatable liferafts, 80
Instruments, navigational, 131–135
International Regulations for Pre-
    venting Collision at Sea, 56
International Uniform Buoyage Sys-
    tem, 112
International Code of Signals,
    297–300
Isobars, 251

Kedge anchor, 34–36
Kelly's Eye, of trawl, 40
Knots and splices, 11–17

Latitude, 179, 184
Leadline, 131
   'arming' the lead, 132
   marks, 131
Leaks, repair of, 108, 109
Lengthener, of trawl, 40
Lifeboats, (RNLI), 67
Lifelines, 247
Liferafts, inflatable, 80–85
   associated equipment, 82, 83
   boarding, 82
   emergency stations, 80
   launch procedure, 80, 81
   procedure on board raft, 84, 85
   righting, 81
   sea anchor, 82
   stowage, 80
   use as shelter ashore, 85
Light characteristics, buoys, 119–120
Light and sound signals, 284–288
Light signals on vessels, 276–283
List and loll, 238
Logs, electro-magnetic, 133
Logs, impeller and pressure, 133
Logs, patent and taffrail, 132, 133
Longitude, 178, 179, 184
Loran A and C, 198–200
Lows, 250, 251

'M' Notices, 97–99
Man overboard, 97–99
Grounding, (stranding) procedure, 99
   assisting vessels, 100
   beaching, 101
   insurance company, 100, 101
   jettison of gear, 100
   use of anchors, 101
Marks, trawl warps, 44
Mayday, 56, 289
Mercator charts, 162
Mercury barometer, 140
Messenger wire, 43
Meteorology, 249–265
   anticyclones, 259, 260
   Beaufort Scale, 260–262
   Buys Ballot's Law, 255, 257
   cyclones and anticyclones, 250
   dangerous quadrant, 254

   depressions, 251
   fronts, 250
   influence of the sun, 250
   isobars, 251
   prevailing winds, 258, 259
   sea areas, UK, 267
   sky and weather notation, 264
   storm centre, action taken, 254, 255
   swell states, 263
   terminology, 252, 253
   tropical storms, southern hemisphere, 256, 257
   visibility scale, 264
Metacentric height, 232, 233
Mines, torpedoes, bombs etc, 96, 97
Mooring, 32, 33
Morse Code, 298

Nautical almanac, and tables, 170, 171
Navigational aids and equipment, electronic, 183–201
   Decca Navigator, 197
   echometer, 197, 198
   Loran, 198–200
   Omega, 200, 201
   radar, 187–197
   radio direction finding, 184
   satellite navigation, 201
   VHF radio
Navigation, astronomical, 165–182
   meridian altitude, 171–176
   sight reduction tables, 181, 182
   stars and planets, 177–181
Navigation, buoyage systems 112
Navigation, coastal, 151–164
   angles on the bow, 159, 160
   bearings and cross-bearings, 151–154, 157, 158
   bearings and soundings, 159
   charts, 161–164
   effects of the tides, 160
   fix by station pointer, 154
   range-finding by sextant, 153, 154, 158
   running fix, 156
Navigational instruments and appliances, 131–150
   aneroid barometer, 139

automatic steering gear, 148, 149
barograph, 141
electromagnetic log, 133
gyro compass, 137
handline and lead, 131, 132
hygrometer, 143
impeller and pressure log, 133
magnetic compass, 134–137
mercury barometer, 140
patent log, 132
pelorus, 150
sextant, 143–147
station pointer, 147
thermometers, 141–143
Net drum, 48
Netsonde, 48
Notices to Mariners, 202

Officer of the Watch, 202–209
at anchor, 208
duties of OOW, 202, 203
keeping the log, 206, 207
keeping the watch, 204
lookouts, 205
'M' Notices, 202
Notices to Mariners, 202
personnel, 207
pilots, 208, 209
restricted visibility, 204, 205
taking over the watch, 203
Oil, use of, for quelling waves, 69
Omega, 200
Otter boards, 46

Parbuckle, 23
Pelagic trawl, 46, 47
Pelorus, 150
Pole star, 179
Position reporting, 68, 69
Powerblock, 48, 51
Propeller, side thrust and pitch, 212, 213
Propeller, variable pitch, 221
Purchase, 18–24
Purse seining, 50–51

Quarter rope, of trawl, 42

Radar, 187–197

appreciation, 195
control setting, 193
interpretation, 194
limitations, 187, 188
operation, 195
position fixing, 189
racon beacon, 191
ramarks, 190
reflectors, 190
types of radar: ship's head up; stabilised, North up; true motion,
North up; true motion, head up,
191, 192
training, 196
Radio direction-finding, 184–186
Radio equipment, 183, 184
Radio navigation aids, 183–201
Radio, UK Code of Operation, 69
Regulations for preventing collisions at
sea, 56
Reporting position, 68, 69
Requisition of other ships, distress, 57
Rhumb line, 163
Rigging slings and spans, 25, 26
Righting moment, 232, 234
Rocket line-throwers, danger to tankers, 72
precautionary signals, 72
Roll and righting moment, 232, 234
Ropes, artificial fibre, 27
Ropes, knots and splices, 11–17
Ropes, strength of, 25
Ropes, tow, 27
Royal National Lifeboat Institution,
(RNLI), 67
Running fix, 156

SAM suits, survival, 85
Safe working load of ropes, 25
Safety and survival at sea, 56
Safety of Life at Sea, International Con-
vention for, 57
Safety of Life at sea, obligations and
responsibilities, 57
Satellite navigation, 201
Sea areas, UK, 267
Sea anchors, 34
Sea states, 263
Seine net fishing, 49

Seine net fishing, by trawl, 49
    cod seine, 49
    haddock seine, 49
    plaice seine, 49
Sextant, 143–147
    adjustment and errors, 145
    use of, 146
Shelters, Iceland, 69
Ship handling, 210–231
    effect of wind, 215
    going alongside, 214–217
    going alongside anchored vessel, 225–227
    in harbour, 210–212
    pivoting point, 224
    pooping and quartering seas, 229–230
    propeller pitch and slip, 223
    roll and pitch, 227–229
    rudder, effectiveness of, 224
    rudder, going astern, 225
    shallow water conditions, 220
    ship handling at sea, 227
    stern to tide, 219, 220
    transverse thrust, single screw, 212, 213
    turning circle, 224
    turning in heavy weather, 230, 231
    variable pitch propellers, 221
    use of anchor, 217–219
Ship's log, 206, 207
Sight reduction tables, 181
Signals, additional, for fishing vessels, 289
Signals, breeches buoy operation, 78, 79
Signals, distress, 56, 289
Signals, International Code of, 297–300
    by flag, 297, 298
    by Morse Code, sound or light, 298, 299
Signals, light, on vessels, 276–283
Signals, running into danger, 79
Signals, sound and light, 284–288
Signals, visual, ships in distress and shore stations, UK, 74–79
Skipper, when to call, 206
Stability, basic elements, 232–248
    centre of flotation, 238

centre of gravity and buoyancy, 232, 233
conversion table, 245, 246
effect of additional deck gear, 236
effect of ice, 235
effect of lifting with derrick, 236, 237
effect of weight of pelagic catch, 236
free surface effect, 242
GM, 234
list, 238
loll, 238
metacentric height, 232, 233
moments, 246, 247
relative density, 246
righting moment, 232, 234
suspended weights, 243
Systeme Internationale (SI) units, 244, 245
transverse stability, terminology, 232–234
Station pointer, 147, 148
Steering gear, automatic, 148, 149
Stern trawling, 46
Stern trawlers, stability of, 238
Stoppers, 9, 10
Storm centres, 254, 255
Stowage of fish, responsibility for, 44
Strop, use of, 14
Superkrub otter boards, 46
Submarine telegraph cables, 301–307
Suspended weights, 243
Système Internationale (SI) units, 244, 245

Tackles, 18–24
Tackles, pull, calculation of, 21
Taffrail log, 132, 133
Thermometers, 141–143
    Absolute or Kelvin scale, 141, 142
    Centigrade scale, 141, 142
    Fahrenheit scale, 141, 142
    conversions, 142
    hygrometer (wet bulb), 143
Tides and tidal streams, 121
    definitions, 124, 125
    depth calculation, 125–130
    influence of moon, 121–123

navigation in estuaries, 128
neap tides, 122
spring tides, 121
tidal streams, 130
tidal variations, 123, 124
tide tables, 125
Towing another vessel, 102–108
Tow legs, of trawl, 40
Trawl doors, (otter boards), 40
Trawl gear, rigging and working, 40–48
coming fast, 45
Delagic trawl, 48
German flying gear (bang-up), 44
hauling the trawl, 43
parts of the trawl, 40
preparing to shoot the trawl, 40
shooting the trawl, 42, 43
stern trawling, 46
towing the trawl, 43
trawl warps, 42, 43
Turning, (side trawling), 43
Turning in heavy weather, 230, 231

Urgency signals, 60, 61
cancellation, 62
Mayday, 60, 61
Pan, Pan, 60, 61
'Securite', 60, 61
silence periods, 61

Variation, compass, 135
Vertical sextant angle, 153, 154
Visibility scale, 264

Warps, trawl, 42, 43
Watchkeeping and ship handling, 202–209
Weather (meteorology), 249–265
Weather states, notation, 260–265
Whipping, rope, 15
Wire splicing, 16, 17
Wind strength, Beaufort Scale, 260–262
Wings, of trawl, 40

Zenith distance, 174

Other books published by Fishing News Books Limited, Farnham, Surrey, England

Free catalogue available on request

Advances in aquaculture
Advances in fish science and technology
Aquaculture practices in Taiwan
Atlantic salmon: its future
Better angling with simple science
British freshwater fishes
Commercial fishing methods
Control of fish quality
Culture of bivalve molluscs
Echo sounding and sonar for fishing
The edible crab and its fishery in British waters
Eel capture, culture, processing and marketing
Eel culture
European inland water fish: a multilingual catalogue
FAO catalogue of fishing gear designs
FAO catalogue of small scale fishing gear
FAO investigates ferro-cement fishing craft
Farming the edge of the sea
Fish and shellfish farming in coastal waters
Fish catching methods of the world
Fish inspection and quality control
Fisheries of Australia
Fisheries oceanography
Fishery products
Fishing boats and their equipment
Fishing boats of the world 1

318

Fishing boats of the world 2
Fishing boats of the world 3
The fishing cadet's handbook
Fishing ports and markets
Fishing with electricity
Fishing with light
Freezing and irradiation of fish
Handbook of trout and salmon diseases
Handy medical guide for seafarers
How to make and set nets
Inshore fishing: its skills, risks, rewards
The lemon sole
A living from lobsters
Marine pollution and sea life
The marketing of shellfish
Mending of fishing nets
Modern deep sea trawling gear
Modern fishing gear of the world 1
Modern fishing gear of the world 2
Modern fishing gear of the world 3
More Scottish fishing craft and their work
Multilingual dictionary of fish and fish products
Navigation primer for fishermen
Netting materials for fishing gear
Pair trawling and pair seining – the technology of two boat fishing
Pelagic and semi-pelagic trawling gear
Planning of acquaculture development – an introductory guide
Power transmission and automation for ships and submersibles
Refrigeration on fishing vessels
Salmon and trout farming in Norway
Salmon fisheries of Scotland
Seafood fishing for amateur and professional
Stability and trim of fishing vessels
The stern trawler
Textbook of fish culture: breeding and cultivation of fish
Training fishermen at sea
Trout farming manual
Tuna: distribution and migration
Tuna fishing with pole and line